Wainwright's Secret Lakeland

Volume 1:
Northern, North-Western and Central Fells

Chris Stanbury

Published by Sigma Leisure – an imprint of
Sigma Press, Stobart House, Pontyclerc, Penybanc Road
Ammanford, Carmarthenshire SA18 3HP

British Library Cataloguing in Publication Data

A CIP record for this book is available from the British Library

ISBN: 978-1-85058-926-6

Typesetting and Design by: Sigma Press, Ammanford, Carms

Photographs: © Chris Stanbury and Stan Hawrylak

Cover photograph: Ladyside Pike on the ridge from Hopegill Head
© Stan Hawrylak

Printed by: TJ International Ltd, Padstow, Cornwall

Disclaimer: The information in this book is given in good faith and is believed to be correct at the time of publication. Care should always be taken when walking in hill country. Where appropriate, attention has been drawn to matters of safety. The author and publisher cannot take responsibility for any accidents or injury incurred whilst following these walks. Only you can judge your own fitness, competence and experience. We strongly recommend the use of appropriate Ordnance Survey (or equivalent) maps.

Foreword

Chris Stanbury is a sinner come to repentance. His last book was *The World of a Wainwright Bagger*. OK, he wasn't at the extreme end of that black art and he took my sending him up a bit in *After Wainwright* – trainspotters with altitude sort of stuff - with remarkably good grace. But now he's back with a finer book that draws its inspiration from the asides and hints and gentle appreciations of peace and silence that breathe between the main ascents of AW's *Pictorial Guides*.

Of course the secret Lakeland of Wainwright's time is less secret now. There are simply more people on the hill, but what Chris proves comprehensively in this gently written book is that solitude can be found if you put your mind to it; if you take Wainwright's advice to follow your nose not just the guide book. The places he visits are not honey-pots and all the sweeter for that. What he finds in the process is the beating heart of the mountains. There's a lot of space out there if, like Chris, you take the trouble to go in search of it.

Eric Robson

Dedicated to Stan, my best friend and quite simply the best walking companion anyone could ever have. Thank you for the many thousands of miles we have walked together and the hundreds of summits we have shared.

Contents

Introduction

There are over sixteen million visitors to the Lake District each year. That is an enormous volume of people vying for their own experience of an area that is only about 50 miles from north to south and 35 miles from west to east. Admittedly these sixteen million folk do not all invade at once. Summer remains the most popular time for visitors. In addition the majority of these sixteen million won't be fellwalkers and will limit their knowledge of Lakeland to a ferry across Windermere, or a trip to Grasmere. However it is an unquestionable fact that the Lake District is popular, perhaps in the view of many walkers too popular. Moreover, in an age where life's demands seem to conspire to make existence more and more stressful, there is little doubt that the Lake District will become increasingly popular over the coming years, as more and more people look to refresh their spirits among the fells.

Now I would be among the first to say that every one of those sixteen million has a right to enjoy the Lake District (barring the minority that litter and destroy, or those who contrive to spoil the enjoyment of others). However, I would also be among the first to admit that there is little pleasure to be had from climbing say Scafell Pike from Seathwaite Farm, if the crowd of people walking around you is more reminiscent of a crowd heading to a Premier League football match, than to the summit of a mountain. There are many reasons why a book comes to be written, but one of the reasons for this book is that I wanted to stop just moaning about crowds on the fells and see if there was an alternative experience to be had. I am glad to say that in this task at least, I succeeded.

Oddly enough it was on completing the walks for my first book, *The World of a Wainwright Bagger*, that the genesis of the idea for this book occurred. I was sitting on the summit of Mellbreak with my long time hill walking companion Stan. We had just completed a twenty year journey that had taken us to the summit of every single one of the 214 Wainwright Fells. The celebration of that final summit, including a champagne moment, was followed by a little sadness and reflection, but also by a tremendous desire for more. Dedicated fell baggers are a breed obsessed. They love the Lake District and cannot imagine a time when they will hang their boots up. They crave to explore for as long as they can and when they are old and the sands of time stop them from even doing their laces up, they long for an afterlife with an endless number of fells to climb.

So the initial spark of an idea that both Stan and I readily agreed upon, was that we should do the 214 Wainwright fells all over again. The journey had been so good, why not repeat it? There were fells climbed in the rain that begged to be visited in clear conditions and other fells done in summer that instantly suggested themselves as great winter walks. And if, perish the thought, the desire to bag something new overcame us, there were still a number of Wainwright's Outlying Fells to be done. Yes there would surely be enough variety, enough fresh experiences, to keep us going for the next twenty years and more.

However, there was one thing lacking from our plans. It was not quite enough to have only a vague idea and plan stretching out into the future. I baulk from admitting it but the bagger within me, who had enjoyed working towards completing the 214 Wainwright Fells and gradually ticking them off, still wanted some kind of structure going forward. The conversation on Mellbreak became more ponderous and thoughtful, as we both searched our minds for that definitive idea that would signal the very start of a new era in the fells, where another era had just ended. As often is the case it was Wainwright who provided the idea. In one of those sudden moments of revelation it occurred to me that while we had bagged all the fells, a lot of them had been done via high level ridge routes from one fell to the next. I could not say for instance that I really knew Grasmoor, or Wandope or a number of other fells, because I had not as such climbed them for their own sake, but had included them either on the way to, or from, some higher or grander objective. So the plan emerged to try and do as many of the fells as possible by alternative routes described by Wainwright, or as separate independent climbs.

There was an immediate joy to think of climbing Blencathra, not by the popular Sharp Edge or Halls Fell route, but by the more secluded Gategill Fell or Doddick Fell, or even the lonely canyons, such as Doddick Gill, that split the buttresses of this famous mountain. So once back at my home in the flatlands of Kent, I substituted being in the fells for a study of the fells. I took each of Wainwright's seven *Pictorial Guides*, as well as his guide to the Outlying Fells and methodically looked through them for new and interesting routes of ascent, the routes that appeared as if they would be less popular. A sobering truth soon dawned upon me. There were more than just a few such routes, more than fifty or even a hundred. In fact there were around two hundred routes. It was humbling for someone who had spent years doing all the fells and prided myself on a good knowledge of the Lake District, to realise that here was the key to a deeper and richer knowledge of the fells. Yes it was humbling, but it was also invigorating. Here were enough walks to occupy a number of years. Here was the life enhancing agenda Stan and I had been seeking. An agenda not governed so much by reaching and touching a summit cairn, although all the routes described do that, but more by the journey to reach that summit and the qualities of that journey, be they solitude and silence, crags and drama, or hidden idyllic beauties.

It also occurred to me that as these routes I was choosing were not the time honoured routes to the summits of the fells, my desire to try and find the Lake District away from the crowds, the secret Lakeland, would hopefully also be satisfied. I was hoping to find a Lakeland that was much the same as it was in Wainwright's time. Having now done the first third of my journey through secret Lakeland, I can honestly say that these 50 miles by 35 miles of landscape have a Doctor Who's Tardis type quality. In three dimensions they somehow contain more space than you would ever have thought possible from simply looking at a two dimensional map of the area. At times the peace and isolation of these walks has made the journey seem like travelling through a parallel Lake District, from a quieter era forty or fifty years ago.

However there was a conundrum and a worry in this agenda of uncovering secrets. Had I not been a writer and had the desire to put my experiences into words, in the hope that others might read and enjoy them, I could have been content to just do the walks and keep the secrets to myself. These places really do represent a kind of final frontier of peace and solitude in a crowded area and so there has been a little reluctance to write such a book and thereby broadcast the hidden places. However my conscience in this regard has been eased by two things. Firstly, all the routes I was to write about were already to be found in Wainwright's *Pictorial Guides* and I was simply grouping them together. Therefore anyone who wanted to had access to them already. It was not as if I was revealing the secret of alchemy to the world, or the location of the Holy Grail. Secondly, I figured that even if many thousands of people read my planned *Secret Lakeland* trilogy of books, there were over two hundred walks for them to do and 365 days in a year, so it was unlikely that any individual walk would increase that much in popularity on any given day. However, if I may give a piece of advice for these walks, it is that they are walks best enjoyed either alone or with perhaps one or two kindred spirits. The very essence of secret Lakeland is that parties of walkers would spoil that hard won solitude and peace, both for you and for others.

Of course having decided upon which walks to include in theory, I then had to decide on a kind of benchmark for a secret walk to merit its inclusion in this trilogy of books. It would be perfectly possible for some battle hardened Goliath of a walker, to climb the tourist route up Skiddaw at night, in a blizzard, in winter and for that walker to encounter nobody. Any summit or walk can be experienced alone, either by sheer luck or in appalling conditions. That does not in itself make for a secret Lakeland walk. Therefore a valid benchmark should seek to test the routes during the times of day that most walkers would walk and in weather conditions that would not turn the average walker away. There is no absolute guarantee anywhere in the Lake District that any route up a fell will be achieved without meeting a soul, but the routes described in this book are those on which one is least likely to meet anyone. For instance on the three routes up Knott described in these pages I encountered no-one. On numerous other walks I met just the odd fellow solitary walker. On just a few of the walks, done mainly in the summer months, I met a handful of people, but these walks still made it into this book due to their relative lack of people compared to the hordes on other fells that day. Above all, while doing the walks for this first book of three, I have been pleasantly surprised by how many of these alternative routes really are hidden gems. It has given me a fresh perspective on the Lake District and many times I have felt like Wainwright must have felt experiencing these same walks some fifty or more years ago, when his descriptions show a Lake District often devoid of walkers. Some of my original list of walks did not pass the benchmark of secrecy, although one notable example is nonetheless described in this book, as an example of when secret Lakeland went wrong.

As for the nature of the terrain on these walks, it ranges from the easiest of grassy, gentle walks, that could probably be done in trainers, to walks that are steep, uncompromising and pathless to some fairly full-on scrambles. I have always figured that if Wainwright could do it then so could I, but at times I have found myself in particular situations of exposure or extreme direness of terrain that have caused me to reappraise my respect for Wainwright as a walker and wonder whether it was worth risking my life for this project. There are some walks in this book that are best done in dry weather and outside of the winter months. However, if you do chose to do the more challenging walks in winter then the usual safety caveats apply that you must wear crampons and take an ice axe. One or two of the walks seem to have been untouched since Wainwright walked them and are somewhat exercises in masochism. You can rest assured though that any such walks are described frankly and with due health warnings and by a walker who is no he-man. I am certain however, even only one third of the way through my task, that it will prove to be at least, if not more, challenging than the 214 Wainwright Fells. Even if you do decide to give the toughest walks described here a miss, there are still more than enough straightforward secret Lakeland walks to give any walker a new lease of life and a fresh perspective of the fells. Indeed on many walks I have seen a fell that I thought I knew quite well as a totally new entity. It was as if I was climbing a different mountain.

So are there any rules to doing these walks? The simple answer is no. Whereas with the achievement of the 214 Wainwrights one has to touch the summit of every fell, the achievement of the secret Lakeland task is more governed by cerebral pleasures, by the act of walking itself and the quality of that walking and, of course, by the solitude. Some routes are definitely for ascent only, due to either steepness of terrain, or the kind of rare beauty of terrain that is best experienced when fresh at the start of the day. Other routes simply cry out to be done in descent, due to their ease or speed. Where possible I have tried to link one Wainwright route in ascent, with another in descent, to make some delightful circuitous walks that are rarely done, but which I hope give you the joy they gave me in accomplishing.

It soon became clear that one book could not do justice to the wonders of secret Lakeland. Above all I did not want to rush this wonderful task. Additionally the pressures of work and having three lovely children to bring up, mean that the task will be a longish one to complete. So I have decided on three volumes with two years to complete and write up the walks.

It would be amiss of me at this point not to thank those people who wrote to me, or e-mailed me, to say how much they enjoyed my first book *The World of a Wainwright Bagger*. I can honestly say that the satisfaction derived from these comments has inspired me to press on with this new project. As with my previous book I would stress that this book is not a guide book as such. It does describe the walks accurately and in some detail, but not with a view to being used as a practical field guide, rather as a means to hopefully inspire others through a series of essays or stories about the walks. As a nod to guide book format, I have divided the book into three sections relating to the geographical boundaries set by Wainwright in his guides. I have also listed the relevant volume and page they appear in Wainwright's seven *Pictorial Guides.* The rest of the secret Lakeland routes will be revealed in the subsequent two volumes and a full list of all the routes, numbering around 200, will be included at the end of Volume Three.

Although I have created this *secret Lakeland* list of walks and have written about them as they are to be found in the crowded 21st century, I owe a profound debt to Alfred Wainwright. It is within his guides that I have discovered these hidden riches of Lakeland. As with most things to do with Lakeland fell walking, he got there first!

As instigator and writer of this new list of walks, I have had to do all the walks (with one exception) and I hope that others will also take up the challenge of doing them all. It does not bother me, and it should not bother you how long it takes you or how you do them. As long as you enjoy these walks and are enriched by the experience, that is all that really matters. As a little enticement though, to those up for the task, you should know that in completing all the secret Lakeland walks to be described in this trilogy, as well as the 214 Wainwright fells, you will have gained a knowledge of the Lake District that few can match and none, apart from perhaps AW himself, can surpass.

opposite: *Approaching Burn Tod and Hause Gill*

The Northern Fells

'I felt I was preparing a book that would have no readers at all, a script that would have no players and no public'.
Alfred Wainwright, *Pictorial Guide to the Northern Fells*
Personal Notes in Conclusion

So wrote the great man in his concluding notes to the *Northern Fells Guide*, which he completed in the autumn of 1961, some fifty years ago. For two years he had wandered these fells time and time again. Yet outside of the famous mountains Skiddaw and Blencathra, he saw only one person on all of the other twenty-two fells in the guide. Even that one person was only seen at a distance. He did not actually meet them as such, much to his delight one imagines.

When I first set out into these fells, some 30 years later in the early 1990s, there was only a slight and subtle change to the experience Wainwright had. Yes I did encounter the odd person, but nearly always a fellow solitary walker. We would meet, greet, exchange a few words and then depart and give each other back our solitude. Such encounters were quite rare and I nearly always had the fells outside Skiddaw and Blencathra to myself. Hours on end were had in my own company. At times I felt like the happiest man on earth and at other times, generally in poor weather, the loneliness felt acute and a little threatening.

In the twenty years since I first climbed the fells Back O' Skiddaw, which oddly enough coincide with the twenty years since Wainwright's death in 1991, I have noticed something of a sea change in the popularity of the Northern Fells. They have definitely increased in popularity. That is not to say that out here a walker will encounter the types of crowds that are attracted by Scafell Pike and Helvellyn (accept on Blencathra and Skiddaw). These days it is unlikely, if you follow the normal ridge routes and the usual routes of ascent, that you will encounter no-one. During the course of researching this book, I encountered a party of people on the East Peak of Lonscale Fell, a favourite retreat of mine where I had met no-one on five previous visits, and a similar crowd on High Pike. It is a trend that will probably increase in the future as the quieter appeal of the Northern Fells tempts those who want a little solitude, away from the more dramatic but busier peaks to the south. One can only hope that in another twenty years from now solitude can still be found in this wonderful area of rolling wilderness.

However, despite the increase in volume of people on these fells, my mission was to find those routes in the Northern Fells that remained pretty much as they were when Wainwright first climbed them. With this mission now accomplished I can honestly say that there are still many lonely places and routes, where there is a high chance of having a walk entirely to oneself. In fact my journey through the secret places of the Northern Fells was something of a revelation. The Caldbeck and Uldale Fells provided a number of routes of ascent and descent where not a soul was encountered. For mile after mile on lush grass and heather paths, I walked as though in heaven. Here I came across not just rolling, glorious terrain, but such wild drama as Roughton Gill and the beautiful stony ravine of Hause Gill. It was indeed like Wainwright had walked and very little had changed. Classic routes of ascent and no little drama were also found on the East Ridge of Bannerdale Crags and the tough and steep North East Ridge of Lonscale Fell. But perhaps the biggest surprises were had on those two old and popular favourites, Skiddaw and Blencathra. Outside of the crowded main line up Skiddaw and the nearest as popular route over Ullock Pike and Longside Edge, there are a number of glorious routes up and down Skiddaw where I met almost no-one. Skiddaw's vast northern backside hides the Barkbethdale and Southerndale approaches, both as wild and in their own way grand as anything Skiddaw has to offer. Lonely miles can be tramped on Hare Crag and Sale How. The south-west arête of Skiddaw Little Man, though intimidating from a distance, is on close acquaintance just a wonderful steep climb, in a great situation and with a bit of mild scrambling. Similarly, outside of the honey pot routes of Sharp Edge and Hall's Fell, Blencathra offers an altogether quieter, but almost equally dramatic experience on the ridges of Gategill Fell and Doddick Fell, while the deep canyons in between the ridges, such as Blease Gill, offer rough and confined scrambling for walkers who like that sort of thing, but with a health warning for those that don't (more on this later).

Above all my wanderings in these fells reaffirmed my enduring love of this area. If the Lake District is my home from home, then the Northern Fells are my favourite room within that home. This cauliflower shaped massif is wholly separated from the neighbouring fell masses and groups by a ring of flat land. The Southern Fells merge into the Western Fells and the Eastern into the Far Eastern, with only deep valleys in between, but the

Northern Fells stand isolated and unique, a separate kingdom offering a separate type of experience. The flatter areas surrounding the Northern Fells massif are as much a part of the appeal of the area as the fells themselves. To the north of Skiddaw and the Uldale and Caldbeck Fells, is a delightful area of small villages and hamlets, a place that time has largely forgotten. Wandering the quiet lanes and footpaths in this area has been almost as great a pleasure as walking on the fells themselves. South of Skiddaw is a low level traverse on quiet roads and paths that takes in such charming settlements as Applethwaite and Millbeck. Quiet corners and signposts, leading into lonely routes, abound all around this massif. Nearly always the reward was out of all proportion to the effort and expectation.

I have, however, been somewhat dismayed by the number of new and growing cairns that keep popping up in the Northern Fells, where there were none or very few in AW's day. Even as recently as 1991, when I first walked these fells, they were still at the most very modest adornments. Cairns have their place and can sometimes be useful as guides for navigation, but there are already more than enough cairns in the Lake District, without the need to embellish cairns on the likes of Knott and even erect an entirely new cairn on Mungrisdale Common of all places. The summit pictures in the Wainwright guides that depict these fells are sadly an anachronism. All walkers who love this area should think of themselves as guardians. No one can own these fells. Mountains and landscape that are eons old cannot be owned. But in the short span of our lives we can do our best to be guardians of the landscape, to tread carefully and not litter the wild places with rubbish or unnecessary cairns, to make as little noise and intrusion as possible, to leave the landscape as we find it, so that others that follow in our footsteps in the future will find it so. In this spirit I hope you enjoy these walks as I have.

The Many Faces of Skiddaw

Skiddaw provokes mixed emotions, from those that doubt its status in the hierarchy of Lakeland's Fells, to those for whom it is a beautiful Queen of mountains. I make no apologies for taking the latter view. Skiddaw's name means simply 'shoulders', so let's not dwell on that. But, if Skiddaw lacks the crags and rough edges of those fells at the heart of Lakeland, its smoothed, air-brushed contours still make for a form that undeniably pleases the eye. Respect is also due to Skiddaw from a geological point of view. Its slates are the oldest rocks in the Lake District, far older than those at the volcanic heart of Lakeland. If man, whose total existence on this Earth is a mere ripple on the ocean of Skiddaw's history, cares to criticise her, then I doubt she really cares.

There is no denying however that whatever camp you sit in regarding Skiddaw and its merits, it is a popular mountain. Its rounded, accessible appearance, the fact it is the easiest of Lakeland's four 3000 feet peaks, and that it has a car park at 1000 feet to ease the total ascent, are all homing beacons to the hordes. So why does friendly, tame Skiddaw deserve even a mention in a book about secret Lakeland, let alone a whole chapter? Well that is the nature of things secret; they are well hidden and take a little finding. But browse a map of Skiddaw, or better still study the Skiddaw and Skiddaw Little Man chapters in Wainwright's *Northern Fells Guide* and suddenly a whole new world of exploration opens up on Skiddaw's flanks. In some places it is a world without paths, a world of solitude. It has been a surprise to me, as I have wandered away from Skiddaw's time honoured routes, to find another Skiddaw totally apart spiritually from the traditional concepts of Skiddaw and yet a world geographically, at times, almost within spitting distance of the popular routes. It is probably true of most complex mountain forms, that 90% or more of the people who climb them occupy 5% or less of the surface area of the mountain in doing so. That leaves 95% for lovers of solitude. So here are some of my favourite secret and lonely routes on and off Skiddaw.

While Skiddaw and Skiddaw Little Man have separate chapters in the *Northern Fells Guide* with good reason, they are nonetheless joined forever at the waist and it is rare that I will climb Skiddaw without a visit to the summit of Little Man. The superb view alone is justification. But having pored over the pages of the *Northern Fells Guide* for a number of years, I knew that there was a way of ascending Skiddaw Little Man that did true justice to this fell, instead of just including it as a detour from Skiddaw's main line. This route would prove one of the finest of the secret Lakeland routes in this volume. It has the three key ingredients, drama, solitude and the essence of adventure.

When viewed front on, the south-west arête of Skiddaw Little Man looks impossibly steep for it to be a mere walker's route to the summit. Yet closer acquaintance shows that appearances are deceptive. It is steep and it does require a little scrambling, but there is nothing here to horrify the seasoned fell walker. Wainwright describes this as a 'fine-weather route' and 'a scramblers route pure and simple', so heeding the great man's advice I chose a perfect day in May to make my first ascent.

If ever there was a peerless blue sky day, with literally not a cloud around, this was it. Even better, a band of rain had passed through the night before, leaving a Lakeland of utmost clarity, yet warm and devoid of all but the lightest breeze. There is nothing finer than sitting at a guest house breakfast table, knowing the weather has done as forecast and that a planned walk is at your mercy. Such were my feelings this glorious morning as I made my way through the fields and lanes beneath Skiddaw and the picture postcard,

The approach to the seemingly sheer South-West Arete of Skiddaw Little Man

whitewashed village of Applethwaite. Half a mile later, I arrived at the next village of Millbeck and here the route proper begins.

A tree shaded path runs behind the back of the houses before opening out onto one of the most verdant, grassy and welcoming paths in the district. Almost immediately the south-west arête appears looking grey and formidable, dominating the narrow valley ahead. Ignoring the more popular route up onto Carl Side, a lower path runs invitingly into the very heart of Skiddaw. The Mill Beck weir is soon reached and this is a delightful place to stop. It was only mid-morning, but already the early summer heat made for an instant decision to take walking boots off and dip my feet into the little pools of water beneath the small cascades of the beck. It was here that my secret Lakeland desires took an early blow, as first a solo middle-aged male walker and then a young couple reached the weir above me before heading in the same direction that I was going.

I have never been one to rush walking, preferring to allow enough time for a walk and to be able to stop when the mood takes me, or even to vary the route if so desired. If at all possible time should never be harrying one through a walk. But there is something about the prospect of drama ahead, a mixture of excitement and the tiniest hint of foreboding that makes even a rest lover like me want to push on. As I headed onto a narrow shelf path, leading into what I call the womb of Skiddaw, I could see the three people about a hundred yards ahead of me. However, this part of the path is quite narrow and has some nasty drops down to the beck, so my focus was necessarily on the ground beneath me, rather than the walkers up ahead. They could only be going one of two ways, either the South-West Arête route, or on to Skiddaw via Carlside col. A larch tree marks the branching off point to cross the beck and start the haul onto the arête. A simple tree, noted by Wainwright when he first came this way in 1960, but easily overlooked by anyone who was unaware of this secret route. Was it selfish of me to hope the three walkers ahead would pass the larch tree without a glance? Perhaps, but then there are enough places in the Lake District where one can guarantee meeting people, for it to be reasonable for all of us to hope for a little time on our own when it has been purposefully sought out. Today I was in luck, as first the man and then the young couple headed straight past the larch and up towards Carlside col. As I reached the tree, there was no-one behind me and no-one ahead on the arête.

The crossing of Mill Beck, easy though it was physically, symbolised in the mind a passage into a different Lakeland. This was Lakeland as Wainwright would have known it. There was little though in the early stages of the climb to inspire a continuation of such mystical thoughts. Instead the first 500 feet were an unrelenting pathless haul, through short bracken and heather. I recall, from my school days, a rather self-satisfied physical education teacher of mine extolling that there was 'no gain without pain' as I badly attempted some seemingly pointless, lung collapsing exercise. Well this was the 'no gain without pain' part of the arête, although unlike the PE lesson, I rather enjoyed this type of exercise, alone, toiling away, gradually lugging myself into a wonderful position of solitude. It is impossible to climb many hills over many years without having some measure of masochistic enjoyment in this type of slog.

Before long, as it always does, the fun bit started. At around 1700 feet the ridge begins to form and the steepness of ascent lessens. From this point onwards it's a delight all the way to the summit of Little Man. As the rocky crest commenced, I found a perfect shelter for one person, nestled into a large rock. Here I could look back at the plunge towards Millbeck, with ever expanding views towards Coledale, Newlands and Derwent Water. The next 800 feet or so should be savoured, for here one can climb a narrow ridge of flaky rock, in a wild and dramatic situation, yet totally alone and with the fantasy feeling that no-one has ever been here before. Having viewed the awesome appearance of the ridge from below, it was somewhat surprising to find that there were no hidden terrors up here. Although pathless, the ridge is easy in comparison with the likes of Striding Edge or Sharp Edge. There is a little sense of exposure, but it's at the very mild end of the scale and more an enjoyable sense of height and awesome surroundings than anything to cause panic. The ridge is a curious intermingling of sharp little rock upthrusts, which give the impression of a Stegosaurus' armoured spine and delightful grassy patches, perfect to recline on and think about nothing in the sunshine. The bilberries, which Wainwright says thickly carpet the ridge, were at this time of year merely nascent shoots and leaves.

It's a shame that this delightful part of the ridge does not last for longer and is soon replaced by loose slate and stone as the final pull to Little Man is made. This is one of those climbs where the summit cairn only comes into view at the last second of the climb. There is therefore no gradual transition from secret Lakeland to popular Lakeland, but instead a rather rude awakening. It was odd to have the rug of solitude so quickly pulled from under me, after an intense period of time basking in its comforting arms. One moment climbing alone, the next that oh-so-familiar cairn on Little Man, adorned with half a dozen other fell walkers. This was to be the short and popular middle section of an otherwise lonely day; as walkers were here as expected, I did not mind too much. The view from Little Man is one of the Lake District's finest and it was therefore with an inward wince that I overheard one lady say on reaching the summit "It's not very impressive". Compared to the Lhotse face of Everest, perhaps not! I consoled myself that this would be one person who was unlikely to climb Little Man again. While the summit of Little Man is a popular place, it is not as frequented as its glorious view and proximity to Skiddaw would suggest. I would say only about a third of people who ascend Skiddaw via the main line, make the small detour to the summit of Little Man. A shame for those that pass by but a bonus for those that linger.

Having ascended Little Man, it was an obvious kind of pilgrimage to climb the parent fell, Skiddaw. I'd like to say I've been on Skiddaw's summit more times than I can recall, but unfortunately being a bagging type, I have a database which lists among other things the number of ascents made, so I could tell you how many times, if you were interested. Let's just say more than 15 and leave it there. And out of all these times, including blizzards, rain and lashing winds, I can recall few calm, sunny and warm experiences on Skiddaw's lofty summit ridge. Today was one of these rare occasions. It was a time to bask rather than cower and to take my time, rather than just touch the cairn and dive into the nearest available shelter. Yes it is popular, but is there a mountain that has a finer feel of height above the surrounding landscape and a greater sense of distant view as one looks out towards Solway and the hills of southern Scotland? Although Skiddaw and Little Man are only separated by a thin neck of land and by a couple of hundred feet in height, they are entirely different in their mountain flavour. Little Man, on the one hand, has a small summit and a view predominantly of and into mountains. The summit of Skiddaw is by contrast a massive whaleback, with several distinct summit undulations and cairns, the best feature of the view being the vast stretch of plains to the north and the huge height plunge down to Bassenthwaite Lake. For me Skiddaw is a place of pilgrimage, where it all began for me in terms of high mountains and where, if I could choose, I would have my ashes scattered.

The generous scale of Skiddaw's summit means that one rarely feels crowded by people even when there are dozens on the summit ridge. On this day I had my few moments by the highest point, with the so familiar weather beaten trig point and squat, rounded viewfinder, and then for a hit of solitude decided to visit the North top and cairn. Here there is another substantial shelter, which sees far less human traffic than the other shelters, because for the majority of people the true summit is as far as they want to go. There is nothing wrong with that. I rarely visit the north cairn, as the weather is usually too hostile on Skiddaw's summit to be bothered. Today as I entered the shelter for a bit of calm contemplation, I was greeted by one of my pet hates on the hills. Some walker, who had made the effort to carry a water bottle all the way up Skiddaw, had not been bothered to make the lesser effort of carrying it back down. Instead this two litre spring water bottle lay in the North top shelter, an affront to Skiddaw. Now I am quite used to finding bottles and wrappers and other odds and ends on the hills; in fact I carry a plastic bag in my rucksack to collect such wantonly abandoned detritus. But this was worse. This was not the kind of thing that even an environmentally conscious fell walker would want to carry off a fell. You see while the bottle had been drained of its original contents, the walker who had left it up here had obviously been in need of relieving himself (not being sexist but logic dictates it was a him, this is Skiddaw summit ridge after all, not a place a lady is likely to choose for such an activity!) and not having the willpower or care to resist the urge for the 45 minute descent from Skiddaw, had felt it necessary to urinate into the empty bottle. Like Sherlock Holmes, I considered the thought process at work with mounting incredulity, as it became obvious to me that having committed this act, he then committed the heinous crime of simply leaving his 'mess' at the north cairn, a place others were likely to visit and certain to find this disgusting object.

I was not going to carry this bottle of filth off the mountain and I certainly was not going to sit in the cairn beside it, so it was time to leave Skiddaw and head again for remoter, less spoiled environs. I had decided when planning this walk months before that I wanted to make special time for Sale How. I had only visited Sale How once, some 18 years earlier, but even then it had struck me as the sort of place where solitude was highly likely. 18 years on and far from bolting Sale How at the end of a long walk, I had decided that I wanted to pay a kind of homage to the place, to see what happened if one simply sat there for as long as time allowed.

At the uppermost fence that crosses Skiddaw's mainline, I left the time honoured route to head for Sale How. The first immediately noticeable change from 18 years before was that a clear path had now been trodden by countless feet and I could see its reasonably wide course winding all the way to Sale How. If any path to Sale How had been there 18 years before, I had failed to find it. It was yet another example of how, over the generation of years that I have been climbing in the Northern Fells, a network of paths up each fell and linking each fell has appeared. I suppose these days the Sale How route to and from Skiddaw has become more popular, both as a good quick way down to Skiddaw House and the Cumbria Way and also as an easy route up to Skiddaw from Skiddaw Forest.

It was not long before I arrived on Sale How. Both on a map and when viewed from any direction, Sale How appears as little more than a rounded blob of land, bolted onto the side of the grey-blue whaleback of Skiddaw's eastern slopes. However, as I was to discover, for those who make the time to stop and stay, this place has an indefinable quality that one can best label 'atmosphere'. At first my lonely reverie did not quite go according to plan. After the surprise of the path to Sale How, I was now in for a shock. As I reclined on the summit, warm and dry in mid May, I was conscious of a sound I vaguely recognised but seemed somewhat out of place. Moments later the sound took form as a Scottish Terrier dog, panting its way towards me, followed not far behind by an equally out of breath owner struggling up Skiddaw's slopes on his mountain bike. It was perhaps not quite the last thing I expected to see on Sale How. The Four Horsemen of the Apocalypse might have been the very last thing, but this was certainly up there with them. Or perhaps I was just expecting more of Sale How than I should have. Maybe I was still romantically living in 1990.

Today though I was as immovable as Sale How itself, for I had time on my side and I wanted that rare feeling of connection with a place. The minutes slipped by; I sincerely hoped that no-one else would disturb me. A glance behind showed the biker and his dog now some distance away and no-one else coming from Skiddaw summit towards me. A look down towards Skiddaw House also revealed no sign of humanity. The joy of aloneness consumed me as I lay back on the dry grass, with my eyes closed and my ears listening. So often on walks we don't really take time to listen to the landscape. Those who rarely stop have the constant backdrop of the noise of their own feet over the land. What you discover, if you take the time to listen, is that what at first appears to be silence and solitude, has its own natural noises and inhabitants. First there is the sound of the grass and the heather being blown by the wind, a noise that ranges from a faint whisper to a louder rustle and is only silent on the most windless of days. And this day on Sale How there was a natural symphony of half a dozen skylarks above me. I have often loved the treble twittering these birds make. It seems to encapsulate the wild places in sound. But never before today had I lain for a full twenty minutes with my eyes shut and my mind switched off to everything but this world of sound. After a while it was no longer random noise, but subtle little variations on the same warbled notes. I felt truly privileged to be the sole recipient of this effortless sextet. For a few moments my mind was emptied and I entered that rare state of oneness with the landscape, where self vanishes and becomes no more than another stone, or blade of grass, or whisper of wind on Sale How's flanks.

The views from the highest point, while not bad towards Skiddaw Forest and Lonscale Fell, are restricted in distance by higher fells. Its summit is adorned by a few stones and rock splinters and a couple of posts a hundred yards away. For most it will just be a utility on the way from Skiddaw to Skiddaw House. But to me forever more it will be a magical place.

Before reading Hugh Walpole's Herries Novels, Skiddaw House had merely been a grey walled former shepherd's bothy, more latterly turned into a youth hostel. It had perhaps always struck me as a little sombre in appearance and with its ring of trees also perhaps a little out of place in the heart of Skiddaw Forest. However, having recently read Walpole's *The Fortress*, Skiddaw House would now forever be associated with a fictional meet-up between enemies John Herries and Uhland Herries, where Uhland ends up shooting John, before turning his gun on himself and blowing his own brains out. It's odd how brilliant fiction can almost embed itself in the mind as a quasi reality. People go and hunt for 221B Baker Street although there never really was a Sherlock Holmes. Walpole's love of the Lake District landscapes shines through in his vivid descriptions. He is to Lakeland fiction what Wainwright is to Lakeland fact. Both men loved this small corner of the world and it shows.

It was now late afternoon and the day had reached that wistful reflective stage, which the heart wants never to end, while the body merely craves sustenance and rest. I passed beneath Lonscale Fell's crags, fearfully black now the sun had gone behind them. I was alone, but I had thought all my thoughts and I needed a little company. So on went the MP3 player, my companion back to Keswick. I had met no-one since the cyclist and his dog on Sale How. I had become used to being alone and now that the time of day had come when walkers seemingly vanish from the hills, I could expect to be alone pretty much all the way back into Keswick. However, it was not to be. The harmonious strains of Sibelius were rudely interrupted by a rather irritated raised voice from behind shouting 'Excuse me!' It was a mountain biker, whizzing his way round the side of Lonscale Fell. Now I don't mind mountain bikers. I've been one myself many times, including an exhausting ride to the very top of Mount Keen, the most easterly Munro in Scotland. It was more the attitude that I was some kind of annoyance interrupting this fluorescent lycra-lout's progress that irked me so much. This was not a velodrome; this was a walker's route and cyclists should above all respect the fact that people have been roaming these paths for centuries. Wainwright, who was used to having these Northern Fells to himself, would have hated such an intrusion and attitude. Still these little episodes in a hill walker's life soon pass and as I rounded the corner with the Vale of Keswick, washed with sunset glow, beckoning me back to creature comforts, I reflected on a day on a popular mountain, happily mostly spent in solitude.

'Ask a Barkbeth sheep what the north-west ridge of Skiddaw is like and it will reply without hesitation "C'est magnifique"'. So wrote Wainwright about one of Skiddaw's most hidden and secretive places. Indeed the vast acreage of Barkbethdale and Southerndale are the types of landscape sheep can graze for the duration of their natural lives in a worldly ovine paradise. The impression provided by Wainwright however is that what suits sheep does not necessarily suit the fell-wanderer. The difference I would suggest between when Wainwright wrote his guides in the 1950s and 1960s and today, is that more often than not he had the fells to himself, so for him perhaps the type of solitude and peace to be found on the North West Ridge was less of a rare commodity than it is nowadays. Today such a route beckons those who prefer to be alone. At the same time, while the north-west ridge does not compare for drama to Sharp Edge, I consider it is nonetheless a worthy route to the summit of Skiddaw and has charms less obvious but nonetheless as appealing, for those that seek them, as the most famous of Lakeland routes.

Perhaps the finest way to tackle any 3000 feet mountain is to traverse it from Point A to Point B, rather than the circular routes often demanded of the car traveller. One of the best ways to achieve this, and at the same time earn yourself a carbon footprint Brownie point, is to make use of the excellent Lakeland bus services available. Go to the Keswick website, check out the section called 'Getting about' and you will have access to every bus route timetable you could ever wish for. Make sure you check the timing of your intended bus back and be sure to carry a timetable in your rucksack. You never know when bad weather or weary limbs may necessitate an early exit from the hills or a change of plan. Also, a bus can deliver you to surprisingly far flung corners of the Lake District, a welcome boon for the walker keen to explore Lakeland's secret places, but a profound misery if you miss the last bus and find yourself stranded miles from nowhere. You will at least have the compensation of knowing you are exploring the Lake District in the very same manner as Wainwright himself all those years ago.

The bus stops at Chapel on the A591, which is as close as a bus gets to the start of the north-west ridge. From now on, I would be reliant solely on leg power to get back to Keswick, my starting point. From here you can take your choice of quiet country roads or some equally quiet footpaths through the fields surrounding Chapel Beck, to the start of the route proper at Barkbeth. These fields and indeed this whole area have a feeling far removed from the popular hub of Borrowdale or Langdale. It was no surprise to come across a solitary young deer grazing in this pastoral idyll and equally no surprise when the animal, having seen my hulking six foot frame approaching, bounded Bambi-like away, vaulting sizeable field boundary fences with apparent ease, as it disappeared into the middle distance.

The previous few days had been warm verging on hot and I now had a Lake District induced sun tan, as well as the odd raw patch where I had omitted to slip-slap-slop with the sun cream. So it was a welcome relief that this day was overcast and breezy, although of good visibility. Skiddaw's massive summit brooded in the cloud, a giant yet familiar presence. It would be windy up there, as it nearly always is. The cloud might even linger. Yet I felt confident in the hands of my old friend. In the foreground the scattered screes of Randel Crag were lit up like diamonds in front of Skiddaw's grey summit. Barkbeth is nothing more than a farm and a couple of houses. Once past this last sign of habitation, the tree-lined path leads high up above Southerndale Beck to a magical traverse that is all too soon over, as the trees give way to the vast acres of Skiddaw's gigantic backside. At a sheepfold down by the beck, a fine path heads towards Southerndale and another up Ullock Pike, whose presence now predominates. Three or four walkers were heading up Ullock Pike, bound for the fine route to Skiddaw by Longside Edge. By contrast no-one was heading my way, which now branched off from the main track, on a thread of a path towards Little Knott and the North-West Ridge of Skiddaw.

Little Knott is nothing more than a tiny excrescence on the immense façade of Skiddaw, yet it has a certain definition to its highest point and is undeniably in a wild and grand location. The whistling wind increased in intensity, lending this forgotten knoll an even lonelier feel, as the coarse grass rustled and whispered its primal tune. From here I spotted the cluster of boulders that Wainwright calls a 'little Stonehenge'. I can't really see this stone ring catching on as an alternative to the real thing in Wiltshire, but it does again demonstrate Wainwright's fastidious nature when it comes to picking out any and every natural feature. Trying to locate these sometimes worthy and sometimes innocuous details from the guides certainly lends an underlying purpose to a walk. Great Knott, which succeeds Little Knott as the ridge continues, is actually less worthy, being merely a grassy swelling on the ridge. It does however provide striking views ahead to the next section of the ridge, which dips before climbing steeply up to the impressive Randel Crag. Here also the feeling of being hemmed in by mountain grandeur, a slightly claustrophobic feeling, is generated by the impressive sweeping flanks of Ullock Pike and Long Side to one side and the even more impressive grey screes of Gibraltar Crag and Broad End to the other.

It was somewhat surprising, but also quite pleasing, to find a clear zig-zagging path up Randel Crag's flaky face. This path did not last much beyond Randel Crag though and petered out in a grassy plateau. This plateau, with Skiddaw's final 700 feet slate slopes rising above it, is a peculiar place. Like a little piece of moorland elevated to 2,300 feet. It is a good place to rest and take stock before tackling the unremitting slog that lies ahead. This plateau is only a few hundred feet from the crowded summit of Lakeland's fourth highest mountain and yet it is a contender for the wildest, most forsaken, yet strangely tranquil and compelling places on Skiddaw's massif.

And so to the final, seemingly interminable, scree slope leading to Skiddaw's summit. I expect the attitude to this labour will vary from person to person. Some will find it tedious or demanding in the extreme, a feat of masochism, and will wish they had never been persuaded by the author to try this route. Those who are supremely fit (the author not included) will probably gallop up it and wander what all the fuss was about. My feelings, however, were that this was a kind of labour of love for an old friend and also that it was a privilege to be in the midst of the colossal final rampart of Skiddaw's summit ridge, a place not far from Skiddaw's main tourist line in distance, yet infinitely removed in mood. Wainwright describes the ascent as being 'not unpleasant' and the slate as soft and yielding. However, as with all scree slopes, it is a case of a few steps up, followed by a few steps sliding back down. The easiest method I found here was to zig-zag up the scree and also to keep to the odd patches of more stable grass to be found. Just as the privilege of my situation was beginning to become a little stale and the convex nature of this slope was beginning to resemble some unending punishment from the realm of Hades, I spotted the summit cairn through the mist, a matter of a hundred yards distant. Pain turned instantly to pleasure (an oft repeated hill walkers experience), as I realised that through some luck and some common sense I had scored a bulls-eye on the summit cairn that Wainwright mentions as the only reward for this slog.

I was now in a place where the summit cairn of popular Skiddaw was within a stone's throw (or perhaps within a slate's hurl would be more appropriate). For all I knew, there could have been fifty or more people crowding round the Skiddaw trig point at that moment. However, nestled on these scree slopes, in a pathless place where few tread, I still had my solitude and also a magnificent view northwards to the Cumbrian Plains, westwards down to Bassenthwaite and across to Coledale that was within an iota of being a fine as the summit view. The summit remained in cloud, yet a hundred feet or so down from the summit I was privileged to still have the view. So a place that I would be hard pushed to ever positively identify again cried out to me for a stop, as I looked to eke out every last second of time without meeting a soul.

I had started this walk at 11 o'clock in the morning but by the time I finally reached the trig point on Skiddaw it was nearly five o'clock on a late May afternoon. A route that had taken me six hours to complete could have easily been done in half that time. But that would perhaps miss the point. This was not about rushing. My body had still had plenty of good exercise and, at the same time by refusing to rush, I had given my mind the space and time to truly absorb the landscape and so be replenished and refreshed. There was also the added bonus to reaching Skiddaw at this comparatively late hour. The crowds that had undoubtedly been there perhaps only an hour before had all but gone and I had that rare privilege of being on one of Lakeland's popular quartet of 3000 feet mountains on my own. Well almost.

The cap of cloud that had draped Skiddaw's summit for the entire day still held fast. From below it had appeared a stagnant object, unmoving and unyielding. Once within this cap, it showed itself to be an ever evolving entity, as it rolled and folded across the summit, driven by a brisk wind. Every so often the cap would slightly relent, to reveal a window of plunging views down to Bass Lake, or a portion of Cumbrian Plain, but for the most part it cocooned me into its essence. At such moments one could almost imagine that there was no Keswick, no rest of the Lake District, no World, no-one but me and the summit of Skiddaw. It is a not unpleasant feeling, perhaps because it is just an illusion, a temporary detachment from civilization. I was therefore quickly jolted out of my self-indulgent reverie, when a man's voice called out 'How Do?' from behind me; an ageing fell runner, who had swiftly and suddenly appeared out of the gloom, just as swiftly became a dim shadow and was gone.

The slightly abstract nature my walk was acquiring continued as I took the time honoured and often busy route from Skiddaw to Skiddaw Little Man, without a soul around. Even the fell runner did not make a re-appearance, although as he was doing a pace about twenty times my own, he was probably back at the Gale Road car park by now.

I briefly halted on Skiddaw Little Man and looked down upon the bristly fin of the south-west arête having now climbed that route. I had often stood here before and thought how awkward this route looked, but now I knew this was but an illusion. Although steep, the south-west arête was an easy scramble and a totally enjoyable one. Usually Skiddaw Little Man was followed by a descent down the tourist route, but today I had other ideas. I had not yet finished with secret Lakeland.

Skiddaw Lesser Man gets a bit of a rough deal. I doubt many people tarry long here although the view is scarcely less worthy than that from Little Man. This day, however, Lesser Man held more of an excitement for me, for it was the starting point for another new detour into the remoter recesses of Skiddaw. Wainwright's description of my route down to Applethwaite revealed something of particular interest, that there were three distinct zones of vegetation that I would encounter. The first of grass, down to 2000 feet, followed by a zone of heather taking me down to 1500 feet and finally a zone of bracken below 1500 feet. The initial zone of grass was a plush surface to walk upon and progress was quick. It was a fine thing to still have wonderful views of the Vale of Keswick and Derwentwater from such a secluded place. Then I hit the heather zone. I once read that there is more heather in the British Isles than on the rest of the planet. Heather is a vital part of our wild landscape, a beautiful thing when in purple flower and often a fine springy thing to rest upon. Thick clumps of heather, however, are not a fine thing for walking over and on this zone of Lesser Man's southern face there is clumpy heather in profusion. Two legs were not made for such terrain. Heather is deceptive for a walker. You could try and bound over its carpeted surface only to find yourself snapping your leg in some hidden pothole. There can be no sense of trust in one's footing on such terrain and unless care is taken, finishing the day without injury of some kind is about as good as one can hope for. I laboriously and tentatively made my way across the heather zone. The 500 feet of grass descent above had taken a few minutes, but the 500 feet of heather took an age and all the time the short cut bracken zone below and the sylvan paths towards Applethwaite teased me, close yet seemingly unattainable. So awkward was the terrain that I stumbled and went head over heels with my rucksack ending up over my chest instead of my back! That thankfully was the worst of it and happily there was no-one present to witness my slightly embarrassing tumble. The whole experience has left me with a bit of a love-hate relationship with heather.

Thankfully being May the bracken was not high and progress below the heather was straightforward and much quicker. Without the middle heather zone this would have been a very quick and accommodating route down from 2500 feet. Back in enjoyment mode, I located the 'curious mound' that Wainwright illustrates, yet another of those obsessive details that would have been bypassed without a Wainwright guide to hand. According to Wainwright, this was not a natural mound, but he did not elaborate on how it came to be there. My mind ran away with all manner of fantastical explanations. Could this be an ancient burial ground or perhaps the site of a UFO crash?

Having negotiated the deep and surprisingly steep trough containing Applethwaite Gill the rest of the walk was pure pleasure. It had turned into a glorious May evening, and even old Skiddaw herself had now finally shaken off her cap of cloud. The deep evening hues of light accompanied me as I finished my walk past rhododendron bushes and through a little wood, to Applethwaite and the minor road beyond. The remainder of the walk consisted of a road tramp back to Keswick, but my mind was enriched with golden memories and with soul charging solitude the tarmac slipped past easily enough.

The north-west ridge of Skiddaw bisects two of the most peaceful and unassumingly beautiful valleys in the Lake District. These are Barkbethdale and Southerndale. The in-car temperature gauge registered minus one Celsius as Stan pulled into the little car park between High Side and Barkbeth. Yet the intense sunlight, pure blue sky and distant haze felt more like spring than winter. At one end of the car park a footpath leads into a glorious pasture land. Every little muddy pool was covered in ice, but the going was easy and gentle and the wide grassy path verdant as it slowly meandered past some wind gnarled trees, through one gate then another and on towards Southerndale. For a short distance a broad sledgate path winds above Southerndale Beck, in the kind of scene that beckons the walker onwards. The path then descends to cross Southerndale Beck, before bifurcating. The right hand path heads into the depths of Southerndale. It would be the last of Skiddaw's recognised routes I would climb on my exploration. Looking down into Southerndale was looking into my future. It was for another day, different conditions and who knows what kind of experience.

On this day however Stan and I branched left at the confluence of paths, bound for Barkbethdale. The path becomes less distinct before trending round the base of Little Knott and the north-west ridge. Looking back, the Ullock Pike ridge dominates the scene, slender and knobbly in appearance. Before long though it disappears behind the nearer north-west ridge; a scene of peace and idyllic beauty now lies ahead. A grassy track heads down Barkbethdale making an unerring course for the deepest shadowed flanks of Skiddaw's backside. The path is so gently inclined here and the scene so wildly serene that every step is a joy. It is an oddity that this path lies so close to the start of the route up the north-west ridge, at times just a few yards away and yet the experience is so different. The north-west ridge is a high walkway to Skiddaw, all space and air; the Barkbethdale track by contrast leads seemingly into nowhere, destined to abruptly end beneath the rotten scree slopes of Skiddaw. However, a glance at the Wainwright guide reveals that at the very head of Barkbethdale a narrow trod traverses the face of Skiddaw beneath Broad End. From a distance this trod looks absurdly situated but, as is often the case, a scene viewed head on and two dimensionally from a distance is typically less dramatic and somewhat more benign on closer acquaintance.

The head of Barkbethdale was so dominated by the sheer wall of scree above that it was in shadow, even on this day of brilliant and intense March light. Here there are two options. Either you can take the narrow trod, which we did, or if you are feeling masochistic you can tackle a direct scree fan leading unerringly to the North Col of Skiddaw, amid scenery reminiscent of Frodo Baggins final ascent of Mount Doom from *The Lord of the Rings*. Being slightly unhinged fell walking types, Stan and I were sorely tempted by this purist line of scree and boulder, but decided to leave it for another day, to come back and climb as a footnote to this corner of secret Lakeland.

The narrow trod which had seemed to slant across a near vertical face when we had first set eyes on it, turned out to be nothing more than a pleasant heather flanked path, gradually trending upwards. Now at 2000 feet the feeling of height above the landscape that is so characteristic of Skiddaw began to encroach upon our senses. The slender spire of St John's Church near Bassenthwaite stood proud from the green fields and pastures far below. Before long the narrow trod path joins several others at a crossroads. The way continues over Broad End and to Skiddaw's fairly dramatic North Col. Here we encountered our first and only people on the climb from High Side. From the North Col, the summit of Skiddaw appears more graceful and slender than one is accustomed to, rimmed by a line of shattered crag and scree called Gibraltar Crag. Patches of late winter snow rimmed the line of the crags, lingering out of reach of the sun's searching rays. Looking down the scree fan that forms the alternative route up from Barkbethdale, the terrain looked awkward but perfectly doable, although it is easier to look down on something from above than to contemplate it from below.

A final short and exhilarating pull leads first to the north top and then the main summit of Skiddaw. Here again were the oh-so familiar shelter, the trig point (that had provided the foreground for countless photos over the years) and the squat viewfinder. These items were as familiar to me, perhaps more so, than the items of furniture in my own home. They were dear inanimate friends. Their companionship seemed to always be associated with happiness, excitement and exhilaration. It was too hazy for the classic Skiddaw panorama. Solway and Scotland only existed in the mind's eye. Although it was not classic, it was an unusual view, particularly into

A glorious track leading into Barkbethdale

Lakeland, where the very lack of clarity turned the fells into row upon row of smudgy blue outlines. A line from the poet A.E. Housman came to mind, although I accept Housman was not referring to the Lake District. Today these truly were 'blue remembered hills'. I can never tire of the summit of Skiddaw. Every time it is different.

In descent we were to take another secret Lakeland route, first retracing our steps to the North Col and then taking a path that faithfully followed a fence back to the Cumbria Way path at Dash Falls. This proved another quiet route with no encounters of the walker kind. The path made for an excellent and quick descent and is in fact best is descent. This route would be quite tiresome and relatively unrewarding in ascent. However, it also gave me a chance to revisit and reappraise the summit of Bakestall. I had only been there once before and came away with the impression that it was scarcely worthy of its 'Wainwright' status; it had seemed to me little more than an appendage to Skiddaw. My second visit, if not elevating Bakestall to my top ten Wainwright summits, or even top hundred, did nonetheless convince me that the first impression had been rather too harsh. The view this time was enhanced by the early evening colours. Broken cloud hung over Little Calva and Great Cockup, as little patches of golden light danced across the brown flanks of the Uldale fells. With Dash Farm below enfolded in sheep pastures, it was a timeless scene that I will not easily forget. Is it perhaps the case that an impression of a fell is as much about our own mood and the weather as it is about the topography of the fell itself? In the right conditions any fell can leave an indelible imprint on the memory. That is why they are all worth climbing and if possible more than once. Bakestall has a further surprise, one whose nearby presence is oddly sensed, although not seen, from the summit. This is the eerily named Dead Crags. Only once firmly on the Cumbria Way and beneath the crags, can one appreciate their dimension and drama. Outside of Blencathra these are the finest crags the Northern Fells have to offer. In evening shadow their name seemed quite apt. Bakestall was continuing to work its spell on my mind. The last few miles back to the car were firstly on the pleasant broad track of the Cumbria Way and then on the quiet road past Barkbeth farm. As a final treat the orange orb of the sun set beside Sale Fell and lit the sky up in a red sea of cloud waves.

So to my final new route on Skiddaw, up via the valley of Southerndale and down over the slopes of Hare Crag. Southerndale had been calling to me from before I even thought of the idea of doing these secret Lakeland walks, from before I had even completed the Wainwright fells. On a number of occasions I had looked down from Ullock Pike or Long Side into the wild and dramatic enclosure of upper Southerndale. Surrounded by walls of mountain, it always looked like a dead end, impossible to escape from. I knew, however, that this was a deception, because Wainwright shows that there is in fact a perfectly straightforward, if rather steep and at times quite loose, route out of Southerndale.

   I was on my own for my climb of Skiddaw via Southerndale. It was a cloudy October day, but forecast to be largely dry and with only a moderate wind. Clouds hung oppressively over the fells, forming a uniform wall of grey above 2000 feet. Above that line would be a different, sequestered world. After an encounter with a road full of cattle, the double decker bus dropped me off at Chapel, with its small church. This is the church of St John, built in 1879 on the site of a former medieval chapel and renowned for its delicate slender spire, which I had previously spotted on a number of occasions from high on Skiddaw. From where the bus dropped me, I used various minor roads to get to High Side, where the routes to Southerndale and Barkbethdale both begin. The first section of this path is along a tractor track. When I had done the earlier walk up Barkbethdale with Stan, this track had been hardened by a heavy overnight frost and was easy and firm ground for walking. That was in early March. Now it was October, after a weekend of torrential rain. The tractor track was a mire of thick mud. Every step was a floundering chore. Stepping away onto what looked like firm grass was a false hope. The cattle had churned up the grass so badly that it was full of watery hoof marks that sunk beneath one's feet. A sign on a gate said simply 'Bull in Field' which served only to exacerbate my discomfiture. I could just imagine this scene from a nightmare, with a bull looming ever closer behind me and my legs stuck fast in mud. I was glad to escape the mire and get away, higher up onto a sinewy path beside some twisted trees. Soon this track became wide, grassy and a lot less muddy and despair was soon replaced with joyful anticipation of what lay ahead.

At the second of two walls that are crossed by a gate and a stile a man was rebuilding a collapsed dry stone wall. For all the hundreds of times that I had admired these walls, I had never actually seen someone working on them. I could only have gratitude to this man for keeping his corner of Lakeland looking as it should do and preserving the old traditions. It was particularly odd to see this man rebuilding the wall, given that the path up Southerndale that I was to walk upon is a sledgate path, formerly used for bringing down stones from the head of the valley for the building of such dry stone walls. It was also one of those quirky encounters that are either fated or mere coincidence, depending on your own standpoint. This was to be the nearest I came to an encounter with a person all day. The path was now a joy as it headed deeper into Skiddaw's bowels, crossing Southerndale Beck which was in vigorous temper after the recent deluge. I had walked this far before, but now my route branched off into Southerndale itself. The sledgate path was a fine thread of a track, a little wet in places, but generally excellent. A couple of hundred metres above me were Little Knott and Great Knott on Skiddaw's north-west ridge. Yet the feeling here was again totally different. Instead of a gradual rise into open spaces, this was a path that seemingly led nowhere, that became ever more confined and dominated by the fells above. At the head of the valley, the final steep rise up to Carlside Col was still in a dense, thick mist. It merely added to the intense loneliness and slight foreboding of the scene. It was, though, thrilling in its dark drama and I had no desire to head back. Rather I felt drawn in, like a child that cannot resist a mild danger purely because the senses rail against it. The twilight gloom ahead was contrasted by the ever expanding view back down the Southerndale valley which was starkly beautiful and now bathed in a watery sunlight. Southerndale has an immensity of scale and is as secret a place as any in this book. This scale was highlighted by my companions on the walk in – dozens of brown hairy caterpillars. Having spotted a few of these charming little creatures, I decided to count them as a way of gaining height without noticing the effort too much. In a short space, of perhaps five hundred metres walking, I counted 114 caterpillars. This was just in the immediate vicinity of the path I was walking on and led me to wonder how many thousands of caterpillars there must have been that day in the entire Southerndale valley. Nature scatters her seed liberally and only the fittest will survive. Such is the struggle of life. Solitude derives from an absence of people not wildlife, which teems in abundance everywhere one goes in the Lake District and only ever intrudes on one's consciousness in a good way. On a later trip to the Kendal Museum, I found out that these were moth caterpillars. Of the 114 I had counted, how many would survive to fulfil their biological destiny?

Soon enough I rounded a bend in the sledgate path and there was the dramatic head of Southerndale ahead of me. To the left the flanks of Skiddaw rose in an unabated sweep of 1500 feet. To the right Long Side threw down a seldom seen dramatic spur of rock, split in two by a little hidden gully. Fingers of mist swept over the mountain flanks around, becoming denser and more channelled towards Carlside Col, the direction I was heading. A brief parting along the Longside Edge ridge, 900 feet above me, revealed a party of half a dozen walkers. It made the loneliness of my situation more acute and yet in some ways more magical. I stopped by the beautiful little cascades of Southerndale Beck, at the very head of the valley, and contemplated the scene ahead of me. I knew from reading the Wainwright guide that the final ascent up to Carlside Col was easier than it looked. The trouble was that under a thick grey mist, I could not see how it looked and that was fodder for the imagination. I knew it would be slippery going after the recent rain. I hoped the route finding would be easy, as I did not want to veer too far to the right and get onto the crumbly rock walls of Long Side. As long as I stuck near to the beck, I knew all would be well. I was not fearful, just nervously excited. I crossed the beck, making for the ruined fold on the other side. I entered the thick mist and for a while used the nearby beck as a guide. It was then that I suddenly lost my footing in a slippery patch of mud and scree and found myself, face down, summarily dumped to the ground. It would have been no more than slightly annoying had there not been an upright and rather pointed stone directly underneath me, which my sixteen stone weight crashed down onto. For a while my belly, where the stone had hit me, was painful and numb. A walker of lesser girth than me might have ruptured something vital! As it was, this was to be one of the few times in my life I have been glad of a little extra natural cushioning! The next day, to my consternation, I discovered a huge purple bruise about four inches across, but luckily that was the only damage done. I decided to stop for a bit, just to check I was OK. Slight concern turned suddenly to wonderment as nature turned me outwards from my inward thoughts. In a matter of seconds the mist parted, revealing the full length of Southerndale bathed in a pallid, translucent sunshine. Mist played with light for the next fifteen minutes or so, repeatedly parting, then closing, in a wondrous spectacle. Gone were thoughts of injury and loss of pride. I was living more vividly than ever I can remember. Also, to my delight, Carlside Col was revealed ahead and I could now see an easy line onwards, which served to dispel the demons of doubt which had plagued me. I was now certain of the way ahead and soon reached the Col as the mist, once again, started to encroach on my surroundings. It is odd how from the main path between Long Side and Skiddaw the route down into Southerndale is curiously hidden and would be quite difficult to locate, although it's not a route suited for descent.

Even in mist the Wainwright summits of Long Side and Carl Side were too near and too tempting not to visit. There was a further brief parting of the mist on Long Side, which revealed the silvery waters of Bassenthwaite far below. No such fortune on Carl Side, whose cairn gradually appeared out of the gloaming and whose flat, mist enshrouded summit could have been at ground level, rather than at over 2400 feet. I passed Carl Side tarn, which on a previous visit was frozen solid and backed by a snow covered Helvellyn ridge. Today it was a gloomy steel grey entity, backed by a pea soup mist, but beautiful in an eerie half-world way. The final pull up onto Skiddaw seemed interminable in this dark cloud-bound world, where one patch of slate covered ground in front of me was pretty much the same as the next. I started to wonder whether the summit shelter and viewfinder would ever appear, or whether I would be condemned to endlessly slogging up shifting screes. The mind plays out odd fantasies in the mist. Dependable as ever, Skiddaw's summit furniture eventually appeared, complete with the customary gale force wind and spitting horizontal hail. I wondered why I loved this mountain so much, when around seven times out of ten the view was obscured. Yet love her I did, in all her moods.

There was no-one on the summit and nothing to tempt me to stay for more than a cursory bite to eat in the shelter. Then it was off for Hare Crag, descending first to Skiddaw's north col (thick mist), then over slippery moss and marshy heather (more thick mist) and eventually to the little rising of ground that is Hare Crag (yes in mist). I would have liked to provide a more detailed account of open space, wide vistas and glorious relaxing stops, as had been my joy on Hare Crag's neighbour, Sale How. Instead there was little point in stopping. Everything around was wet, particularly so a marshy area encountered just before gaining the Cumbria Way path. A boot full of peaty water, but little else, was my reward from this trip over Hare Crag. I can

The imposing terminus of Southerndale

certainly say this was secret Lakeland in abundance; I felt about as utterly removed from civilization as at any time researching this book. Pity, for in dry, clear weather I think I would enjoy Hare Crag a whole lot more.

Having joined the Cumbria Way path it was a five mile walk back to Keswick. The mist did clear slightly, but only to a more general rain. Not perhaps my finest walk up Skiddaw, but I could never forget Southerndale and the glorious parting of mist from its upper reaches.

So having explored all the routes onto and off Skiddaw, I am now as sure as anything that there will always be somewhere on this huge entity where a person can sit alone for an hour, with a great view spread before them and empty his or her mind of care or concern. I have indeed enjoyed my time crawling ant-like over Skiddaw's broad acreage and experiencing its other, lonelier sides. I am a firm believer that however many hundreds of peaks one chooses to bag, a walker should have at least one mountain that he or she knows intimately. Such intimacy can often be missed, dashing from one tick to another. With Skiddaw this familiarity has not bred contempt, it has merely bred love.

Mixed Emotions on Binsey

Binsey is the last northern outpost of Lakeland before the fells blend into the Cumbrian Plain stretching away to the Solway Firth. It is also an outsider in the Northern Fells group, the other Northern Fells being closely packed together in a roughly circular area. Binsey lies outside of this circle and as befits an outsider, it has a different feel and flavour from the rest of the Northern Fells. It is a little independent island of a fell, hemmed in on all sides by narrow quiet lanes, pastureland and tiny hamlets, like a moat round a castle. It has a fantastic view and fine summit of rocky outcrops and ancient cairns. Binsey is an outpost, but it is certainly not an outcast.

I had become friends with Binsey many years before I began my research for *Secret Lakeland*. I had climbed it several times and experienced it in the warmth of summer and the chill of winter. Yet it had always been by the short and standard route from Binsey Lodge, a simple quarter day stroll, enhanced by the surprisingly extensive view from the summit and the pre-historic atmosphere of the place. Binsey is small in stature, yet I was surprised to discover that there were a further two ascent routes described by Wainwright. I decided to join these two routes together to make a grand tour of the fell and its surroundings. I have never found Binsey to be that popular, but at the same time I have on a number of occasions met walkers on the 'standard' route up from Binsey Lodge. My aim now was to see whether these two new routes would provide a more solitary experience worthy of secret Lakeland.

I began my expedition at the Castle Inn Hotel, a typical, picture postcard Lakeland waterhole and also a stopping point on a number of bus routes. On this particular morning, the only passengers to alight were myself and another man, who clearly wasn't headed for the fells, dressed as he was in chequered blue and white trousers and white tunic. Unless he was intending to cook up a stew on the summit of Binsey or was an escaped lunatic, things were looking good for the solitude prospects! For me, the bus is the preferred option, if practicable. I would always prefer to be without a car as I find that walks tend to be longer and more varied as a result, with a greater sense of freedom and adventure. The car too often provides the temptation to just drive to where the climb begins, do the climb and head back down again, in so doing missing out on some of the ambient charm a gentle stroll to the base of a fell often provides.

Unfortunately the road from the Castle Inn to Uldale is distinctly lacking in charm of any kind, being a busy thoroughfare for local traffic. At the first available opportunity, I decided I would leave the road, on a footpath headed for High Bewaldeth, shortcutting a corner from the original route. Now I tend to have a rule about low level 'shortcut' paths through fields that I have not walked on before. All too often in the past I have used a low level path to cut off some road walking, only to find myself floundering through boggy fields, meeting a dead end after a total lack of signposting or even chased by crazed, homicidal farmers driving ATVs. Taking the safer option these days is typically the preferred option. I have become far more circumspect and discerning when making such decisions. I examine the terrain looking for boot prints, checking for distinctness of path or perhaps a little yellow arrow indicating the way across the fields. If none of these clues are evident, I tend to continue on the road. However, the path to High Bewaldeth, I concluded, looked to be on reasonable terrain, enough to at least make an attempt. This was a decision I would swiftly regret. With my very first step down from the stile, my right leg sank deep down into a patch of sludgy brown bog. As the slime oozed inexorably into my sock I let rip a volley of one word profanities, as if this was going to help in any way, other than to startle a few sheep. I made a rapid and rather ungainly retreat back over the stile in the resolute direction of the road. I know such an attitude did not conquer Everest but I did not fancy floundering through muddy fields, when a much easier, albeit longer, alternative existed. A twenty year old version of me would have carried on regardless of bog, bulls and angry farmers. Now in my forties, I have come to realise what I most enjoy about walking. Such is the freedom of walking alone.

Today I was to have some reward for my decision to shirk the footpath, as within a few hundred metres of re-joining the busy Uldale Road, I turned off onto a very minor road heading towards High Bewaldeth. This was much more like it. It had a green strip of grass down the middle, the tell-tale sign of a lack of motorised use. Its environs were lovely glades of early autumn trees, through which tantalising glimpses of Binsey could be seen. Under a bower of trees, a gurgling stream tumbled down to the road. Ahead was a charming cottage, diminutive in stature, like something from Hansel and Gretel. The road had become narrower and narrower and now two gates were stretched across this little strip of tarmac, separated by about ten metres. I had that odd but unmistakeable feeling that I was entering someone's property, rather than a public place. Surely not though? The map still showed a minor road here that passed straight through High Bewaldeth. So imagine my bewilderment when I reached the second gate and found that the road ended and was replaced by no more than a rough farm track through a field. How could the road vanish? I had little choice but to carry on, as to do otherwise was going to mean a huge detour to get to the ascent starting point at Bewaldeth. The farm track did eventually become clearer at a house called Riggwood, but some barking dogs in kennels did not make me feel any more certain of the legitimacy of my route. I was quite relieved however to emerge onto the familiar road beneath Binsey, heading towards Bewaldeth. Bewaldeth itself is no more than a few houses and a phone box, by a road leading to the A591. I had made this circuitous route to avoid a stretch of main road walking, figuring that although much longer, it would be more than compensated for by its charm. It had been a mixed blessing; the quarter of a mile of rain soaked main road walking that now followed, to the start of Wainwright's described ascent from Bewaldeth, certainly did not improve my mood but was a necessary evil.

Although I had not taken the car, I did notice that there was absolutely nowhere to park near the tree fringed path that starts this ascent route. The nearest convenient parking place would, I suspect, be back at Bewaldeth and there seems no way to avoid a little main road walking. Just keep your wits about you. In a way this very lack of parking spaces, lay-bys or a large car park shouting 'come and climb me!' is manna for lovers of secret Lakeland. It is likely to deter all but the most determined of Wainwright followers. The initial path, seemingly landscaped with trees either side, had a wistful charm about it. Wainwright mentions that this lane is cut up by tractors. Today it was also festooned with a thousand cow pats. Despite this my mood could not fail to improve, as a delightful little stream joined the path and the route was now clear ahead onto Binsey. Climbed from this direction, this is a very different looking Binsey. One even wonders whether this really is the familiar rounded shape that has been climbed and seen from a distance so often. It appears loftier here than from Binsey Lodge and also shows off its one point of mini drama, West Crag. This crag would not get a glance were it in Langdale or Borrowdale, but Binsey is very proud of it, so hush.

Once you have passed through the gate ahead, it is all open fellside. The grassy rake of a path winds past a disused gravel pit and up to the ridge, leading onto West Crag and Binsey's summit. So often the moments that we reach a ridge or a col are revelatory, sometimes even better than the experience on the summit itself. Today the ridge of Binsey was a case in point. Mist still lurked over the summit and the ridge had a half-lit

Binsey's shy side on the approach from Bewaldeth

atmosphere about it that was dourly beautiful and slightly eerie. It was however the view towards Solway that captivated the senses. It was not the clearest view of Solway I have ever seen, but it was perhaps the most dramatic and ethereal. In the near foreground grey clouds hung, just a hundred feet or so above the fellside. The edge of these clouds was a tattered line of dark fingers, ever shifting and swirling, charged with atmospheric energy. Beyond the dark brooding mist, glittering light shone on Solway and Criffel creating a stark contrast that was simply mesmerising. I had no desire or need to go a step further, while nature was performing such a wondrous display. For perhaps ten minutes I stood there transfixed. However, such visions are often fleeting. The clouds morphed into an arrangement less pleasing to the eye, the sparkling distant view dimmed and the mist rolled in to obscure the scene. It was time to head for the summit.

It is a subject open to debate as to whether that quality we call atmosphere on the fells is truly engrained in the landscape, like some ancient energy, or whether it is a filter that we place on the landscape through our own thoughts and feelings. Perhaps it is even a combination of both the external and the internal. All I know is that for me Binsey summit has always had a peculiarly ancient feel about it. Not just ancient from a geological point of view but ancient from a historical point of view. The summit ridge is topped by a tumulus, an ancient mound of stones raised over a burial site or grave. Maybe it is just my imagination printing this ancient feeling on my subconscious. Or perhaps the memory of some timeless event is truly imprinted here, imprisoned within the landscape, like a photo on a camera.

I spent most of my time on Binsey immersed in the sizeable summit shelter, for there was a keen wind chill on the open top. When I did venture out of the shelter, it was to take some poorly lit but quite dramatic photos of the cairn, with Over Water and a glowering, cloud enshrouded, Uldale Fells as a backdrop. I also noticed for the first time the private pools on the flanks of Binsey that Wainwright mentions in the guide. I am not sure whether they are man made or artificial but certainly on that October day they were not 'almost completely concealed by trees', as Wainwright describes them, but conspicuously visible from the summit ridge.

My route of descent from Binsey was to be down to High Ireby. The guide showed this as being mainly pathless, for at least the first half of the descent, until a decent rough lane is reached. It was with a free and joyous spirit that I made a pathless trudge over heather, heading towards the corner of a little plantation of trees shown in the guide. My spirit was perhaps a little too carefree, as I ended up on the wrong side of the stone wall, although I did not realise it at the time. I saw a gate at the corner of the plantation and assumed that was the way. I felt somewhat less sure of myself when the gate turned out to have barbed wire across it and a lack of any convenient latch to open it. I began to wonder whether I was trespassing as I instead headed for a pronounced gap in the middle of the small plantation and then through another field. As I approached a second, larger gate, I could clearly see a sign fixed to the other side of this gate. As sure as eggs are eggs, I knew that this sign was going to say 'Private Keep Out', a suspicion confirmed after I had vaulted the gate. I found myself at a little sneck of land, with a ford across a lane and a gorse bush surrounding. I was back on track. This was the little gorse common that Wainwright describes. Sure enough, to the other side of the wall and field that I had trespassed through was a clear and friendly walker's stile. The route was the other side of the wall. So in descending this route from Binsey's summit, just remember to keep to the left side of the clear wall ahead. It will save you that rather watched feeling, when unsure whether or not one's footsteps are on private land.

Secure of my route, I crossed the little ford in this peculiar tiny common and then followed a broad lane into the hamlet of High Ireby. There were views ahead towards Solway, although paling in comparison with the view I'd seen from Binsey's summit ridge earlier. High Ireby is a pleasant collection of houses, clustered round a triangular green. Unfortunately the path through Binsey Plantation, shown with a red dashed line in the Wainwright guide, is a private path with several large signs to tell the walker so. Were this path public, it would make a pleasant walk back to Binsey Lodge. As it is, the road that one has to follow is, at least as far as Ruthwaite, quite delightful. The road hugs close to the plantation and one can get tantalising glimpses into the former estate of High Ireby Grange. The Grange itself burned down some time in the 1950s, but one can still see into the landscaped grounds. Passing here I was reminded again of Hugh Walpole's *Herries Chronicle*. High Ireby Grange and estate could almost be a candidate for the fictional Fortress the wealthy Walter Herries builds, as a symbol of his power over whom he deems the socially inferior members of his family, his sworn enemies, living in nearby Uldale. The road eventually branches away from the Binsey Plantation and heads through a beautiful grove of old trees to Ruthwaite. Ruthwaite was the home of John Peel, the famous huntsman, although there are only a few houses here and no reason to stop.

From Ruthwaite it would now be a further three miles of road walking back to the Castle Inn Hotel, a thought that did not fill me with great joy at the end of the day. I therefore decided to try and avoid some of the road walking, by taking another footpath that leads from the Uldale road, through Park Wood and onto Bassenthwaite Village. I had about an hour and a quarter before the bus home was due. I should easily make it back in time if I carried on the road all the way. But if I took the footpath instead, I would have to walk quickly and steadily. Still it could be done. I saw from the map that the first part of the path was on a farm track. When I reached the start of this path, I rejoiced in being off the road and yet still on an easy metalled track through the fields. It appeared that this would be one of those low level footpaths that I might visit again. Then just before the broad farm track ended, a little sign pointed the way ahead across a rather boggy and unpromising looking field. Not to worry too much, as there was a fence ahead and surely at the fence there would be a stile or gate and a direction indicator. A couple of hundred yards of labouring through the muddy, pathless field led me to the fence. There was indeed a new gate here, but no indication as to whether to go through the gate or not. I decided to go through but found no trace of a path. I began to curse my over optimism that this would be a clear route. Time was getting on and I needed to make a quick decision or risk missing the last bus. I went back through the gate to see if there was a path on the other side of the fence. It was even less promising though, being pathless again and, as an added 'bonus', leading straight through a herd of cows. I had taken this footpath for an enjoyable end to the day and it wasn't one. So I decided to head back and take the road all the way to the Castle Inn. I had wasted twenty or so minutes, floundering around and even the road walk would now be pushing it to be in time for the bus.

However it is surprising how much ground one can cover when time is pressing and I eventually found myself at the bus stop with a gloriously ample five minutes to spare. I checked which bus stop to stand at, as there are two here and had a quick double check of the timetable. Yes, the bus was at 5.15pm. Good. Then, with horror, I suddenly saw the dates that this bus service ran. Today was the 8th October and the bus service only ran until 30th September! The bus I had hurried for did not actually exist. For a few moments despair took hold as all the bad moments of the day crowded in on my consciousness. At best I was faced with a hideously expensive taxi, at worst a very long walk in darkness back to Keswick. It was then that I noticed my saviour in the perfunctory words and figures of the timetable. There was one last bus, at 6.45 p.m, which did run in October. My mood almost instantly lifted. The glories of the glowering clouds and sunlit Solway returned to my mind's eye. It had not been such a bad day. To cap things off I was right next to a bar. Twenty minutes later, my bog ridden self was sitting at a table in the Castle Inn Hotel, sipping a pint and eating spaghetti bolognaise. Life was good.

Lonely Miles Back o' Skiddaw

Knott is an uncomplicated name for a fell. It means simply 'hill'. It has nothing about it that speaks of romance or drama such as the names Helvellyn or Glaramara do. Its name, perhaps more than that of any other Lakeland fell, evokes thoughts of dullness, drabness and the uninspiring. No-one could be bothered to give it a proper name so they just called it what it was, a hill. For a number of reasons though Knott has gradually become a favourite of mine as it has revealed its secrets over successive climbs and made me realise that a bland name does not always make for a bland fell.

In my early years exploring the Northern Fells, Knott called to me. This was in part because I have always had a yearning for off the beaten track places and although the name was ordinary, it also spoke for something that was uncompromising, wild and untameable, that did not conform to picture postcard images of Lakeland. Many, including myself, have been surprised to learn that Knott is actually higher than, say, the celebrated Pavey Ark. The fell, occupying a dominant position, as the King of the Uldale and Caldbeck fells, is a huge entity with a number of radiating ridges. Here was surely a place to discover that must have many secrets.

My first acquaintance with Knott was an out and back bagging exercise from Great Calva, perhaps the least inspiring method of getting to Knott as it crosses some rather boggy ground. Yet although my choice of route was uninspiring, the summit itself lived up to my expectations. True it is as flat as a pancake and is lacking in depth of view. But the view still manages to be enormous and the feeling of altitude impressive. On Knott one feels high. That day Knott was wreathed in a mist that hung just above the summit. From under that mist a view of distance and clarity could be seen, but the dour grey mist only strengthened the uncompromising nature of the place, as did a hailstorm encountered on the way back to Great Calva. Neighbouring Great Calva, with its neat summit and conical appearance, remained superior in my mind to Knott. My next excursion to Knott was via another rather nondescript ridge route from High Pike. Once again I enjoyed the summit of Knott for what it was, but could not say that the fell increased at all in my estimation as a result. It was still what I had expected it to be all along. It had not disappointed, but neither had it exceeded expectations.

During the research for this book though all that was to change, as a reluctant regard for Knott changed into a genuine affection for the fell. I discovered that if you want Knott to reveal its hidden charms, you have to climb the fell for its own sake and not just as an afterthought to another fell. It is the high point of this region and treating it as such has revealed much to delight in. Knott is far more than a flat topped fell with a wide ranging view. Its best bits are well hidden from the summit.

For some time during the planning of the walks for this book, the ascent of Knott from Fell Side had called to me. Fell Side is a tiny hamlet on the far northern border of the Lake District, just a few houses and a farm. It is something of an adventure just to get to Fell Side, let alone begin this walk. The rural country north of the Uldale and Caldbeck Fells is served by few buses these days and the car journey to Fell Side is along the quiet strips of road that skirt this forgotten area. Here exists a part of Lakeland far removed from the tourist honey pots of the more central areas. I imagine that little has changed here since Wainwright's time and the whole area has a pastoral charm and gives a curious feeling to the visitor of having time warped fifty or sixty years, back to a quieter, more relaxed world. Fell Side therefore called out as an ideal place to begin a secret Lakeland walk. Stan gave me a lift to the start point. He had planned to meet me on Knott from a different route. As he drove away I really did feel like I had been transported into the back of beyond. There was no-one around except me.

A minor road leads round the back of the farm and onto a rougher road heading into the folds and corners of these smooth green fells. To begin with there is little impression of the drama to come. Brae Fell dominates to the right, but that was not today's objective. My destination was further in, hidden around a bend in the landscape and seeming more wild and secret for being hidden. The road makes for quick walking and for the type of walking where most of the time one can look at the view around rather than one's boot laces. On this day, with legions of white clouds racing through the sky above and a constantly evolving mix of sunlight and shade crossing the fells, there was a great sense of space and freedom. However, as I crossed Dale Beck and the road became a smooth wide track, this sense of space became more constrained by the encroaching fells. The long arms of Yard Steel and Birk Moss loomed over me to right and left. The beck is charming enough, as is the grassy track above it. But there is a slightly intimidating feeling as one continues towards the terminus of the valley, which is dominated by the rarely seen but rather impressive wall of Iron Crag. My starting point at Fell Side was now obscured by the fells surrounding me. It was as if I had willingly funnelled myself into some dead end trap. There was not a soul about and the ruined mine workings of Roughton Gill, visible ahead, only served to heighten the eerie nature of the place. Where once had thrived an industry, now there were only ghosts and the echoes of the past. I cannot say that I found this place beautiful in the same way I have found so many other secret Lakeland walks. It certainly had a kind of haunting, forgotten beauty about it. Here I also felt lonelier and further from 21st Century civilisation than I did on any other walk in this book.

At the head of the valley the only realistic way out and onto the spacious fells above is a scramble up Roughton Gill or a clamber over the very steep Balliway Rigg. Either option is pretty much pathless and rough. Wainwright suggests Balliway Rigg, if Roughton Gill looks 'too intimidating', but having come to this wild valley head, it would be a shame to miss its highlight. I decided that I would follow alongside the gill where I could and if I found anything that looked a bit dodgy, I would then detour onto Balliway Rigg. Roughton Gill is a series of mini waterfalls, cascades and rock pools set dramatically amidst a scene of heather and grassy flanks. If it were in the heart of the Lake District it would be more celebrated, but as it is you may well have it to yourself as I did. Threads of path make their way alongside and at times slightly scarily above the gill. Some paths seemed to lead to dead ends, at which point a detour away from the exact line of the gill was my preferred choice. There is no set way of tackling Roughton Gill. Some walkers may prefer to keep a higher line above the gill and not get to close to its dangers. On the other hand there are those hill walking types who may stick to the exact course of the gill and indulge in a spot of 'gill scrambling' as I believe it is known. Now I enjoy putting my weary feet into the lovely cold waters of a gill sometimes, but the idea of scrambling in the water and over slippery rocks and greasy, mossy banks is not my idea of fun. However, it is your choice, so indulge in the freedom to make it. That freedom from the shackles of convention is all part of the secret Lakeland experience.

About half way up the gill the sun came bursting from behind the clouds, lighting up a particularly lovely cascade and plunge pool in a glistening display. Gone was the oppressive, slightly forbidding mood of the valley floor, to be replaced by a life enhancing scene. I stared mesmerised by the flowing water for a couple of minutes before noticing, rather tardily, that across the other side of the gill was a large dark hole pierced into the naked rock. I had found one of the two old mine levels mentioned by Wainwright. Knowing the dangers of these levels, which AW frequently reminds us walkers of, I had no desire to cross the beck and explore the level further. Its dark secrets could remain that way.

A crossing of the gill can be made after the last cascade, where the drama peters out into the more familiar heather, grass and marsh of the open fell side. At last I could see my objective, Knott, a quarter of a mile away and just a few hundred feet higher. How much more worthy Knott felt climbing it this way, as opposed to just bagging it from Great Calva or adding it on to High Pike. With the air of relaxation that comes when you know you have overcome a challenge, I found a dry nameless little patch of land and reclined back, doing nothing more for a few minutes than watch the clouds pass above and admire the space and distance of the view around me. In places like this, with vast open panoramas, I find that this very space enters me and gives my conscience a wider, more balanced, outward looking view. It is the exact opposite of the inward, subdued self that one might exhibit amongst the seething mass of, say, Oxford Street in London. Grand thoughts are born from meditation in the hills.

Just a few hundred feet of grassy slope remained now to the summit of Knott. My best mate Stan had walked in from Mosedale and taken a wild route over the flank of Knott given the functional name of Snab, a route that even Wainwright himself does not describe and one which I plan to do some day. Having spent about three hours in utter seclusion, I was eager to have my best friend's company. By a quirk of fate, or perhaps mere coincidence, we both reached the summit of Knott at almost exactly the same time. Although Wainwright is correct that the summit of Knott is as flat as a cricket pitch, I would argue with him that 'no suggestions can be made for whiling away the time'. Admittedly the view does lack the important component of depth, but it has a great feeling of distance and spaciousness. If Wainwright was still alive and active on the fells and we met and got into a discussion about Knott (unlikely given his character), I would provide him with the suggestion for whiling away the time that Stan and I indulged in. You will have heard of children playing snow angels in the snow and sand angels in the sand. Well that day on Knott, Stan and I invented the Knott Angel. With childish delight we lay flat on our backs, formed a star with our legs and arms and simply listened to the chorus of the skylarks and watched the great white clouds above, as they first fused together to close a patch of blue sky and then a few minutes later drifted apart, dragging at their edges great spinning tails of cloud, revolving like galaxies. I am sure AW would have enjoyed this pastime, but each person experiences a fell in their own way. The fact that Wainwright does not rave about Knott does not mean that he is right. There is no right or wrong in such matters and nor should there be.

As Stan had parked at Mosedale, that would be the ultimate objective for both of us. This necessity, however, did not preclude us both taking a new route off Knott, a route that is very fine in descent. A broad grassy path, another joy to tread initially, heads from the summit in the direction of Miller Moss and the Lingy Hut. Towards the hut itself and after the crossing of Grainsgill Beck, the path becomes a little rougher and boggier and here we met the only other walker on either of our days on Knott's flanks, a solo walker with a dog, who passed a few words with us and then headed on up towards Knott, in what was now fading light.

This area's penchant for unusual names continues with a crossing of the minor stream of Arm o'Grain. With an obsessive love for everything Lakeland I wanted to find out the origin of this name. When I did find out, there was one of those groaning moments, when you realise that it is really quite obvious. The main stream or gill here is called Grainsgill Beck. Its tributary, being joined to the larger watercourse, is quite simply the Arm o'Grain.

This route in descent is a particular delight when the heather on Coomb Height is in bloom and covers one huge arc of the scene in purple. Beauty is also in the more distant prospect, with the delightfully inviting valley of Mosedale stretching ahead towards the flatlands. More mining activity is in evidence here, but whether it was my sunnier mood, the company of Stan, or just a plain fact, these old ruins did not seem nearly as foreboding and tinged with sadness as those at Roughton Gill. Path became old mine road, became tarmac road in a gradual return to civilization. Still it is only a very minor road, with just the odd dwelling to keep it company and the remaining mile and a half back to Mosedale is a constant joy in the right conditions.

Mention of Mosedale reminds me that there is also a lonely and quiet route up the fell that starts from here and climbs Knott, via the intervening Coomb Height. The approach march is quite long and it is possible to park at the road end of the valley, but for those that feel a summit should be earned and feel satisfaction in merely putting one foot in front of the other, the full walk will be the preferred option. It's a delightful walk anyway, in early May at least, with the vibrant yellow of the gorse bushes of Carrock Fell's lower slopes to your right and to your left the soft, aural backdrop of new-born lambs, carelessly chasing each other through the fields.

The ridge of Coomb Height, initially disconcertingly distant, gradually with each foot fall, slowly and imperceptibly grows in size. Finally the point is reached when one leaves the tarmac and boot meets rock, grass, heather and bog. A narrow path leads up from the base of the ridge, twisting and turning through the heather as height is gradually gained. Dominant on the left is the back shoulder of Bowscale Fell. Carrying on further up the ridge, the angle eventually eases, heather giving way to grass and wider expanses of sky and fell.

Looking all around, I suddenly realised what a bleak and very isolated position I was in. I had that odd sensation people describe as though someone is walking over your grave. Lover of solitude though I am, I was a little spooked. On a grey day as this was, with the clouds low, there are few places in the Lake District with quite this sense of isolation and loneliness. For a while it plagued my mind, I even became convinced that there was someone, or perhaps something, behind me. I quickened my step accordingly, to escape my imaginary pursuer. All wild imaginings and ninety percent of the time I love the wild and would laugh at this folly, but just occasionally these empty places do affect one in odd ways.

In my haste to be somewhere familiar, I wandered away from the rather indistinct path, trending round to the northern side of the ridge. It was an outcome not without its rewards, for there was an opening panorama looking across the head of Grains Gill Beck, towards High Pike. Suddenly I realised I was on a sheep track and heading round the side of Knott, instead of towards the summit. So I left this fool's path and headed back up to the ridge again, for the final march to the top. Here I forgot my imaginary pursuer and revelled in being alone on the familiar, flat summit of Knott.

My final secret Lakeland walk up Knott was planned to start at the tiny hamlet of Orthwaite and end at the equally tiny hamlet of Longlands. This would necessitate approximately a mile and a half of road walking, either at the start or end of the walk. I have always found that it is best to get any tarmac stretches done at the start of the day if one can, as tired and sore feet do not enjoy the hard unyielding nature of road surfaces. So it was that the car became parked beside the lonely tarn of Over Water – this would necessitate a mile of road walking at the start of the day, but enable the return leg on the road to be shortened to half a mile, a fair compromise. Over Water is a shy creature and unless you have a fishing permit there seems to be little way of actually accessing the shore of the tarn, which seems to be mainly private, although I have never been bothered enough to try and find out. What Over Water lacks close up though, it makes up for when viewed from above, where it appears as a quiet jewel in a peaceful landscape of fields, hedges and trees. I never mind walking down this stretch of minor road. Particularly on a sunny morning this lane has a rural charm, a sense of stepping back in time, that is a characteristic of this most northern of Lakeland areas. Just past the cluster of houses that is Orthwaite, and around a sharp bend, is a large gate upon which is written something like 'Caldbeck and Uldale Commons'. Who would have thought that a simple sign on a gate could inspire such joy? Its sign may as well read 'enter here for tranquillity and lonely adventure'.

Shutting the gate behind you, the route begins as a broad gravel track, but after only a few hundred metres Wainwright suggests a choice of a route A or a route B. Both routes will eventually meet up, but route A is by far the finer. It has both the advantage of a better path and height over the other route. So follow this grassy slanting traverse up between the bracken, steeply at first but before long levelling out into a grand traverse, with Burn Tod and Knott dominating ahead. As the path levels out, a very short detour, a matter of a few feet from the path, takes one to the little collection of sharp rocks that mark the top of Brockle Crag. This is not a Wainwright, or even I suppose a proper summit, but it is a fine place to linger. A place to nourish the soul. It is not a place that generally registers with those familiar with the more famous high places of Lakeland. There are some places, however, that evoke something within the brain and the consciousness of the individual. It is as impossible to sum up as it would be impossible to describe a piece of music using only words. There is something about the arching span of Park Wood below, the side-on view of Bassenthwaite Lake, the opposing heights of Sale Fell and Setmurthy Common and the sweep of flat land down the Vale of Embleton towards Cockermouth, that just clicks for me. Add to that the wonderful peace and pastoral charm of the place and it is to me a recipe made in heaven. When I am old and can no longer manage to toil up scree and boulder to the highest summits, or even make it to the top of Knott, I hope I can still climb the three hundred feet from Orthwaite to the summit of Brockle Crag and here while away the hours in meditation and reminiscence of the years when I cared only about the highest summits and the grandest views.

The path remains pleasant and easy as far as Hause Gill, where a crossing of the water needs to be made. Burn Tod now rises imposingly

The author admires the view from Brockle Crag

ahead and here the stream bifurcates with one arm, now called Burntod Gill, heading away towards the secretive gap of Trusmadoor and the main arm of Hause Gill heading up towards the col between Knott and Great Calva. It is the Hause Gill way that the route heads, taking a faint, grassy path a couple of hundred feet above the gill, which is a little marshy and indistinct at first but soon improves to a narrow, stony path, as the valley walls contract into a delightful ravine. Occasionally a walker finds an unexpected special place, a place that neither the map, nor even Alfred Wainwright in his guide, shouts about. Wainwright simply refers to the 'wild upper recesses of Hause Gill'. Evocative indeed but this narrow defile is about more than that. It is a true hidden Lakeland gem. For a few hundred feet of walking the valley narrows to such an extent that its walls confine a space no more than perhaps thirty feet across, through which both the path and the purest of streams thread, the path continually switching first one side and then the other side of the gill, in a childlike play. As we entered this sanctuary a solo walker passed us, his face lit with a knowing smile. We exchanged comments about the hidden delights of the place. A short while later I found myself reclining in comfortable grass, with one hand resting in the stream on a soft, moss covered stone, as the blissful caress of the cool water rushed over my skin. This was

Stan in the delightful confines of Hause Gill

about as close to Nirvana as I am probably ever likely to get. It is true that sometimes the simplest pleasures can be the most profound.

The only problem with the ravine of Hause Gill is that it is but a brief acquaintance. All too soon you pop out of the ravine and onto the more familiar grassy expanses of the ridge leading from Great Calva to Knott. Hause Gill ravine leaves one wanting more and I shall be returning as soon as I can. The final few hundred feet to the top of Knott were on the old familiar route. Apart from Stan and I, Knott itself was entirely free of people. This made a hat-trick of summit experiences on Knott in 2011 without meeting a single person. Such a succession of wonderful ascents and descents, coupled with a wildness and solitude I have rarely experienced, has elevated Knott in my estimation.

This time we chose a route in descent that I can honestly say is one of the easiest ways down from 2000 feet. The path provides the red carpet treatment for one's feet and you are likely to be alone within this wonderful, golden coloured, landscape. From Knott it is an easy descent and a short pull to the summit of Great Sca Fell. There is not a lot to recommend this summit. As summits go it is one of the poorest in Lakeland, with Wainwright referring to the top being 'as flat as a crown bowling green and several acres in extent'. Despite the large grassy plain of the summit, with not a stone in sight, a person or persons have taken the time and effort to find some stones and form them into a decent sized cairn. Why, is frankly beyond me. The stones must have come from much lower down the fell, or perhaps even from dried up stream beds nearby. It must have taken considerable effort, an effort wasted in my view. Although few would rave about Great Sca Fell, it will always be significant to me. This is not though for reasons of romance, but purely for the fact that Great Sca Fell was my hundredth Wainwright fell.

Before leaving Great Sca Fell's summit topography altogether, a visit should be made to its lower neighbour, Little Sca Fell. Little Sca Fell is living proof that the best place on a fell is not necessarily to be found on the highest ground. Little Sca Fell has altogether more of the feel of a defined summit than its greater sister. The view has the necessary depth to be pleasing to the eye, and encompasses a wide sweep of the Cumbrian Plains and the surrounding fells. A short detour to the edge of the fell reveals a decent plunge down towards Meal Fell and Trusmadoor. It is also from here that Over Water's distant sheet is somehow more aesthetically appealing than from close up.

Having taken in the final summit of the day, enjoy the luxury of the old bridle road heading towards the ravine of Charleton Gill. This next half mile is surely some of the most gloriously free and comfortable walking in the district. The path narrows slightly and becomes a little boggy in places as it reaches the banks above the gill. But it is minor league bog and the route remains a pleasure until the path broadens again as the bridle road continues. Charleton Gill is not as impressive as Roughton Gill, or as confined and beautiful as the upper reaches of Hause Gill, but it has a certain wistful charm and wildness about it. Lower down the gill Wainwright refers to 'a little twisted ridge', which has the name of Saddleback. Anyone expecting anything remotely resembling the architecture of the more famous fell of that name will be disappointed. The Saddleback here is little more than a grassy wedge of land and, presuming I did correctly identify it, will soon be hidden under a canopy of freshly planted trees, in a fenced off area. This area is apparently being replanted to return a part of the landscape to how it must once have been before the sheep and deer mowed it bare. At the moment, with various fences and plastic poles in evidence, it does not look that great a decision, but I am sure in twenty or thirty years time it will be a delight and shown to be a worthwhile project. Hopefully, at age 72, I can still struggle up here and enjoy it!

The old bridle road soon joins the old gravelled road, which leads in a wide curve down to the hamlet of Longlands, where two sheepdogs in a circular raised garden greeted us. Now you have the advantage of having parked the car at Over Water, as it is just over half a mile down a leafy and pleasant lane to get you back to your starting point. Along the way look out for the little snippet of view of the shy stretch of water called Chapelhouse Reservoir. With your eyes fixed to the road and the view ahead you will not see it. However if you wait till the top of the gradient rise in the road, just past Lowthwaite and turn your gaze over your right hand shoulder, you will see the reservoir hidden in a hollow. It is not the grandest stretch of water in the district, but for those like me who enjoy the simple pleasure to be had from locating something on a map it is quite a prized possession. One wishes for a path from the Lowthwaite Road to the car park at Over Water, but there isn't one, so a bit of a dog leg on the minor roads is needed. It is quite satisfying at the end of the day to see Over Water shy and reclusive on the level and know that you have looked down on its finest aspect from 2000 feet.

So I had three trips to Knott in the space of a few months and three times met no-one, apart from Stan, on the summit. That this was probably due more to luck than anything was demonstrated by the two research trips that I did on High Pike and Carrock Fell. On my earlier trip to Fell Side, when headed for Roughton Gill, I had started the walk with not a soul in evidence. This time however there was a minibus in the little car park by the farm, with a group of young school day trippers also headed for the hills. The author was beginning to mutter under his breath about not being able to call this secret Lakeland, when the group, instead of heading up High Pike, continued on the rough road towards the Roughton mine workings. I vaguely overheard them talking about geology and made the inference that they were on some kind of field trip that would perhaps not involve High Pike. It goes to show that solitude can never be taken for granted. On my walk into the recess of Roughton Gill, I had the place totally to myself. However, had I decided to do that walk on this day, I would have ended up playing tag and tail with about 30 school children.

Instead the slopes of High Pike proved as quiet as I had hoped. This ascent is pleasant throughout and with a height advantage of nearly a 1000 feet to start with, there is only a little over 1300 feet left to climb. This was a day of sunshine and showers, in some ways one of my favourite types of hill weather. Provided they are not accompanied by buffeting winds, the showers will keep the air clear and the landscape hues washed to a magical brilliance. Roughly along the 1600 foot contour and close to the path are several fenced off mine shafts, further evidence of the industrial past of this now tranquil corner of Lakeland. I certainly would not advise vaulting the fence surrounding these workings to take a closer look, as hidden dangers lurk in their depths. Before long the dome of the final pull to the summit comes into view and then the collection of oddities marking the summit itself. I'm not a great fan of man-made addenda on summits, but given that they were there on High Pike in Wainwright's time, and together they give the fell something of a unique feel, I suppose I can make an exception. Please though no more cairn building in the Northern Fells and certainly no more stone benches of the type found on the summit of High Pike. The trouble with a stone slab to sit on is that in most weathers experienced in the Lake District it is rather a chilling experience for one's backside. Plus when the wind is roaring it provides little shelter. Not to worry though for there is also a sizeable cairn and shelter up here to hunker down behind, along with an Ordnance Survey column, and further north the site of a beacon and even the ruins of an old shepherd's cottage. All of these semi-permanent artificial augmentations I had seen on previous visits to High Pike but today it was instead the fleeting natural wonders that seized my attention. For to the north were several large shower clouds, like great grey battleships, each one firing its own curtain of rain to the ground below. Between each of these amorphous masses was a peerless view across the Cumbrian plains, with every field and village picked out in detailed clarity. There are not many experiences in life that one can guarantee not to forget and during the course of twenty odd years in the fells I have had hundreds of great experiences, but I hope that this is one that I will truly not forget. The camera could not do it justice, but in the mind's eye it remains clear.

I guess Stan and I were lucky to have this spectacle to ourselves for a few minutes before a group of four walkers with a dog came into view, approaching the summit from the Lingy Hut direction. It was decidedly breezy on High Pike that day so we searched for a sheltered and hopefully warmer spot on the leeward side of the massive shelter and cairn. After no more than a minute of starting on my well-earned lunch, the group of four decided to join us. Fair enough, as they needed shelter as much as we did. However, the lady with the dog sat so close to me that the dog was sitting on my jacket and eyeing up my roll. I am not a great fan of dogs, although I can see why walkers get pleasure having them as companions on the fells. However in my experience it seems that dog owners, who are sometimes far worse than the dogs they own, often misguidedly believe that other walkers are going to have the same enthusiasm for their dog as they do. Such was the case with this lady, who started telling me all about her pooch and how he loved walking the fells and what a lovely dog he was. I am sorry if I seem curmudgeonly, but having climbed a fell, I am more concerned with my lunch and the view than with the vital statistics and achievements of this stranger's mutt. I also resented the invasion of personal space that having the dog within a few inches of my face represented. By nature I am polite, unless severely provoked, but I sometimes long to be the type of person that can just tell someone what they are thinking in a situation like this, rather than just tolerate it. Instead I found myself making polite conversation, whilst an insistent voice within was saying 'just get up and walk away'.

It was not long and at a convenient pause in the doggy talk, before Stan and I did get up and walk away, headed now for Carrock Fell. If you do High Pike and time allows, it is too tempting for most walkers not to do Carrock Fell as well, both for the contrasting view and because these two fells are an obvious pair. Aside from that Carrock Fell is very different from High Pike and indeed different from any of the other fells in this area. Its long ribbons of grey coloured scree, contrast sharply with the greens and browns of the heather and grass that is predominant in this area Back O'Skiddaw. They are in fact more reminiscent of Skiddaw's flanks, on a minor scale of course. The walk between High Pike and Carrock Fell is not the most thrilling, although on a clear day the sweeping panorama is still fine. Milton Hill is a bit of a no-man's land and blessed with a name that is about as exciting as its appearance.

Although higher than High Pike, by a matter of a few feet, Carrock Fell does not, in my opinion, have quite as fine a prospect, although it makes up for this in two ways. Firstly, the summit is a nice little rocky plinth and, secondly, it has a fine view down to the Caldew valley. I was able to appreciate neither of these on my previous trip to Carrock Fell due to an attack by a swarm of giant midges, but today the breeze kept the midges at bay and for a while we again had Carrock Fell to ourselves. Then by a cruel twist of fate, history repeated itself. For the second time that day we decided to shelter, this time in a deep round shelter just away from the summit. For the second time that day we soon had company. The shelter was comfortable for two walkers to recline in, especially when those two walkers were each six feet tall and one of them had a sizeable belly. There was not really room for a third walker, unless perhaps it was a loved one who you could cuddle up closely to. Had I come across two walkers in this shelter I would have left them to themselves and relocated to one of a myriad other natural shelter spots that exist on the rocky summit of Carrock. So both Stan and I were rather surprised when a man, perhaps in his mid fifties, with a large frame and a bit of a belly like myself, poked his head into the shelter and asked, 'Do you mind if I join you?' Now such a question is a bit like someone pointing a gun to your head and asking 'Do you mind if I pull the trigger?' There is only really one answer you can give. To the gun question you have to say 'no', or risk getting blown away and to the shelter question you have to answer 'yes', or risk being seen as rude and entering into an unseemly argument, which is the last thing most walkers want on a day out in the fells. So we were held over the proverbial gun barrel and both answered 'yes', although our voices could not perhaps hide a slight tinge of annoyance. Earlier in the day I had had the dog sitting on my jacket and snuggling up to me, so it was only just and proper that this time Stan had the dubious pleasure of the walker trying to squeeze himself into the shelter, who was almost sitting on him. I guess even now the experience might have been acceptable if the walker had been a nice friendly chap, ready to regale us with his years of experience in the fells and listen and compare our stories. That was not the case. He just sat there, ate his sandwich and said nothing. Generally speaking, misanthropes in the hills tend by their very nature to avoid others. I know this as I can be one. So here was something of an oddity, a misanthrope who wanted company. Having walked with Stan for over 20 years, I could tell that we were both sharing the same thought. It came as no surprise therefore when Stan said, 'I think we had better head on', which is a veiled way of saying that we could not stand a moment longer in this grumpy man's company and wanted to get away from the tension of the situation.

For a while the bad taste of our encounter lingered, as we muttered about how inconsiderate and unfriendly a minority of fell walkers can be – and I do stress a minority. There are many walkers with whom I have had delightful and informative encounters. It's just that generally speaking the slightly weird or curmudgeonly encounters make for better print! We headed back over Milton Hill, but instead of a complete re-ascent of High Pike, we took a broad, gravelly path that trends around the side of the fell. Although this path is a bit of a scar on the grassy environs of High Pike, one cannot deny that it provides a wonderful walkway at just below 2000 feet and the type of terrain where one can walk and absorb the spacious views ahead. This path eventually joins the old mine road leading to Potts Gill Mine and it was here that I had my first encounter with one of Lakeland's more curiously named objects, the Dumpy Stone. This large erratic boulder is something of an anomaly on High Pike, so much so that it gets its own name. Were it in Langdale or Borrowdale it would be in the company of thousands upon thousands of similar or bigger boulders and, like them, would have to suffer the ignominy of being nameless. Out here however, it can bask in smugness, knowing that it has a certain celebrity, having been illustrated by the great Wainwright himself in his High Pike chapter, page 6. I have tried to find a definitive reason for the name Dumpy Stone. Wainwright unfortunately does not provide one. The best I could do was a theory. There is a Dumpy Stone level in the mines hereabouts. The stone may have got its name from dumpy bags, which are a type of large bag used to carry stones and debris from mining. That, I am afraid, is the best explanation the author can offer for the time being, other than the boulder also being dumpy in appearance.

The mine road now skirts High Pike at the 1400 feet contour until it reaches Potts Gill Mine. If you think that the remnants of this mine area have a slightly more recent feel about them than, say, those at Roughton Gill, you would be right. This mine was still being worked for Barytes, used in the making of glass, fifty years ago. Its scars have yet to heal and moulder back into the landscape, as some of the older workings have done. If bound for Fell Side there is now a choice of continuing on a grassy path, that maintains the 1400 feet contour before descending over Fellside Brow, or making a descent from Potts Gill mine down the wide mine road. We decided to take the mine road and then a lower path at 1000 feet. This lower path passes a little covered reservoir. Much to the annoyance of Stan, I feel I have to try to find these features from the Wainwright guides. To walk past a feature is somehow not to complete a walk. The covered reservoir, when discovered, was about as boring as it sounds and Stan groaned, with a due sense of sanity questioning despair at the obsessions of his friend. I think he just wanted to be back at Fell Side and the car at this stage of the walk, rather than tracking down a reservoir, which because it was covered, couldn't be seen anyway! I could hardly blame him.

To many walkers a route description that begins 'the lower slopes are defended by an impenetrable barrier of bracken and gorse' would be enough to make them think twice about ascending that way. However, for a seeker of secret Lakeland this type of description, and the very fact that it might put off other walkers, make it a highly attractive proposition.

These were my thoughts when I chose the ascent of Carrock Fell from Mosedale as one of the routes for this book. I knew that I could be in for a rough climb and that my report might suggest that only gluttons for punishment need apply. I am glad to say however that I was pleasantly surprised by what I found.

There is a small grassy parking area just outside Mosedale from which the route begins. Soon a track leads behind some houses on towards the metalled road that leads down Mosedale valley, to the Skiddaw Forest wilderness in the distance. You only need stay on this road for a few hundred metres, and I would suggest at this point keeping a constant eye on the bracken, heather and scree slopes above, as you will need to find the best line up the fell. The first 500 feet of ascent are the toughest. Particularly when the bracken is high, the fragments of path may be totally obscured, which is why I would recommend this walk for spring. At this time of year it should be possible to pick up a thread of a path, rising up towards the scree line. If you can locate it, the climb will be a lot easier. In the early stages there is some prickly gorse, so the wearing of shorts is not advised, unless you enjoy physical pain. Higher up is a relatively easy, but rather tiresome trudge through scree. It's not particularly unstable scree, but rather awkward nonetheless, as the path seems to vanish and then reappear spasmodically. However, trust me, above this scree are treats for wilderness lovers worth persevering for.

Following the initial scree toil, a large dry stone bield appears. This is a lovely spot to get one's breath back. The views are not especially dramatic, although the crags above Bowscale Tarn are well seen. This place is less about the view and more about atmosphere. The floor of the bield has a lush grassy covering, almost carpet like. To recline here and spend a few minutes thinking about nothing is to escape. The bield has that odd, ghostly quality of abandonment. Here you could remain undisturbed, from dawn till dusk, forgotten and insignificant. The relatively busy summit of Carrock Fell is just 800 feet above and the popular road above the banks of the river Caldew is just 500 feet below and yet here, in between, is another world. And as you rise from your repose to carry on, you will see that it is indeed an odd world, yet eerily and quietly beautiful. Here is the plateau, the 'strange landscape of scattered blocks and boulders in heather' that AW describes. For the lover of landscape photography, several of these boulders make for great foreground subjects. In the Northern Fells, on a clear April day such as this, it was a joy to survey our surroundings: heather and grass mingling pleasantly in alternate brown and gold glorious crystal clear views across to the Pennines, the ever present shrill of larks crying from high above. There is now a reasonably clear path which leads to a situation of drama above the crags and where we found a wonderful little rock shelter, with a plunging view down to Stone Ends farm. From here it is not far to the familiar stone ring of the hill fort and tumulus that marks the summit of Carrock Fell. Aside from a little roughness in the early section, this route of ascent had been a joy, in unfrequented and unusual surroundings.

This time we were undisturbed on the summit of Carrock Fell. However there may have been a good reason for this. Until we reached the top the wind had been no more than a breeze, but on reaching the summit the full force of a northerly gale hit us. It was one of those occasions where the summit is touched momentarily before diving into the nearest shelter. Even though the wind was strong, had there been a couple of walkers in the shelter, Stan and I would have simply carried on and left Carrock Fell for another day, unlike the misanthrope from our previous visit. Walkers deserve their little bit of space. Luckily the shelter was free from anybody and we indulged in that slightly smug feeling of hiding from the raging elements 'outside'. The walk over Milton Hill was a battle against the wind, although at the same time quite exhilarating. The golden flanks of High

The strange plateau on Carrock Fell

Pike ahead and the thought of another sizeable shelter there kept us going. High Pike again had a few people milling around on top of it, but the wind was too strong to indulge in conversation and besides one of them, to our amusement, had his woolly hat blown off by the wind and was rushing after it.

It was only once we were bedded down on the leeward side of the massive shelter, that we suddenly realised the spectacle of the northern panorama. From these Northern Fells, clarity of view can usually be benchmarked by whether one can see the Solway Firth and into Scotland. If you can make out the hill of Criffel, the first sentinel of Scotland, then that usually indicates a reasonable clarity. If you can make out the Galloway Hills behind Criffel that usually indicates exceptional clarity. On this windy April day on High Pike, we witnessed the finest clarity into Scotland we had ever seen, and after 20 odd years of fell walking that is saying something. A huge arc of Scottish coast stretched into the far distance. Scotland's version of Lands End, the Mull of Galloway, could clearly be seen approximately 70 miles to the west of us. It was, however, the view into the Scottish interior that was most astonishing. In October 2010, just a few months before this walk, I had climbed Tinto, an isolated hill of 711 metres, which sits in Lanarkshire, just south of Glasgow. It is an odd phenomenon that having climbed a hill or mountain one then much more readily recognises it in a view from another mountain, even if that mountain is some miles away. Now we could see a distinctive hump way in the distance and seemingly to the east of the Galloway Hills. We both speculated that this might be Tinto, some 70 miles distant. We knew from our planning and study before we climbed Tinto that you could see the Lake District on a clear day from that hill. It therefore stood to reason that on a similarly clear day you could see Tinto from the northern Lake District. It was here that modern technology came to our aid. While I still always carry a paper map, it is now possible to have the entire collection of Ordnance Survey maps of Britain displayed on one's mobile phone. To know exactly your location on that map is a brilliantly effective tool for the hill walker. Often, I take a couple of minutes from my busy working day to simply study different parts of the country; places I have been to before, places I would like to go to, as well as places I will probably never go to. Since it would of course be impossible to carry the paper versions of all the Ordnance Survey maps in your rucksack, it's the only way to confirm the identity of distant objects on clear days. As such, Stan and I were able to plot a course from our location, in a direct line leading unerringly to Tinto. I have often regarded strong wind as the unseen enemy of a fell walker, but today the battle was worth it for the realisation that we could see deep into the Southern Uplands of Scotland.

Apologies in advance for the Health and Safety lecture, but while GPS and the capability to have all the Ordnance Survey maps on your phone is in my view a great addition to a hill walker's kit, the batteries on these advanced mobile phones tend to only last about a day or even less, depending on usage. Batteries fail, technology fails. It only takes a bit of rain inside one of these phones for it to stop working. So always carry a good old fashioned O.S. map and compass and don't forget to use them every now and again to keep your skills honed.

On this occasion, we had another route planned to get off High Pike. This was the Red Gate route, which branches off the main route between High Pike and Carrock Fell at a crossroads of paths, just short of Milton Hill. We thereby missed the chance to cross Milton Hill for the fourth time in recent months. A real shame! The Red Gate route appears to be so called because of the red colour of the eroded soil near the top of the route. This is a lovely grassy path leading into sublime pastoral scenery. It is the easiest route up and down Carrock Fell. Unfortunately our minds were rather blinkered to the pleasures of the path as we struggled down through the strong winds, which having aided the clarity of the view to Tinto, had once again become our enemy. Carrock Beck was crossed at a spot that would be lovely in calm and warm weather, but we were too wind battered to appreciate it and headed onto the rough mine road on the other side of the beck. Now we could march at near enough four miles an hour, back to the Mosedale Road and the car. Or so Stan must have been hoping. I, however, had other ideas. Near to the Driggeth Mine road was another of those Wainwright minutiae that I was keen to locate. Willywood Well is a spring and another of the Northern Fells' rather peculiar names. Now Stan is not one for confrontation but I could see his face drop when I said that the spring was described as 'difficult to locate'. For a little while I floundered around in some marshy nothing of a place next to the road, while a chilled to the marrow, weather beaten Stan looked on, trying in vain, to conceal his irritation. Then amidst the marsh I found a couple of stones from which a rather puny trickle of water was emanating. I declared that this must be the spring at which Stan cried out a sarcastic 'Hooray! Can we go now?' and marched off down the path. All I can say is that I may have found Willywood Well, but to be honest it was hardly worth finding and certainly not worth annoying my best mate over.

It was when, a few hundred yards later, I mentioned the Howthwaite Stone and whether we could locate it, that Stan finally cracked. He was heading back to the car and I could go and look for the stupid stone if I wanted to, especially as locating it would mean heading in the wrong direction and our ears were by this time in danger of dropping off, due to the biting wind. I conceded that friendship should take precedence over looking for Wainwright trivia, continuing instead on the mine road with Stan, headed now for Mosedale and the car. The Howthwaite Stone would have to wait for another day, although at least for now I have the next best thing, which is a picture of it on High Pike chapter, page 6 of the *Northern Fells Guide*. The last couple of miles along the road back to Mosedale were a delight as we finally got out of the worst of the wind, now enjoying a spell of evening sunshine. Although the odd car comes along this section, the road has large patches of velvety grass moorland at its verges, which can be used if a car passes by. Perhaps the prettiest spot is a footbridge and ford crossing Carrock Beck, where a delightful grassy verge provides the perfect place to sit and reflect on the day to the sound of rushing water. This was the last of the walks Back O'Skiddaw to complete my research for *Secret Lakeland* and I could only reflect that although these parts are becoming more popular, there are still many routes and vast swathes of land where, with a little luck, one is likely to be alone and often in wonderful surroundings.

The Children of Skiddaw

Skiddaw has sometimes been described as a great mother mountain with her children (the lower satellite fells) arranged at either side, like a family photograph. The popular Latrigg, with its ten minute stroll to the summit from the Gale Road car park, is sometimes known as the 'cub of Skiddaw'. Latrigg is the celebrity child of Skiddaw. Although its darkly wooded flanks are a favourite haunt of mine and contain some secret niches and nooks, it is not secret Lakeland terrain. However, there are other very worthwhile offspring, such as Lonscale Fell and Ullock Pike, which have routes where an absence of people is the norm. Climbing the routes I have already described on Skiddaw, and those of its subordinate junior fells, gives a proper sense of just how enormous the Skiddaw massif is. Using the Ordnance Survey map, I counted all the one kilometre squares and bits of squares to calculate a total surface area of Skiddaw. Not a very scientific method I'll admit but nonetheless a worthwhile approximation. The Skiddaw range occupies 36 square kilometres. That is a lot of space in which to find peace and solitude.

The Dodd Wood car park would not suggest itself to many people as the starting point for a secret Lakeland walk. A route that begins with a large car park, public toilets, a tearoom and several way marked routes through the woods, does appear to be the opposite of what this book is about. However the ascent of Long Side from Little Crossthwaite visits some surprisingly lonely and uncompromising places. The Dodd Wood enterprise no doubt provokes mixed reactions among fell walkers. Wainwright himself described the tree covered Dodd as a 'little wretch' stunted by its covering of trees and disowned by the parent fell Skiddaw. Personally though I am quite fond of Dodd and its wood, even though it can be a very popular place, with sometimes hordes of ill equipped walkers making their way to the summit, no doubt encouraged by the fact that it can be reached by a way marked route. However there are enough paths and tracks in Dodd Wood for there to be quiet corners, forgotten routes and darkly hidden recesses.

Dodd Wood at the beginning of March is a very different experience to Dodd Wood at the height of the tourist season. As Stan pulled into the car park, it was clear we'd managed to beat the rush – it was deserted. Perhaps the weather had put some people off; it was the sort of grey, drizzly day that even the most optimistic of people would concede was unlikely to brighten up. On the plus side though, the wind was light and the rain, although persistent, was not coming down in a torrent. We began the walk by following the way marked Green Route, something of an anathema to the ethos of secret Lakeland, but actually very charming and quiet on this misty, atmospheric day. Although the Green Route initially heads in the opposite direction to Dodd, have faith, for after a steepish ascent the path doubles back on itself and then makes a lovely traverse of the woods. Here the path is a glorious shelf between steep and dark banks of trees. I have always loved walking through these forest tunnels and, with wisps of mist hanging in the boughs of the trees, it was a delight.

The Green Route eventually lands a walker onto the summit of Dodd. When Wainwright was writing the *Northern Fells Guide*, little concession had been made by the, then, forestry enterprise for walkers wishing to visit the top of Dodd. The summit was covered in trees and Wainwright described it as 'a place to visit – and flee from'. The cairn was hard to locate and the view could only be seen either by those who were seven feet tall or by those who could jump high enough to snatch a little peek over the trees. Even in 1990, when I first climbed Dodd with my brother Peter, it was a difficult summit. I remember various red signs warning of danger from tree felling and only being able to gain the summit by slow and awkward progress clambering over felled trees. Things are altogether different in 2011 and the difference, I feel, marks both changes in the philosophy of the forestry enterprise towards visitors and also the increase in popularity of the Wainwright fells. These days there would be an outcry if a Wainwright summit was barred from access by fallen trees. Nowadays the Green Route leads one easily to the summit of Dodd. Dodd summit has been shaved of its covering of trees; just a few stubbly remnants litter the fell side. A broad gravel path now leads to the top. The view is now spacious, with the deep plunge down to Bassenthwaite Lake being one of the finest exposed situations in the Lake District. The summit of Dodd no longer represents a place of solitude as it did in Wainwright's time or when I first climbed it. But surely only a curmudgeon of a walker would prefer the old Dodd, deprived of its wonderful view. I for one would rather share such a view with a few people, than struggle over felled trees only to see nothing!

All of which digresses somewhat from the route up to Long Side and readers will start wondering where secret Lakeland has gone to. Well fear not, Stan and I were about to well and truly head away from way marked trails and colour coded routes. Where the Green Route meets the main forest road, the Wainwright guide indicates to follow the forest road towards Long Doors before doubling back on oneself at a slightly higher altitude, on a higher forest road. However, it occurred to Stan and I that this was quite a circuitous way of getting to a point that could much more quickly be reached by just taking a straight, pathless line up through the trees. So with a sense of excitement we left the path behind. Now hereabouts, the trees are not solely the densely packed conifers that are found lower down and in other parts of Dodd Wood, but are a more varied and well spaced assortment of trees. This enabled a fairly straightforward, if very steep ascent to be made, with a pleasant carpet of pine needles and leaf mould making for easy terrain, with just the odd slippery foothold. I accept that this kind of pathless scramble will not be everyone's cup of tea, but it is undeniably secret Lakeland. At one point Stan and I just stopped and took in the secluded and sequestered atmosphere of this place, away from the beaten track. From a practical point of view, it made sense as well. It was only a few hundred yards of this pathlessness before a steep man-made bank was climbed and we found ourselves on the higher forest road. The Green Route is now long since left behind and this forest road has an unfrequented feel about it which increases as it gives way to a rough forest track. Once designed for vehicular access, this track has clearly fallen out of use, as nature is well on the way to claiming it back for herself; there is grass and heather growing down the middle of the track and an overgrown, unkempt feel, although it is still at this stage an easy route for a walker. It was along this section of track that we stopped and sat by the verge, admiring the mist swirling around the shaven head of Dodd and the grey waters of Bassenthwaite Lake below us, barely visible in the gloom. A magical spot, far removed from the colour coded routes and the familiar images of Dodd Wood. Unfortunately the magic did not last and the next section of walking comes with a bit of a health warning. If you enjoy pathless thrashing through fledgling trees, an awkward fence to negotiate with and a pathless heather flank to follow (all steeply inclined) then this could be the walk for you!

The reason for the track mouldering back to nature became clear. It no longer led anywhere and gradually petered out into a no-man's land of sapling trees. We tried more in hope than expectation to follow a vague sort of track, but this did no more than circumnavigate Long Side, rather than head upwards. We could see the forest fence that the guide indicated we had to cross and we were not getting any nearer to it by following this fool's track. Only one thing for it and that was to just make for the fence, over steep and rough heathery ground. The fence was a little higher and more awkward than it had appeared from a distance and negotiating it, while avoiding the snaring of various delicate parts of the anatomy, would prove to be a combination of judgment, experience and luck! Having crossed the fence we surveyed the remaining 600 feet of wild terrain leading to the crest of Longside Edge. The only way of making it slightly more bearable was to have frequent stops and turn one's back away from it, in the vain hope it would look a little more inviting once we had got our breath back. It didn't, but at least we were, on some level, enjoying our foray into an undeniably wild and unfrequented corner of the Skiddaw massif. There was a certain masochistic enjoyment to be had from thinking of ourselves as tiny ants on that great steep flank of Long Side, a flank which from a distance looks imposing and almost sheer. The place had atmosphere in spades, but I still prefer writing about it, in retrospect and comfort, than actually being there doing it! Of course the reason walkers put themselves through this kind of suffering is for the reward at the end. Our reward was the dramatic moment of emergence onto the Long Side Edge ridge, with GPS enabling us to score a bulls-eye on Ullock Pike summit.

An awkward obstacle on the steep flanks of Long Side

I guess it would have been an even greater reward for our pathless slog if the summit of Ullock Pike had offered up a clear view. Instead we were presented with thick mist and drizzle, again. However, we were just glad to be there with all thoughts of our heather trudge now behind us. It was at this moment, just as we had resigned ourselves to our viewless world of mist that a gaping hole in the gloom appeared, revealing a sweeping plunge into Southerndale. It is a subject of much debate between Stan and I, and perhaps among most fell walkers, as to whether it makes for a finer summit experience to have a 360 degree clear view or whether a sudden parting of mist to reveal a dramatic and unexpected portion of the view is better. It would be nice to have the best of both worlds, where you reach the summit in mist and it gradually clears over the course of half an hour, to reveal the majority if not all of the view. Such debates will continue to rage in the mind of us walkers. I would not want it any other way, for it is the variety of summit experiences that makes fell walking so endlessly enjoyable. There are some mountainous countries, in hot stable climates, where it hardly ever rains and where you can pretty much guarantee a view on any day. I personally prefer the unpredictable weather experienced during a lifetime of walking in the British hills.

It was a grand spectacle over Long Side and on to Carl Side, with the mist sometimes obscuring the view totally and then suddenly tearing apart to reveal vistas of Coledale or down into Southerndale. Our route down started on the familiar and often walked route down to Millbeck. Secret Lakeland had now been left behind. From White Stones we descended to the Long Doors col and so back onto the popular 'Green Route' trail on Dodd. However, as we descended the western shoulder of Dodd, even this normally popular route was devoid of people and we had a delightful traverse, high above Bassenthwaite Lake, to take us gently back to the car.

Lonscale Fell has for many years been a favourite fell of mine, a place I habitually associate with loneliness and relaxation. It is, therefore, not that surprising that this fell contains a number of what I would call secret routes. Perhaps more surprising, for those who simply think of Lonscale Fell as a bland shoulder of Skiddaw, is the quality and even drama of these secret routes.

Although Lonscale Fell is generally about the more subtle attractions of heather and grass, just like Bannerdale Crags it has its own secrets. Few travellers along the busy A66 can have failed to notice the fearful drop of crags from the summit of Lonscale Fell and from this angle it appears a most graceful and almost separate fell. However, this steep face of Lonscale Fell actually contains a perfectly safe, although a little exposed and very dramatic, route onto the fell. This is the north-east buttress of Lonscale Fell and is a secret gem of a place. In one respect it perhaps out ranks any of Lakeland's many more famous ridges in its sense of isolated situation and comparative height above the surrounding terrain. Walking along the slightly exposed and rocky section of the Cumbria Way beneath Lonscale Fell, the drops down to the Glenderaterra Beck and the sense of height, are already impressive. Once you head off the Cumbria Way path and make your way up the steep end of the north-east buttress, this sense of height increases with every hard won step. The bodily motions to be experienced going up the north-east buttress are more akin to scrambling than walking, but a type of scrambling that is less to do with rock, than with hauling oneself up extremely steep heather slopes. A little over half way up the north-east buttress, a full appreciation of the vertiginous situation can be made. Far down below, the grey path of the Cumbria Way winds its way into Skiddaw Forest; even further below, the Glenderaterra Beck makes its sparkling progress, while across this yawning chasm squats the massive hulk of Blease Fell, lending the situation an even greater sense of space and exposure. In four ascents of Lonscale Fell by this route so far, I have met no-one and felt truly at one with the ridge and its fantastic situation.

The ridge eventually flattens and trends above some fearful crags to the fantastic East Peak of Lonscale Fell. Although in height this is not the true summit, which lies on a flat area to the west, East Peak is in my view the spiritual summit and also the finest viewpoint on Lonscale Fell. The true summit, although a few metres higher, lacks the sheer drop that gives East Peak such a fine sense of a worthy mountain top. Over the years, I have perhaps spent a dozen hours of my life relaxing on East Peak, but maybe only a few minutes on the true summit of Lonscale Fell.

East Peak is a fantastic place for a quiet, peaceful contemplation of the Northern Fells. In many visits to this place I have rarely encountered a soul. From this airy vantage, the immensity of Skiddaw Forest can be truly appreciated. Looking into the heart of the Northern Fells the predominant colour is the brown of the heather, but it is surprising how beautiful and varied this brown can be, as it ranges from deep browns, to light browns, to sandy browns, depending on the vagaries of light and shadow. This landscape is perhaps at its finest on days of alternating sunshine and cloud, when the sun lights up areas of the heather in fleeting hues of gold, while the shade colours other areas a more sombre, dark brown. But this is not just a view into the wildness of the Northern Fells, it is also a fine view into Lakeland, especially down the natural rift of St John's in the Vale towards Thirlmere and beyond to Loughrigg Fell. This is the geological fault line that divides the Lake District in a north to south direction.

The north-east buttress of Lonscale Fell is a tough and punishing, but very rewarding climb. However, there is a route up Lonscale Fell that is even rougher, requiring an even greater level of single mindedness and determination. This is the ascent via Whit Beck. This is one of the few walks in this book that is not listed as a route of ascent in the Wainwright guide, which simply says, 'Whit Beck has fine scenery, but is too rough to use as a way up.' In some regards though, this is just as logical a way up, and no more horrendous, than say using Doddick Gill to climb Blencathra.

Whit Beck is a tributary of the Glenderaterra Beck, which is a river well known to those that have walked along the Cumbria Way into Skiddaw Forest. Of all the ways to climb Lonscale Fell, there is none with quite this sense of adventure. There is nothing more liberating that climbing a mountain across seemingly virgin territory, a rough wilderness where every foot of ascent must be fought for. In New Zealand they call this "bush-whacking" and its unwritten code is hard slog.

The route starts from the junction of Whit Beck with the Cumbria Way path. Fragments of path lead away up into the gill alongside the beck. The going becomes increasingly rough, with loose gravel and rotting driftwood at the waterside which serves to make progress awkward and at times meticulous. I was forced to make several crossings of the beck, as I climbed upwards, the ground alongside the water becoming on occasions impossible to negotiate. As these obstacles were eventually surmounted or circumvented, I worked my way further into the insidious tentacles of the mountain, into nature's embrace.

On a wet day, with impenetrable grey clouds overhead, the sense of solitude was intense. This is odd, considering that the main line up Skiddaw is at all times only a hundreds yards or so away from Whit Beck, at the top of the steep bank to your left. Yet here there is utter contrast and the people who are doubtless heading up Skiddaw may as well be climbing in another Universe. It felt completely alien to be here, cocooned in the womb of Lonscale Fell.

I fought my way upwards through cambered slopes, carpeted with thick heather, infested with bog. It was arduous and difficult going but strangely satisfying as the inches were gained. Soon enough the angle eased as I came across a line of fence posts, but the ground remained unremittingly squelchy. Just as the topography became more featureless, I was cloaked into a thick, grey blanket of mist. The only beauty here was in the notion of my solitude and separation from society. Often that is beauty enough.

Soon Whit Beck disappeared underground at its source and I felt a slight sense of losing a companion. Even though I had yet to visit the familiar summit of Lonscale Fell, I felt that the highlights of the day were behind me. I could not have been

Deep in the folds of Whit Beck

more wrong. Resting briefly at the summit, I noticed the cloud above me thinning, revealing a milky sun through the murk, although the mist remained unbroken. I continued on down to the edge of a forbidding precipice north-east of the summit. It was at this moment that a great tear appeared in the cloud and I was gifted with a sudden and dramatic view into Skiddaw Forest. This was a wonderful and unexpected reward after the arduous trudge to get here. Soon enough nature drew down her veil and we became strangers again. It had been worth it though, for the hidden intimacy of Whit Beck and that moment of revelation in descent. It almost goes without saying that I had met no-one.

Wainwright's route 'C' up Lonscale Fell (Lonscale Fell chapter, page 4 of the guide – used above in descent) was also my route of choice on a dark, glowering and very snowy winter's day. This route, which follows a fence almost all the way to the summit, is fine in descent but is a bit of a slog in ascent. The convex nature of this climb means that Lonscale Fell's summit and even the subsidiary East Peak, remain hidden until pretty much the end of the climb. Some heavy snow falls over previous days made this climb even harder going. The snow cover was uneven – for a few steps just a couple of inches in depth, the next steps wading knee deep, my legs filling with lactic acid. Plenty of stops were required, to get my breath back and allow my legs to recover, but also to look back at the sombre, yet striking views of the central and eastern Lake District fells, the snow and ice reflected a gun metal grey under the scowling leaden skies. East Peak, a place I had spent so many hours reclining upon in warm weather, was today a bitterly cold place, with no shelter from a piercing wind. My body was telling me to get down to somewhere less Arctic, but I was rooted to this spot, taking in the seldom seen prospect of Skiddaw Forest and its beloved surrounding fells, under snow. Gone for a day or two were the familiar browns and gold. Today all was white, silver and grey. Normally the beauty of Skiddaw Forest is enticing. Today it was a harsh beauty.

Following an extremely brief, hypothermic stop on the featureless true summit of Lonscale Fell, I headed down towards Skiddaw Forest via the delightful little ridge of Burnt Horse. This normally grassy route is very steep as it heads towards a sneck of land, lying between Lonscale Fell and Burnt Horse. Today it was a steep slope of thick but uniform snow. I had two choices. Either to slowly pick my way down this sharply angled descent, which did not seem like much fun, or to substitute feet for backside and slide down, which was distinctly enticing. Decision made, the next few seconds were a combination of heady, adrenalin fuelled rush as I shot down the mountainside on my bottom, before abruptly coming to a halt in a snow drift with a spontaneous vocal outburst of exultation. Yes, the cold had now seeped far into my underpants, but it was worth it for those few moments of exhilaration.

Burnt Horse is another place where I have often spent happy hours in contemplation. It generally has a wild but welcoming feel about it and is distinctive enough in my view to be a proper little hill, rather than just dubbed an offshoot from Lonscale Fell. Today, snow-covered under sulky heavy cloud cover, it was not quite so welcoming. It was at least sheltered from the bitter wind, although it was still well below zero. I needed a good stop, after several hours of more of less continuous tramping. So with two balaclavas on and thick gloves with hand warmers inside them, I took in the atmosphere of the place. Somehow, silence under snow is even more profound than other types of silence. Normally if we listen intently to the silence of a spring or autumn day, we can eventually hear something, bird or insect life, or the distant rush of water. Today the water was frozen and the wildlife, if it had any sense at all, was long since gone from this place. This was utter, uncompromising, silence.

By the time I had descended from Burnt Horse, I was chilled to the core. The Cumbria Way path leading back to Keswick is normally a joy to tread, but today it was a harsh place of raw wind. Ice was liberally scattered across the path and in some places, where the path became rocky and hugged to the fell side, high above the Glenderaterra Beck, it was more than a little dangerous. It was with some relief that I rounded the shoulder of Lonscale Fell and found myself back at the gate and fence that had marked my start up Route 'C' earlier in the day. Then I had been filled with joy in the snowy winter weather. Now I just needed to be warm. When I finally immersed myself in a hot bath at the B&B, it was a moment of profound bliss but also reflection, as I ruminated on the day's adventures. Lonscale Fell is truly a bastion of secret Lakeland and long may it remain so.

Blencathra - An Adult's Playground

Blencathra is an iconic mountain. Worthy of being in anyone's top ten list of Wainwright fells, its sweeping views are familiar to almost everyone that has walked in the Lake District. Its climbs via the popular routes of Sharp Edge or Hall's Fell are among the showpiece ascents of the Lake District. These attributes in themselves are enough to ensure front page status for Blencathra. Yet there is far more to this fell than meets the eye. Wainwright devoted 36 pages of the *Northern Fells Guide* to this one fell, more pages than for any other fell in all of the seven *Pictorial Guides*. This is partly due to the view, to which Wainwright devotes eight pages, but also to Blencathra having more routes and more diversity of ascents than any other fell in the Lake District. In total, Wainwright describes no fewer than twelve routes of ascent. Two of these, via Gategill Fell and Doddick Fell, are narrowing ridge routes, glorious climbs that give away little in terms of drama to their more famous near neighbours Sharp Edge and Hall's Fell, although are far less popular. Then there are the canyon routes of Blease Gill, Gate Gill and Doddick Gill, some of the roughest most uncompromising walking in the Lake District, contrasting with the easy grassy going of the lonely route by Roughten Gill. I remember as a child, I used to love play areas and the best were those with the most variety of slides, tunnels and climbing frames. I often think that as adults, fell walkers are indulging in something of the childish wonder of play. That to me is part of the reason why fell walking is so relaxing and invigorating. We regain contact with the simple pleasures of life that we used to enjoy unfettered as children. There is no better example of a fell walker's playground than the multi-faceted Blencathra.

Blencathra is also known on the Ordnance Survey map as Saddleback. While Saddleback describes the pronounced saddle of the summit ridge well, I don't know anyone that prefers this name nor have I ever heard it used. Wainwright refers to Saddleback only once in his 36 pages on the fell, a brief reference that speaks volumes for the great man's own preference. Blencathra is a far more beautiful name and is also the older name of the two. Its name derives from *blaen* meaning a bare hill top and *cathra* meaning a chair. Not quite the romantic origin you might imagine but a beautiful name nonetheless. Thankfully these days the word of Wainwright is pretty much final when it comes to the Lakeland fells and as he clearly preferred the name Blencathra, this name has become the popular name since the guides were published. The name Saddleback is dying out, but it is a death that will have few mourners. I could no more think of Blencathra as Saddleback than I could imagine Helvellyn having an alternative title, such as Whaleback.

Unless I am particularly rushed for time, which I try never to be when it comes to walking fells, I like to start ascents of Blencathra's massive façade from Keswick. There is a feeling of adventure leaving the car behind and simply using leg power to both walk to the base of, and then climb, a great fell. The track along the old railway line from Keswick also makes a beautiful start to a walk. So much more complete as a walk than just parking at the base of Blencathra and heading up. Mind you, the Keswick Railway Footpath did not exist when Wainwright wrote the *Northern Fells Guide* and this may be the reason why Wainwright does not describe an ascent of Blencathra from Keswick. The Railway Path is popular at almost any time of year. It is not secret Lakeland. However, its delightful combination of trees, bridges and fields, the moods and shifts of the River Greta below, from swirling cauldron to calm and still, plus the dead flat nature of the walking, makes for a grand start to any walk. There are places as well where side paths lead away from the flat straight course of the former railway track. Seek them out and you will find quiet and solitude just a stone's throw from the cyclists, joggers and walkers.

My first ascent of Gategill Fell began with the Railway Footpath. It is four miles' walking to Threlkeld where the route described in the Wainwright guide begins. This is one of the few stretches of four miles in the district where it is possible to actually average four miles an hour, although there are so many delightful places, calling for a quick stop that only the most time conscious of walkers will march without pause. Gategill Fell looms behind Threlkeld, resembling an ancient pyramid. On days where Blencathra summit is shrouded in cloud and mist, Gategill Fell seems sinister, as if threatening to crush or swallow the village below. On bright days it is just an inviting and benign friend. Whatever its mood, one cannot escape its presence when passing through Threlkeld. Sitting near the top of the fell is the rocky knoll of Knott Halloo, one of the Lake District's more quirky names. It sits like a wart on the brow of Gategill Fell.

Where Threlkeld village ends and abuts onto the open fellside there is a popular car park, and at the far end of that car park a footpath beckons you into the small and sometimes muddy gorge of Kilnhow Beck. This path joins a broad and grassy path which leads for some miles along the base of Blencathra, a stunning low level walk which I describe later in this chapter. A number of people were traversing this path and a shepherd was rounding up a flock of sheep, although I could see no-one on the great upward sweep of Gategill Fell, rising at an uncomfortably steep angle ahead. It was a warm, sunny day and I needed a pause before tackling the monstrous slope now towering over me. By the sparkling lower cataracts of Blease Gill I found the perfect grassy ledge to recline upon and prepare myself for the climb ahead. If in forty years from now this is as far as I can walk to, it won't be such a bad thing. Unfortunately the current version of me, aged 39, now had to get ready for slog mode. Up to the junction of two walls there was a pleasant path leading to the two small rock shelters and the remnant of wall pointed out in the guide. That was 400 feet of ascent done. The next 700 feet up to Knott Halloo, however, was an unremitting haul through gorse and heather, with virtually no path to guide the way. I fooled myself that my regular stops were to look at the ever expanding view and not instead the symptoms of impending middle age and an ever expanding waistline.

On reaching Knott Halloo it all seemed worthwhile and the slog was forgotten. Knott Halloo may appear like a wart from below but there is nothing ugly or wart-like about it on closer acquaintance. It is a rocky belvedere, with a grassy platform on top, which makes for a perfect seat. Now at over 2000 feet, there is that sense of height that marks the boundary between a hill and a mountain. Below my feet, cars and lorries on the A66 below looked like little insects crawling along in regimented columns, far removed from Knott Halloo in atmosphere, if not yet in distance. Tewit Tarn glistened like a precious stone waiting to be plucked out of the landscape. The ridge of High Rigg was well seen, backed by a snippet of Thirlmere and flanked by St John's in the Vale. All was pastoral and gentle, grass and fields and haze tinged, blue fells. Then I cast a glance onwards towards the ridge and Gategill Fell Top and a different scene greeted me. It was dominated by the angular crags and grey screes of Knowe Crags, where any grass was eking out a perilous existence in the few places it could take hold. This was one of Lakeland's secret vistas and it beckoned me on. Beyond Knott Halloo, a heaven sent grassy path leads to another higher rocky knoll and the miniature Striding Edge that Wainwright mentions. It is a grand situation on this grass and flaked rock fin. It is not a match in terms of scrambling and high drama to the real Striding Edge, but it makes up for this with its peace and solitude. Easy walking along this beautiful ridge continues, with Gategill Fell Top becoming increasingly imposing ahead. Just when you think things might get a little tricky, a line of scree continues to the right of the worst of the crags. It is then just a short hard pull and suddenly your head emerges level with the familiar summit path on Blencathra, like a solo appearance from a trap door on to a crowded stage.

Now, I am developing something of a habit of meeting some of the more, shall we say, oddball walking characters, while on the summit ridge of Blencathra. On an earlier visit a man had spent several minutes asking me what virtually every fell in the view was, until I felt like a human guide book. This time, as I emerged from the scree and onto the summit ridge, I was greeted by a friendly voice saying in surprise, 'Where the heck did you come from?' It was a young man, carrying a small camcorder, and staring at the LCD screen in a manner that told me he was recording. I said a bit about my route up Gategill Fell and how I would recommend it for a lonely walk. I then made the fatal mistake of telling him that I was writing a book about secret routes in the Lake District. He began asking me about my writing, all the time unnerving me by filming the conversation and speaking in a television documentary style manner. It was with a sense of relief that I reached the summit of Blencathra, Hall's Fell, to be greeted by a cluster of thankfully less eccentric walkers crowded round this small neat top. I could now melt into the throng, while my erstwhile camcorder companion conducted a narrated panorama of the view. A short while later, as I stretched out and took in the mighty plunge down to the A66, I smiled to myself at this meeting. Fellwalkers are a harmless species, some are eccentric, some are enthusiastic, some just nod and pass by and some say nothing or are even rude to you, but one way or another they all form part of the fabric of any journey through the fells. Experiences sometimes pleasant, sometimes educational, sometimes amusing, sometimes unpleasant, but very often long remembered.

Walking Blencathra's summit ridge from Hall's Fell to Blease Fell is a constant joy. The path is easy, the views far ranging and magnificent. Blease Fell forms the massive backside of Blencathra and is fringed by the drama of Knowe Crags that I had seen earlier from below. As a route up to the summit of Blencathra it is one of the least interesting, but as a route down and with some recent path improvement, it is about as easy and pleasant on the feet as any descent from 2500 feet can be. There is an abundance of grass on Blease Fell's massive shoulders and I often enjoy getting away from the path here and finding a comfortable place, where I can look down the Glenderaterra Beck towards my beloved Skiddaw Forest and its timeless cluster of fells. Lower down Blease Fell, with the temperature again increasing, I found myself overheating in the full blaze of the early summer sun. It was with some relief that I reached the shelter of trees surrounding the Blencathra Centre. I dowsed my head with water as I crossed the Glenderaterra Beck at Derwent Folds, but it was not enough to keep the heat at bay. So it was in one of those quiet spots near to the Keswick Railway footpath that I finally shook off the heat by bodily immersing my head in the River Greta and then laying back on a grassy bank with the generous shade of an old oak tree above me and cool rivulets of water trickling down my face. Surely this was the perfect end to a day in the fells. It was an ending not to be had by those who had parked at the base of the mountain and would by now be far removed from nature.

Gategill Fell is one of the beautiful ridge routes that sit either side of the celebrated Hall's Fell ascent. To the other side is yet another airy, but relatively neglected way to the top of Blencathra. This is Doddick Fell. If Hall's Fell is finest of these three ridges, with Gategill Fell a close second, then Doddick Fell is still a worthy third place. It loses by a nose and not a furlong over the other two. It is still a very fine route up Blencathra, particularly when combined with the path along the base of Blencathra, with its dramatic close up views into the heart of this complex massif. This low level tour along Blencathra's gnarled hand also provides a chance for an exploratory gaze into the canyons of Blease Gill, Gate Gill and Doddick Gill, before one decides whether to embark on these altogether different and rougher ascents.

Whereas my walk up Gategill Fell had been a relatively short walk, with Blencathra as the overriding objective, my ascent of Doddick Fell was to be a much longer and more demanding walk, with Blencathra merely the highest summit of three visited that day and the reaching of its summit just the start of a 20 mile campaign. There were two reasons for planning this massive outing. The first was just to revel in a massive all day walk in my favourite Northern Fells. The second was age related. For this was to be my first mountain walk upon reaching forty. There was therefore pride at stake. I guess I wanted to prove to myself that I could still do the massive Northern Fells tramps that were a feature of the joyous exploration of my early twenties. There was no reason why the onset of middle age should prevent any walker doing anything, but it is nonetheless comforting to know that on reaching that milestone some great curtain hasn't necessarily drawn down upon one's fell walking ambitions. Mind you, I was recently reading a book about South Pole exploration and apparently while those in their early middle age may no longer be the most fleet of foot and athletic, they do apparently have the most stamina for long and arduous journeys, hauling a sledge over

Antarctic wasteland. I hoped that what app-lied to exceedingly fit men racing to the South Pole, might also apply to this slightly over-weight and slight-ly fit, fell walker. To accompany me on this massive hike I had Stan with me, by a few months the younger side of 40 and also a lot leaner than me. Together we would motivate each other if weariness set in.

Starting the walk from Keswick at 10 am meant that we planned, and in fact wanted, to finish with our head-torches on, even though the late September daylight meant that it would not be fully dark until around eight o'clock in

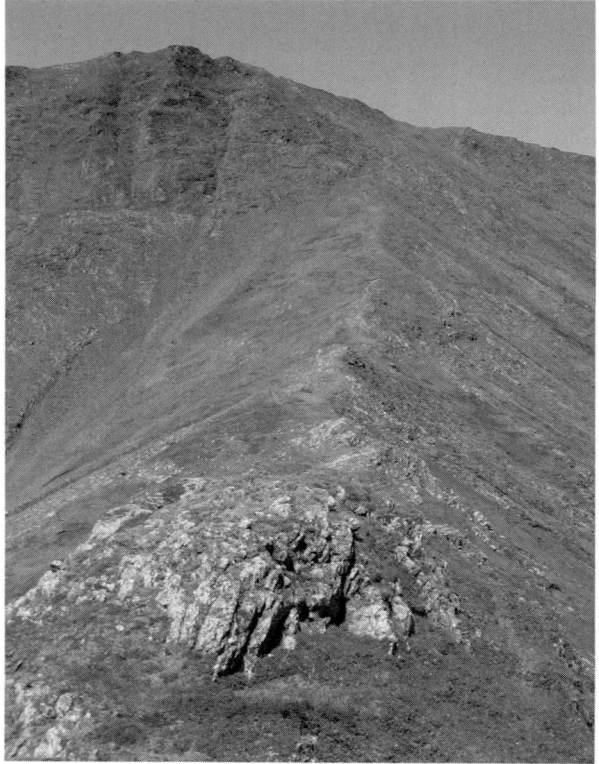

A glorious day on Gategill Fell

the evening. Morning mist hung over the wooded confines of Latrigg, like a harbinger of approaching autumn, as we walked the four miles along the Keswick Railway Footpath to Threlkeld. There was a pleasant coolness in the air that also spoke of gradual seasonal changes afoot. However, the forecast told us that by midday it would be a pleasantly warm and largely sunny day, before the cold returned for a clear evening and night. It is only a short climb out of Threlkeld to Blease Gill and its delightful watercourse. Although impressive, there is much better to come. For a while the path along the base of Blencathra takes a pleasant course through verdant fields, beneath the imposing presence of warty topped Gategill Fell. A large gate beckons you into the drama of Gate Gill. A weir provides an easy crossing of the gill, but the eye is drawn to the stunning backdrop rising in seemingly vertical drama to Blencathra's summit, flanked by the rocky turrets of Hall's Fell. There is nothing but savage mountain chaos here. Anyone who claims that there are no mountains in England should be brought here. With the rocky drama that lay before me, I contemplated with a shudder the fact that there was actually a route up Gate Gill, although this was hard to believe considering what I was faced with. I knew I would have to go further into the bowels of Blencathra than ever before to complete my own list of secret Lakeland walks. The low level path now leads along the base of Hall's Fell before diving into the narrow claustrophobic recess of Doddick Gill, less rocky but just as wild in its bracken and heather cloaked depths. I made another mental record for a future walk, but for now was quite glad that it was Doddick Fell rather than Doddick Gill that I was climbing up.

A steep pull up the lower wedge of Doddick Fell leads to a magnificent viewpoint at roughly the 1400 feet contour. Wainwright describes this view as 'an awe-inspiring scene and the finest close up of the mountain'. Directly ahead is a 1500 feet sweep of bracken and crag leading to the triangular summit of Hall's Fell. One feels humbled in the mountain's presence. Further along the ridge are two rock turrets, which are somewhat less impressive than the name might suggest. However on Doddick Gill it is not so much the scrambling that will impress, for there is very little of that, but the wonderful views both up to the mountain and down to the surrounding fields and pastures, along with the delightful grassy path cutting through the brown swathes of heather. Today there were legions of clouds stacked over the Pennines, forming neat rows, but lazy and unthreatening without a wind to blow them onwards. The trees in the fields way down below had a dirty green hue, tired of the life they rejoiced in when they were spring fresh, now they waited weary of heart for the onset and decay of autumn. My own heart was racing as we reached the top of Doddick Fell and looked down upon the great curving brown snake of the ridge we had climbed. We had met just two people in ascending Doddick Fell and they were heading down. It was, however, two more than I had met that other day on Gategill Fell.

The summit of Blencathra was still a rather dispiriting 600 feet of ascent away, although the two dimensional side profile of Sharp Edge and the dark waters of Scales Tarn below kept the interest going and the feet plodding. I must confess though that about here I began to wonder for the first time about the miles that still lay ahead. 'Take it in sections', I kept telling myself, 'one chunk at a time'. This is easy to think but harder to trick one's weary body to accept. Somewhere inside me though was a

Time for a pause on Doddick Fell

steely pride and determination. It would be so easy now to head down
Blease Fell and back to Keswick – harder but much more rewarding to
head out to Bannerdale Crags and Bowscale Fell. A lengthy stop on the
summit recharged my aching limbs. The summit of Blencathra was a busy
place, but as we headed out towards Foule Crag and Bannerdale Crags the
people began to thin out like morning mist. Even so I was surprised to
see a group of four walkers heading out across Mungrisdale Common, as
their route of descent from Blencathra. In Wainwright's day, and even
when I started fell walking some 20 years ago, you could more or less
guarantee meeting nobody on Mungrisdale Common. These days it is
becoming quite popular as a route off Blencathra.

Heading out towards Bannerdale Crags there is a rocky promontory, a
divine perch set above the abyss of the River Glenderamackin and with
perhaps the best view to be had of Sharp Edge and the distant matchstick
forms of people heading along it. Not a place that Wainwright raves about,
but nonetheless a place more worthy than many a summit. From this
point onwards, for another six hours out in the Northern Fells, we met

only a further four walkers. However as an idea of how the traffic has increased in these parts, I met just one solitary walker on an identical walk some 16 years before. Some readers might wonder why this seemingly small increase in walkers in these parts bothers me. I suppose it is because there should perhaps be a place where one can go and pretty much guarantee being alone. Imagine being Wainwright, who wrote in the concluding Personal Notes to the *Northern Fells Guide* that aside from people he met on Skiddaw and Blencathra he saw only one other person while preparing his guide and that was at a distance on Carrock Fell. So in two years of walking, Wainwright saw just one person outside of Skiddaw and Blencathra. These days you will still meet less people in the Northern Fells than in other areas of the Lake District, but you are unlikely to be on your own. Wainwright's way of experiencing these fells has gone. His comment that he 'felt like he was preparing a book that would have no readers at all', comes from a lost past, as more and more people head into the Northern Fells to try and escape the more popular places, with fewer and fewer people finding the solitude they seek elsewhere. There is no answer. I believe that everyone has the right to experience these places and the right to roam. At least everyone except those who leave litter! However, as this book hopefully demonstrates, there are still places where solitude can be expected if not guaranteed, but those places are becoming like rare flowers and need to be treasured (shame on you for exposing them! – ed). Respect them as an endangered species and go alone or perhaps with one other friend, not in clumsy, noisy parties.

Bannerdale Crags has a flattish summit, but a wonderful view. The view east is perhaps finer here than from the summit of Blencathra. As we approached Bannerdale Crags we saw two other walkers on the summit, enjoying their time alone. Rather than encroach on this, Stan and I decided to hunker down amongst some coarse grass, a hundred yards or so short of the summit, where we could not be seen in order to give these people their bit of time and space. It seemed the decent thing to do. Perhaps this is the future of fell walking, timed tickets for your few minutes of solitude. After fifteen minutes or so they left and we had our own moments undisturbed to enjoy the summit, with its fine view across the M6 corridor and to the distant Pennines. A few feet away from the small summit cairn, the ground drops away to the pronounced East Ridge of Bannerdale Crags. Seldom climbed, the East Ridge is without doubt secret Lakeland terrain. As I stood looking down on the ridge, I recalled a previous climb of this lonely spine.

My walk then began at the tiny but attractive collection of cottages and farm buildings that is Mungrisdale. Whereas some walks need a few miles of leg work to get off the beaten track and into the wild and lonely places, this walk could boast solitude from the very start. After just a few yards I left the minor road, having shut the gate behind me, unlocking the door to a world of peace and silence. That day started cold with ice formed on the path, but as the sun rose into a clear blue sky, the day became surprisingly warm for early November. Ahead of me was the huge pyramidal end of The Tongue; to the left the rising sun was keenly highlighting the East Ridge of Bannerdale Crags, defining its lonely drama. Eventually, by the junction of the River Glenderamackin and its tributary Bannerdale Beck, I left the good low level path and took a minor thread of a path, which widened to a grassy promenade as it led to the base of the East Ridge. Even though the human traffic has increased in the Northern Fells over recent years, this promenade is still one of those places where you don't expect to meet anyone and I didn't. The intense silence was only interrupted as I began walking up the East Ridge proper, as the noise of broken slate clanking beneath my feet awoke the place from its ancient slumber.

Although the East Ridge looks quite fearsome when viewed from a distance, it is in fact a very easy but nonetheless highly enjoyable route. There are no awkward obstacles to be overcome and its charms are more to do with its situation and solitude than with any real sense of exposure, or rush of adrenalin. It is quite simply a divine place to be. About half way up the ridge, providing a good excuse for a stop, is a ruined stone hut. This is a remnant from the workings of the Bannerdale Lead Mine and a reminder that, even in the wildest parts of Lakeland, the ruins and remnants from an industrial past are ever present amongst the fells. However, as with many other ruins in Lakeland, the hut now almost seems to have become an organic part of the ridge it sits upon. I sat in the hut, hoping for a few minutes to bond with the hut and the ridge in organic unity. The minutes I spent there, although not time spent on a summit or gaining a new tick, were some of the most precious and life affirming I have spent in the fells. I had passed over two hours entirely alone, a rare thing in modern Lakeland. I can recommend the East Ridge of Bannerdale Crags, but the experience will be richer if you go alone.

Back from my reverie of a day gone past, Stan and I took the wonderful spacious romp, around the rotten rim of Bannerdale Crags, to the summit of Bowscale Fell. I had last been on Bowscale Fell sixteen years before and that time I had wanted to have a glimpse of Bowscale Tarn, before heading back to Keswick. This time I was to head further out from the starting point in Keswick and descended by a steep grass rake to the shores of one of the last sizeable tarns that I had yet to visit. It was half past five in the afternoon and Bowscale Tarn was now in full shadow, while in contrast Carrock Fell, behind us, remained bathed in the most clarity enhancing evening sunshine. Every scree and bracken patch on the massive grey flanks of Carrock was illuminated. There was no-one else by Bowscale Tarn, no sound apart from the soothing lapping of water against the banks of the tarn and the occasional plop of a fish. The magic of nature was in the air and it seemed just a small stretch of the imagination to think those immortal fish of legend might be the ones we heard. There was a stillness here that lured our tired limbs to stay, like the call of the Sirens. It was an awfully long way back to Keswick and to tear oneself away from this magic seemed lunacy. But the magic was not quite strong enough and sense prevailed as we headed down towards The Roundhouse. This curious building is actually more hexagonal than round in shape. It was here that our spirits were lifted by the sight of a red squirrel leaping from fence post to fence post. It was that time of evening when the people head off the fells and nature re-emerges from the shadows.

Stan and I still had a long way to go and having had a fairly easy time of things with plenty of stops, decided now to get our heads down and march, military style, without stopping to Skiddaw House, a distance of just over three miles. It was a kind of challenge I suppose, but it was odd how the legs gradually became less tired and their actions became almost motorised. As the sun dipped below the fell line, Skiddaw Forest assumed the deep brown colours of dusk, with only the highest inches of Mungrisdale Common still bathed in a reddish gold light. It's a long tramp from the Roundhouse to Skiddaw House, or seems so when you have already covered a considerable distance. At one point hopes are lifted when you round a bend to see Skiddaw House in the middle distance, but it seems to take an terribly long time for it to get any closer. The final killer at the end of this unremitting march was the short sharp uphill pull to Skiddaw House itself. It was the sort of little piece of uphill walk that one would think nothing off when fresh in the morning, but was a hellish treadmill at seven thirty in the evening.

At last we made it to Skiddaw House and it was time for a well earned stop. I had recently taken to carrying a pack of glucose tablets in my rucksack for a quick energy burst. Now after 15 miles of fell walking I was about to give them the ultimate test. I consumed four of the tablets, had a ten minute rest and a drink after which I did actually feel ready for the final five miles. These five miles from Skiddaw House to the Gale Road car park and back to Keswick had been tramped by me dozens of times over the years. I knew every twist and turn of the path. Yet I was about to experience this stretch of walk as never before and there was enough excitement in that to keep mind and body going. It was dusk and only a matter of time before it would be completely dark and headtorches would be required. We decided, in the kind of simple childish play that is part of the essence of freedom in the hills, to refrain from using the headtorches as long as possible, until it became impossible to proceed any further without them. The huge black face of Lonscale Fell glowered down at this tomfoolery. At around eight o'clock that late September evening sense gave way. It was getting to the stage where our pupil widened eyes were barely able to make out the path ahead. Had we been placed here from the comfort of our living rooms it would have seemed totally dark. It was time for the headtorches to go on.

There is a wonderful mixture of the magical and the slightly scary about walking with headtorches. Once they go on, everything outside of the little bubble of light they create is an alien world of deepest black. It was strange to see the so familiar Cumbria Way path lit up by the artificial white light. Strange also to see the tiny dots of car lights travelling along the A66 still some way off and some way below. We wondered whether anyone travelling on that road might be looking out into the Northern Fells and wondering what the mysterious lights were. In reality they probably realised it was just a couple of slightly crazy walkers. Eventually we rounded the corner and headed down to the familiar crossing of Whit Beck. Several sheep gazed at us, looking distinctly unimpressed, their eyes glowing zombie like, in the glare of the headtorches. This stretch of walk from Skiddaw House back to Keswick is ideal terrain for someone wanting to try out night walking. The path is excellent and for the most part quite smooth and there is no trouble route finding.

As we joined the tourist path up Skiddaw at Shepherd's Cross, we turned off the headtorches for a moment, gave a few seconds for our eyes to adjust to the dark, and then witnessed a glorious display of stars with none of the light pollution that can detract from such a spectacle in urban areas. My body was worn out after nearly 20 miles and 11 hours of walking, but my mind still took everything in and knew that this was a moment to treasure for a lifetime – an experience that I wanted to repeat again and again. Before long the twinkly lights of Keswick could be seen below us and at twenty past nine we finally reached the town centre. Tired though I was, it was a happy tiredness. I had known deep down that reaching forty should be no barrier to doing massive walks, but it was reassuring to prove it to myself. I resolved to do the same walk when I reach fifty. There was one drawback, however, to finishing the walk so late. The fish and chip shop had closed!

The ridges of Blencathra provide some of the finest high level secret Lakeland tramps in this book. By direct contrast the routes to Blencathra via Blease Gill, Middle Tongue and Doddick Gill are at times as near as a walker gets to the kind of torture inflicted in the ancient Greek realm of Hades. The Roughten Gill route is an exception, being easy angled and grassy. It makes a half decent route for descent, after the horrors of the other gills. There are, no doubt, some people who will relish these walks, in part for the challenge and in part because they love rough and uncompromising walking. It is for those of my readers that I have included these walks in this book, for they are undoubtedly secret Lakeland in both nature and terrain. There is some of this desire to pit myself against a rough challenge in me, although I'd rather be doing so scrambling high on a ridge, than crawling around in a canyon. I don't mind pathless walking, in fact a lot of the time I love it, but here pathless becomes often simply unpleasant. Wainwright himself does not particularly seem to have enjoyed walking in these gills by his own account of them. For a time I struggled with whether to include these routes in this book at all. However, I eventually decided that secret Lakeland by its very nature would, at times, also be uncompromising Lakeland. If you do all the other walks in this book and pass over these gill walks on Blencathra, you will have missed very little that is enjoyable. The author did not have this choice and gained a considerable number of grey hairs as a result. Whatever your decision, you have been warned!

I decided to tackle Blease Gill first, for the simple reason that having read Wainwright's words about all three gill routes on the face of Blencathra, this seemed the easiest, in relative terms. Having to do these walks whenever holiday dictates, I did not have a lot of choice as to the weather for this walk. During the course of researching this book I have had more than my share of luck with the weather Gods. The day I climbed Blease Gill, however, was not such a day. The top 600 or so feet of Blease Fell were covered in the kind of dark grey cloud that spoke of permanence. As I departed the bus at Threlkeld and looked up towards Blease Gill, this forbidding backdrop did not exactly fill me with desire at the prospect of climbing into it. Blease Gill was in spate. Indeed, people on the pleasant low level path, along the base of Blencathra, were having to make a detour up stream to cross the gill. My route initially headed the same way as the route to Knott Halloo and Gategill Fell. I half wished I could just abandon the cause and do Gategill Fell, whose familiarity contrasted in my mind with the unknown, black depths of the canyon that I was heading for. Around here the Wainwright guide told me that I should branch off from the route up Gategill Fell and on to a track along a rising wall above Blease Gill. Don't expect much from this track. It is not easy to find and once found is little more than the width of a sheep track. The rain that had fallen over the last few days also made this track slippery. To the left was a steep grassy bank, suddenly ending in a plunge down to Blease Gill. A slip on the track could have led to nasty consequences. My heart wanted to hurry this bit and get it over with, but my head knew I had to take my time and take care.

Before long I came to the place where Blease Gill split into two smaller tributaries. It was a wild scene that presented itself. I was now deep in the heart of Blencathra, whose grey, crumbling walls rose steeply around me. Believe it or not there are three route choices here. One route follows the left hand split of the beck upwards, through grass and scree to the ridge between Blease Fell and Gategill Fell. Another route follows a ribbon of steep grass, which leads to the ridge, just to the right of Gategill Fell Top. The third choice is to follow close to the right hand split of Blease Fell and head steeply up into a little canyon. Each of these three routes led up into the mist, which had now lowered slightly, to about 2,000 feet. This did not help matters and merely added to the feeling that I was entering the unknown, possibly never to return. The canyon route was described by Wainwright as the most direct route and the most interesting. So it was with a due sense of dread that I began to toil up the scree and heather towards the narrow canyon. On entering the canyon I also entered the mist. In a strange way this actually helped as it made me focus on the immediate, rather than become too concerned with what lay ahead. Cocooned as I was, I had no sense of my insignificance on the vast steep face of Blencathra. I could not be overwhelmed or frightened by the exposure or situation. It was just me and the rough ascent of the canyon. This is a strange little place between rock walls and for one of the few times on these Blencathra gill walks, I found myself rather enjoying the climbing. At the top of the canyon make sure you incline right as Wainwright suggests, to avoid the scree slopes. By doing this I found myself before too long on the familiar ridge from Knott Halloo to Gategill Fell Top. I was completely enveloped in a grey and slightly damp mist, but I still let out a little whoop of joy at having made it to this point. Suddenly I felt safe again. The scree climb to Gategill Fell Top was soon accomplished and I found myself on the top, with absolutely no view. I now realised that I had not stopped once all the way from Threlkeld to Gategill Fell Top. It was odd how the adrenalin just kept me going without more than a quick pause for breath, all the way up Blease Gill and on to Blencathra's summit ridge. So I now gave myself a full fifteen minutes, with nothing to look at, focused entirely on the rather squashed ham roll in front of me, but feeling oddly relaxed and totally removed from civilization. It was when I made out the murky form of a walker, approaching Gategill Fell top from Blease Fell that I decided it was time to move on. I don't know what became of this fellow solo walker, but I never saw him again that day.

The summit of Blencathra was chilly and damp. It occurred to me that this was the first time I had got to the top of this famous mountain and not seen the glorious view. Lucky indeed, considering this was the tenth time I had climbed Blencathra. It was also the shortest stop I had ever had on this summit. There is little in the way of shelter here and after less than two minutes I left, making a beeline over pathless grassy slopes, on the dull rear end of Blencathra, heading for Roughten Gill. It was not a pleasant descent to begin with. The grass was very uneven and incredibly slippery. Several times I fell onto my backside and let out an involuntary profanity. It was only when I stopped by a sheep fold, finally beneath the line of the mist, that I realised how utterly secluded I was. All around were grassy flanks, heading up into enclosing walls of grey cloud. Even Mungrisdale Common looked sinister. A new fence had been erected by Roughten Gill and a new plantation of sapling trees here looked a little underdeveloped and ugly. In thirty years time they will probably be beautiful. I contented myself with looking from a distance at the falls of Roughten Gill rather than climbing over the fence and down to the watery banks of the gill to have a closer look. At the point where a new gate entered the fenced off plantation, a grassy path began and from here my spirits gradually rose, in harmony with the ever improving path. Before long the grassy track joined the superb low level route which headed back to the Blencathra Centre. I had so often looked at this path from the Cumbria Way or the north-east buttress of Lonscale Fell and thought how pleasant it would be to walk upon. Now I was here and it did not disappoint. Across the Glenderaterra Beck, the towering wall of Lonscale Fell looked immensely impressive, a sight to rival some of the most dramatic in the Scottish Highlands. The day had improved a little and the mist had risen to just skirting the top of Lonscale Fell's east peak, lit up pink and orange by the setting sun. Soon I passed an impressive waterfall, which tumbled directly down to the path, before reappearing beneath it. By the time I reached the Blencathra Centre it was almost dark and by the time I reached Derwentfolds it was completely dark.

Ahead lay a mile and a half of walking along the minor road through Brundholme Woods. This was a prospect that would normally fill me with joy at the end of the day, for these woods are one of my favourite places. However, on this day, the prospect was rather unsettling. I am very used to walking in the dark on my own, with the headtorch lighting up the path for me. Normally though my night walking is done in open spaces, where the oddly comforting lights of houses and cars can be seen and where sometimes the headtorch can be turned off, to reveal a million stars in the heavens, or even a moon to illuminate the landscape. The night walk through Brundholme Woods was different. This was not just your average type of darkness. This was intense pitch black darkness. To make matters worse, I soon encountered a tall sign and a gate in the middle of the road, where no sign or gate had ever been before. It was a warning that the road was subsiding. I rationalised that this was probably just a warning for cars, but the fantastical combination of utter blackness and the road perhaps suddenly giving way beneath me, was not a pleasant one. I carried on, the headtorch creating a small channel of light in the midst of seemingly endless nothing. My step was quick, but every step was the same. Nothing altered, just lit up tarmac to about five feet ahead of me and then a black void. No lights, no cars and nothing to gauge the distance travelled.

After what seemed like an age of this unsettling monotony, I decided to take a look at my position on the GPS. I was making good progress, which was something. However, as soon as my light narrowed pupils turned away from the strong glow of the GPS, I found that I could make out nothing ahead of me, even with the headtorch on and it took a minute or so of aimless wandering before my eyes adjusted and I could march at a steady pace once more. Then the creatures came. I would have been far better off keeping the headtorch firmly fixed on the road ahead, but I could hear an unsettling rustling in the woods to my right and the temptation to look got the better of me. The source of the rustling was revealed, as half a dozen pairs of ghostly green eyes peered at me through the darkness, perhaps fifteen feet away. I jumped, letting out an audible high pitched squeak of surprise, discovering a vocal range I thought I'd lost at puberty! I was beginning to feel a bit like Mole from *The Wind in the Willows*, beset by strange noises and sights in the Wild Wood. Slight terror turned to thrill, however, when the eyes darted away and the rustling receded into the distance, with a speed and agility that could only have been achieved by deer. Countless times I had walked along this road in the daytime and never seen so much as a solitary deer. Now, in the darkness, a whole pack of them had been right beside me. I carried on into the tunnel of darkness, now happily turning my headtorch to the left and the right, in search for more eyes, but there were no more. The thrill of the deer sighting began to evaporate and it was with a certain amount of comfort and relief, like Mole felt when Badger opened his door to him, that I reached the welcoming streets and lights of Keswick.

For its sustained roughness of terrain the ascent of Blencathra via Doddick Gill takes the number one spot in this book. Other walks have sections of greater difficulty and exposure, but these are just sections. In Doddick Gill there is truly damnation without relief. I guess when Wainwright's description of a route includes such phrases as 'hard scrambling throughout' and 'a route to commend heartily to one's worst enemy' one can pretty much guarantee a tough time. In fact I had found myself putting off this one walk; delaying the moment when I would have to set out into Doddick Gill; trying to think of an excuse not to do this walk or include it in the book. In the end, time caught up with me and I found myself with Doddick Gill and the Middle Tongue route left to do. Middle Tongue seemed easier but neither route particularly appealed. So on a fine day, with thankfully only the gentlest of breezes, I decided to do both walks together, Doddick Gill in ascent and Middle Tongue in descent. It was a bit like the prospect of having a filling and an extraction at the dentist and deciding to have the whole cursed thing done at once. Wainwright suggested that Doddick Gill was 'not for solitary walkers', although I can't see many solo walkers coming here anyway, yet alone managing to persuade a companion to come with them! I was fortunate to have Stan with me, a veteran of crazy scrambles in the Lake District and a proverbial stick to shove me with, if my resolve to complete the climb withered.

   The pleasant walk from Threlkeld to Doddick Gill, along the base of Blencathra, gives little intimation of the horrors to come. The valley containing Doddick Gill curves around the base of Hall's Fell, revealing nothing of the later stages of this climb. The walk begins by making the best line you can along the rough and pathless course of Doddick Gill. This unfortunately means criss-crossing from one side of the gill to the other to avoid swamps, fallen trees and other detritus; in relative terms though this early section is not too bad. Eventually tough heather replaces wet grass. The gill here is too narrow and confined to walk into. Here I can only suggest as Wainwright shows, which is to keep to the right hand side of the gill and clamber up through the steep heather banks. At times you will find yourself literally clinging to clumps of heather to keep your balance. I would not particularly recommend entering the stream bed here, as Wainwright suggests. For unless there has been a prolonged dry period before your climb, the stream bed will be very wet, with slippery moss covered rocks. From here the ravine and scree gully that is the route ahead looks quite horrendous and the way of getting to the ravine, without having to enter the dangerous gill bed, is not at all clear.

It was at this point that my resolve to continue the climb withered. In my sullen mood I felt a bit let down by the guide book. Stan suggested heading up towards Doddick Fell, to avoid the crags ahead of us, more in hope than expectation that there might be a way back to the ravine route from higher up. Here fate was to intervene, her whims allowing me to complete my research so that I did not to have to turn back from one of the walks in this book. Suddenly we came across a faint path leading back towards the Hall's Fell ridge and the ravine route. Not marked in the guide book and who knows when last used, it was a vital piece to solving this dreadful jigsaw puzzle. Having traversed the flanks of the fell, our reward, if it can be called that, was the ravine and scree route on to the ridge of Hall's Fell. The scree gully looks impossible from below, but take heart because firstly you do not have to walk into the gully, and secondly a half decent path can be found here. The terrain is still rugged and steep and there is the best part of 800 feet to climb to meet the ridge of Hall's Fell. The scree gully is an impressive site, with its rotting vertical rock walls and profusion of littered scree. For a while we followed the early stages of this ravine, over loose stones and scree, but took a route out of the gully and on to grassy slopes as soon as we could. At last the key to this route had been unlocked and another 400 feet of steep, grassy climb and suddenly we were at the pinnacle on the Hall's Fell ridge. There were a few bemused walkers watching our exit. I turned to them and said 'never again', which provoked a round of laughter.

Suddenly joy came into my life again. As we carried on up the last section of the Hall's Fell ridge, I could again enjoy views, blue sky and sunshine on my face. There were a crowd of about fifteen people on the summit of Blencathra that day, but in an odd way I rather enjoyed the company. Climbing up Doddick Gill, I guess I got a feel of when the hunt for solitude can become a little boorish, obsessive and extreme. On the summit my thoughts turned to the recently rejected proposal to erect a wind farm at Berrier Hill. If this had gone ahead, massive wind turbines would have spoilt the iconic view from Blencathra. It would have been one step closer to my recurring nightmare of the National Park Boundary becoming ringed with thousands of wind turbines. That little yellow line on the map, which marks the boundary of the Lake District National Park, has become a kind of battle line. To one side of the line and within the park, developers know they are on to a losing cause to try and erect these infernal turbines. However, even a few hundred yards to the other side of this boundary line and it appears to be fair game. Berrier Hill is a mere half a mile or so on the wrong side of the battle line. Some would argue about how these wind turbines would spoil the National Park when they won't be in it. This misses the point. Berrier Hill sits just two and a half miles from the Northern Fells massif and eight from the summit of Blencathra. This area is as much about the views as it is about the landscape itself. What is the point of a bit of renewable energy, in the attempt to save the riches of our planet, if by creating that energy, we destroy an iconic view. We have merely robbed Peter to feed Paul. It was with great gladness that I heard of the decision to reject this plan. I was also proud that I had signed the on-line petition against it and persuaded a number of others to do so. My own personal idea, for what it is worth, is that there should be a ten mile zone, outside the National Park boundary, where such developments are banned. Only in such a radical way will the essence of this world renowned scenery remain preserved.

Today on Blencathra I found myself rejoicing inwardly in the crowd around me. My joy was in the probability that this seemingly disparate collection of people shared something with me. I did not do a straw pole, but I am willing to bet every one of them would have been in opposition to the Berrier Hill wind farm. If all our walking was solitary, and I have sometimes selfishly wished it could be, there would not be enough of us to defend the battle lines.

After the rigours of Doddick Gill, a descent over the grassy ridge of Middle Tongue seemed a relatively easy prospect. After all, I had read that fell runners sometimes use this as a route off Blencathra's summit ridge. This easy prospect was confounded by reality. The grass was steep and the footing loose at times, on eroded soil. I slipped several times, getting a muddy bottom for my troubles. We were lucky to find a faint path going down through the heather at the base of Middle Tongue and avoiding some obvious rocky difficulties. We finally arrived at the confluence of the streams, where they merge into Gate Gill proper. Not far now as the crow flies back to a good Lakeland path. Unfortunately we were walkers and not crows and the remainder of the route was a seemingly never ending chore, trying to chose the right line in the steep and lose bed of the gill. This seemed akin to a labour of Hercules at the end of a long and strenuous day. Mine workings and levels that I would have delighted in taking a closer look at, when fresh at the start of a walk, were wandered by with scarcely a glance. Anything that did not move us onwards to the car at Threlkeld was surplus to requirements. Murder might have been committed if I had suggested to Stan playing 'hunt the Wainwright minutiae' at this point. It was with heart rending delight that we finally reached Gategill. This had been beyond a doubt the toughest walk in this book.

I suppose the best way I can sum up these routes on and off Blencathra is that I will be doing Gategill Fell and Doddick Fell many more times. They have now become beloved favourites. Roughten Gill is a reasonable and safe route to get down from Blencathra. It is also very wild and has the joys of the glorious track to the Blencathra Centre to round off the walk. Blease Gill had some fine, lonely moments in the misty canyon, while Middle Tongue is a bearable chore, practical I suppose, but little else and not good in descent. As for Doddick Gill, I very much doubt that it will bear witness to my presence again, barring bribes for money, or a lifetime supply of ice cream. Such is the uncompromising nature of these routes, of wilderness, that the insignificant concerns of a solitary walker count for very little.

opposite: *High Raise summit in moody weather*

The Central Fells

'There are many swamps, the worst in Lakeland, where walkers seldom venture. It is sufficient commentary that in the course of the eight miles from Greenup to Rakefoot this ridge, although in the very heart of the district, is crossed by two footpaths only'.
Alfred Wainwright, *Pictorial Guide to the Central Fells*
Introductory Notes.

The Central Fells are an odd mixture of celebrated classic fells and those that usually only see the footfall of the committed Wainwright bagger. They comprise the smallest book in Wainwright's Seven *Pictorial Guides*, and reading the above quote a new traveller to the district might be inclined to think that the reason for this is that they are the least interesting group of fells. This could not be further from the truth.

The Central Fells divide into two separate terrains. This, however, is not a linear division but a division between the interior and the exterior of the range. A vast swathe of high moorland dominates the interior. Indeed those miles from Greenup to Rakefoot that Wainwright describes in the quote, are prime secret Lakeland terrain. Any walker wishing to experience the wildest terrain that Lakeland has to offer, will not have a complete knowledge until they have tramped the high level Central Spine between Ullscarf and Walla Crag. This is a classic Lakeland ridge walk, only without the crowds one would associate with such walks. On a glowering day, when the mists are down, you will feel like you are the only person on the planet. On a clear and bright day you will feel like a king or queen of your own private kingdom of space and freedom, high above a temporarily subordinated civilization. In either condition the tracts of bog may put you off a little, especially after heavy rain, but keep going for the rewards are more than worth wet feet and muddy trousers. The summits of High Seat and Bleaberry Fell I consider to be classic summits, poking above the squelchy morass beneath, but all the more worthy for having to be struggled for. As a way of getting on to this central spine, I can heartily endorse the route from Wythburn, via Harrop Tarn and on to Ullscarf. As a walker who had never taken this route before, it was a joy that exceeded any expectations I had in planning it. There are hidden treasures here that can only be found by walking the route and cannot even be sensed from the roadside.

The vast interior of the Central Fells was an obvious resource for this book. However I knew my task would be a little more difficult on the more popular exterior, or rim, of the Central massif. Here moorland and plateau give way to tumbling crags, sheer rock faces and exquisite, pastoral charm. The Central Fells are indeed a two faced Janus. The celebrated Langdale Pikes are often overrun, but even here I found three secret routes, two of which I nearly scared myself to death on and the third of which proved one of the quiet gems of this area. High Raise, the reluctant King of the Central Fells, is usually picked off on a detour from the Langdale Pikes, or from Sergeant Man. However a quiet and thrilling route to High Raise can also be made, via the seemingly impregnable fortress of Eagle Crag and Sergeant's Crag.

The Central Fells also boast a number of Lakeland's most characterful lower fells. Silver How, High Rigg, Grange Fell and Loughrigg Fell, although infinitely charming, do not exactly call out as places where secret Lakeland might be found, but on each of them I found a varying degree of solitude. In particular the traverse of High Rigg and the East Ridge of Grange Fell come with my highest recommendation. They are both beautiful and quiet walks, a combination that is becoming rarer and rarer in modern Lakeland. In summary, very far from being the poor relation of the other fell groups, the Central Fells have something to suit everyone's tastes and many places can be found that are as beautifully wild and eerily lonely as anywhere in the Lake District.

Up Close and Personal with Loughrigg Fell

Some hills are their own islands, without supporting ridges to link them with their closest companions. They are their own separate kingdoms, with their own unique atmosphere. Such island hills are most famously found in Britain in the Far North of Scotland, where mountains such as Suilven, Quinag and Stac Polly rise in independent form. However, in the crowded, jumbly world of the Lake District such hills are less common. A glance through any of the seven *Pictorial Guides* quickly shows how most fells have a ridge route linking to their nearest companions. However there are a few fells that stand apart from their neighbours and have no obvious linking ridges – Loughrigg Fell is one of these.

Loughrigg Fell must rank as one of the most popular fells in the Lake District, having approaches from two of the most crowded tourist honey pots, Ambleside and Grasmere. It deserves its popularity for it is a fell full of variety, of hidden nooks, intimate and distant views and jewel like tarns. Although Wainwright does describe a ridge route to Silver How (so technically it does have a link to another fell), this is more of a walk from one fell to another than a ridge route. This ridge route both crosses a minor road and also drops in height from 1100 feet to around 500 feet, having a total ascent of close on 1000 feet to connect these two fells, which are themselves little more than 1000 feet in height. Loughrigg Fell can therefore, in my view, be considered independent; an island fell effectively cut off from its neighbours by roads major and minor and by the famous waters of Grasmere. And this independence is not just one of geography; it is one of mood and feeling. There is no other fell quite like Loughrigg Fell. It is true that one would be hard pushed to picture a distinct profile of the fell in the mind's eye. Loughrigg Fell is not a glamour model of a fell. It does not call from a distance and through an arresting form beg to be climbed, like Great Gable or Blencathra. Rather its charms are those of exploration and discovery. It is a fell where there seems to be a new vista or feature of interest around every corner.

This characteristic is confirmed by the detailed map of the fell to be found on pages 3 and 4 of the Loughrigg Fell chapter, in the *Central Fells Guide*. Is there any other fell in the district with so many paths to explore? This is an instant clue to anyone with some map reading acumen that this is a place deserving of a thorough acquaintance. Contrast this map with that defining High Tove's area on page 2 of the High Tove chapter and it is easy to see the variety of landscape and features abundantly present on Loughrigg Fell and sorely lacking on High Tove.

Given Loughrigg Fell's popularity, why have I included it in a book about secret Lakeland? On many fells it is quite straightforward to find a secret route away from the crowds. With Loughrigg Fell, however, I knew that I was going to have my work cut out. Devising a route that would do its best to make a thorough exploration of the fell and also try and find some solitude, was an enjoyable challenge. Loughrigg Fell was also a Wainwright I did not yet feel I had done justice to. I had only climbed it once before, during my first round of the Wainwrights. The day I first climbed Loughrigg had not even been planned, but was a second choice after an ascent of the Langdale Pikes was aborted due to high winds and blizzard conditions. So on a chill January afternoon, my face numbingly raw from a bitter Arctic wind, Stan and I found ourselves looking for some reward in terms of a tick, from a poor weather day. Loughrigg Fell was a bagging exercise pure and simple. I remember little of enjoyment as we battled the elements and frequent squally showers of snow, mixed with stinging pellets of hail, whilst being half deafened by the noise of our waterproof hoods being buffeted against our faces. The summit was attained as quickly as possible, without detours, without stops. Once there the full force of a wild January day hit us. I remember a view towards a growling, darkly outlined, Langdale Pikes, as we bade a very hasty retreat from the fell as quickly as our limbs would carry us. I suppose the only redeeming qualities that day were a relative absence of people and the witnessing of nature's elemental fury at first hand.

Several years passed before Loughrigg Fell came into my plans again. I had by now done almost all of the well known Wainwrights more than once and was therefore keen to make a closer acquaintance of Loughrigg. So one quiet evening, I found myself studying pages 3 and 4 of the Loughrigg Fell chapter and trying to plan a circular route from the myriad of paths, a route that would both visit as many as possible of the main features of the fell and also try to avoid the crowds. In addition, and through no other reason than the fun of doing it, I wanted to either visit, or get a good view, of the four main sheets of water that are a feature of the fell. These are Rydal Water, Lily Tarn, Loughrigg Tarn and Grasmere. This time, instead of dashing up to the highest point, I planned the route so that the summit and its view would be teased out until perhaps two thirds or more of the walk had been completed. This day would be a day of small detours, a proper and complete circumnavigation of the fell, where the passage of time was an irrelevance.

By the end of the walk I planned to know much better a fell that I had given scant attention to before.

Then a day arrived that seemed perfect for the fulfilment of the plan. It was the start of March, during a week that had begun with its roots firmly in winter and a fresh plastering of snow on the fells, ending mild with a watery blend of warm, milky sunshine that seemed to breathe of the coming of spring. Such a day, with a lack of any wind, clear views after snow and a wide palette of shade and colour, was perfect for an exploration of Loughrigg Fell.

The route began at a car park just after Pelter Bridge, having headed off the busy A591 artery that splits the Lake District in two. It was a pleasant surprise, especially in this location, to find a free car park. I am sure twenty years ago, when I took up walking in a serious way, that virtually all but the busiest of car parks were free. We now seem to live in an age where every action we do is in danger of being charged in some way. I don't mind paying a certain amount towards the upkeep of the landscape, that's not the issue. But I do wonder how car parks that used to be maintained without any payment, or perhaps with a token fifty pence in a pot, can now cost upwards of five pounds for a day.

So our walk began with the pleasant feeling of something obtained for free! To try and at least begin with an illusion of solitude we began early in the morning, when the majority of walkers might still be devouring their third slice of toast in the bed and breakfasts of Ambleside and Grasmere. Soon after setting off, I spotted the first sheet of water on my list, Rydal Water. Today the water was the very essence of calm, an inverted Nab Scar mirrored on its placid surface. Rather than head right down to the lakeside path, we took a slightly higher path, heading for Rydal Cave. I had last visited the cave some 16 years before, my mood of élan today contrasting sharply with my previous visit. Rydal Cave first time had been part of a 'making do' walk. On a day where my brother Peter and Stan had done the Fairfield Horseshoe for the first time and bagged a glut of Wainwrights, I had hobbled around Rydal Water and Grasmere, nursing a badly twisted ankle. In those days the cave was open to explore and I recall walking into its cooling darkness. This time, our visit was greeted by a fence and sign saying to keep out due to the risk of rock fall. It was tempting to ignore the sign and enter the cave, but we reasoned that it would look pretty stupid calling out the Mountain Rescue to a boulder flattened fell walker who had ignored such an obvious warning. We contented ourselves with a quick photo.

From the cave we headed back on ourselves, taking a more minor path rising beside a wall, heading in a north to south direction across the fell.

This path heralded a quieter side of Loughrigg Fell, as it wound its way among minor summits, outcrops and marshy patches, to reach a prominent cairn with a hint of the view south towards Ambleside and Windermere. Here in the very heart of the fell we took a rest with nothing but the sound of silence, interspersed with the gentlest of breezes, to disturb us. A few moments of secret Lakeland had been found on Loughrigg Fell's popular mass. For a while we experienced the fell as AW must have.

Heading down from the cairn we came to an area which on the revised Wainwright guide is littered and criss-crossed by a myriad of red dotted path lines. This is a kind of walker's 'Spaghetti Junction'. There seems no reason for there to be so many paths here, other than the sheer volume of walkers who over the years have made various detours, in bids to find the shortest or easiest way from one place to another. A small tarn sits in the middle of this chaos of paths. It has nothing of the characteristics of a popular Lakeland tarn and is not even worthy of a name. However, another detour on our rambling tour of Loughrigg led us to a rather more celebrated stretch of water. True, Lily Tarn is probably not in Lakeland's top ten most famous tarns, but it is still one of Lakeland's more worthy small tarns. On that March morning that hovered undecidedly between early spring and late winter, the tarn had a thin layer of ice over its small surface, like the skin on a rice pudding. In the midst of the tarn was a tiny island upon which stood a little tree, revelling in its own isolation. Behind the tarn, was a view to Wansfell dusted with snow like a delicately iced cake. This was the second sheet of water on our tour of Loughrigg.

With something of the nature of a child, having no concept of distance, time or plan and only a knowledge and hedonistic curiosity in the now, we ambled from outcrop to outcrop, each its own lofty vantage point, for views of the undulations of South Lakeland, stretching to the far distant silver blue of the sea. We also caught a fine view down to the gentle meanders of the River Brathay. So immersed was I in the now and our childish world of exploration that I left my walking pole somewhere on the fell and had to re-trace my steps amongst half a dozen outcrops to eventually find it. I tend to sometimes lose sight of the practical on the hills and over the years have lost or left behind articles ranging from gloves and balaclavas to binoculars and compasses. This causes me much personal chagrin as I would never knowingly litter the landscape. If I find such lost property myself, which I frequently do, I tend to carry it off the mountain in my rucksack and I can only hope that other walkers might do similar with my lost detritus. I have no desire to have it back, only for it to be removed from tainting the fells. It's my own stupid fault for leaving it there.

On top of one of the many little summits of Loughrigg Fell

Having assuaged my conscience by retrieving my walking pole, we headed down to a major path by a wall that pretty much marks the southern extremity of Loughrigg. By now it was around midday and even in March there were a number of people on this popular path that leads to Loughrigg Tarn. However, rather than take the low road, our route still had a summit to claim and so we once again headed away from the masses, on a narrow path that rose between a steep stone wall to the left and the flanks of Ivy Crag to the right. For a short while we were alone and had the feeling of having the fell to ourselves. This did not last for very long though as other paths intersected ours at regular intervals, each bringing a fresh batch of pilgrims bound for Loughrigg's summit. We passed several attractive unnamed tarns, each of which had its origin in the glacial movement of ice over the fell in some past ice age. The savage forces of primeval nature, which had ravaged the fell many thousands of years ago, now left behind watery hollows and rocky outcrops. Peace and relaxation has replaced nature's chaotic upheaval.

On a lower subsidiary summit we stopped and had a bird's eye view of the third stretch of water in the plan, Loughrigg Tarn. With a snowy backdrop of Wetherlam, Wrynose Pass and the Crinkles, today it reflected its necklace of trees in steely blue water, reminding me fleetingly of the poet Wordsworth's likening of the tarn to "Diana's Looking-glass, round, clear and bright as heaven". This summit just a couple of hundred yards from the true top, gave us our final moments of solitude for the day. From here we watched the main summit of Loughrigg like a couple of hawks watching a prey, waiting patiently for our moment when the summit would be clear of other fell walkers. But the procession of people coming from Ambleside and Rydal was unabated, so we admitted defeat and joined the plodding procession. Now all this may sound rather antisocial, but I can see no reason why, if a fell walker does not intrude on another's enjoyment, that we cannot all enjoy the fell in our own way. I would certainly never be rude to someone; on the summit that day I chatted to an elderly couple and also took a photo for a young couple who wanted to capture their moment together on the summit. And it was all enjoyably tolerable. I would simply prefer to be alone or with a kindred spirit like Stan.

Nothing however could detract from the summit view that day, whose bright March colours were accentuated by the snow covered heights of Bowfell and the Langdales. Could this be the finest profile of the Langdale Pikes? Loughrigg Fell, with its Central position in the Lake District, sitting in the midst of the great central north to south rift of Lakeland, is a great place to appreciate the shifts in landscape of the Lake District: South Lakeland with its undulations stretching to the sea, the Central bowl of fells surrounding Grasmere, and through the rift occupied by Dunmail Raise, the lurking bulky forms of Lonscale Fell and Skiddaw. South and North Lakeland are so very different. In the south there is a chaos of lower fells, a landscape that is rock strewn and rarely flat. In the north the hills are graceful and lofty, with the great flat Vale of Keswick cradling them. More than the obvious visual features, there is a hard to define atmosphere change from south to north. Little wonder that to some extent South Lakelanders and North Lakelanders have regarded themselves in centuries gone by, and still today to some extent, as separate and independent. Not an aggressive independence, but a pride in their own patch of natural beauty.

Although we were accompanied in descent by a noisy party of teenagers, who seemed to regard fells as the perfect places to shout at each other, there was still time to appreciate the classic view of Grasmere from the lower Grasmere cairn. I consider this the best view of this famous stretch of water, with its tree covered island and pastoral quality. This was the last and grandest of the four bodies of water we had planned to see on our tour.

From here we headed along Loughrigg Terrace, still blessed with gorgeous scenery, but with the feeling that the very best was behind us. At the end of the day we sat by Rydal Water, with the glorious shades of late afternoon sunshine bathing the lake and a bevy of ducks waddling expectantly beside us. Our tour of Loughrigg Fell had perfectly illustrated the meaning of the word Loughrigg as 'ridge of the lough or lake'. In places the fell almost feels like a moated castle. But what of my attempt to find secret Lakeland on the popular flanks of Loughrigg? True, compared to the hours of solitude had from many of the walks in this book it had, to some degree, been a failure. However in taking a leisurely tour of the fell, rather than making the usual beeline for the summit, we had experienced some divine moments of quiet and peace that perhaps the majority of fell walkers, focused on the summit, would probably have missed. And perhaps more than the obvious secrets of loneliness and quiet, I felt that I had imbibed the very essence of a fell that I had hitherto merely bagged. Perhaps such immersion in a place, shunning the popular paths as much as possible, also opens up other less obvious essences of secret Lakeland. So had it been a success? Absolutely!

A glowering and wintery Langdale Pikes and Bowfell from Loughrigg Fell

The Great Central Spine

The Central Fells are uniformly craggy on their perimeter. Here are to be found such celebrated fells as the Langdale Pikes, Walla Crag, Grange Fell and Helm Crag. However this grand outline is in direct contrast to what lies within. Behind the façade lies a vast area of upland plateau, broken only by the gentle swells to the summits of the interior. This is wild and uncompromising country, all heather, grass and bog. Yet although this area does not readily display its qualities, it does have its secret charms of space and peace. There is an almost spiritual calm about treading these lonely miles. It is a pilgrimage of solitude that leaves an indelible imprint on the soul.

This central wilderness is divided in two by the high pass of Greenup Edge. To the south of Greenup Edge, High Raise and Thunacar Knott are the sentinels of a large moorland area behind the Langdale Pikes. To the north of Greenup Edge lies the vast expanse of Ullscarf and on to High Tove, High Seat and Bleaberry Fell. It would be quite possible for a walker to traverse the entire Central Fells range from north to south or vice versa in a single day. This would however be a very long and arduous walk, with little time to do justice to either the Langdale Pikes, or the central plateau behind. For me, High Raise and Thunacar Knott are best explored separately from Langdale or Grasmere. To give yourself enough time to enjoy what will still be a long walk, my definition of the Central Spine is the area of moorland north from Greenup Edge.

Unless an unreasonable amount of retracing one's footsteps is done, there is no way to think of this walk other than a linear A to B walk. Whether you start the walk with Walla Crag or Ullscarf as your first fell is your freedom of choice. Either way you are well served by the bus service that runs from Keswick to Grasmere along the A591. My personal preference was to start with a new secret Lakeland route onto Ullscarf and finish with an evening stop on one of my favourite fells, Walla Crag.

I had climbed each of the five fells on this central spine as part of my round of the 214 Wainwright fells: Ullscarf I had climbed from Stonethwaite along with Sergeant's Crag and Eagle Crag; High Tove had accidentally become my first Wainwright fell on a walk from Thirlmere to Watendlath; High Seat I had climbed from Ashness Bridge and Bleaberry Fell and Walla Crag as a pair from Keswick. I therefore had a little knowledge of the terrain and special atmosphere of this central wilderness, a bit like having listened to a highlights package of an Opera or read an abridged version of a book. I had dabbled in the central wilderness and now longed to link the fells in one long and self reliant linear walk.

For some months before, I had dreamt of the day when I would disembark from the bus at the Armboth Road End stop beside Thirlmere, to piece together another part of the great Lakeland jigsaw of exploration. I now found myself treading the first tarmac mile along the relatively quiet minor road along Thirlmere. It was a muggy day in early June, forecast to reach twenty-five degrees Celsius. No rain was forecast to thwart my ambitions. There was however a concern about keeping cool in the massive heat trap up on the central spine. As will be seen, I had my own solution to this problem. As ever, I delighted in studying the detail of the Wainwright guide in a game of 'find the trivia'. The rain gauge shown on Ullscarf page 6 could be seen from the road and there was no mistaking the giant Binka Stone, whose flat face has been carved out not by man but by nature. Of the three routes up Ullscarf from Wythburn, shown in the Wainwright guide, the route via Harrop Tarn seemed to offer the most variety, being wooded to approximately 1300 feet and incorporating a tarn that I had not got round to visiting but had harboured desires to acquaint myself with for a number of years.

It was sweaty work climbing the zig-zag path following the line of Dob Gill, although the occasional tree provided some welcome shelter. Just before the path crosses a stile and dives delightfully into the coolness of the forest, I saw a couple of people approaching behind me. When I am hot and sweaty, the last thing I want is to have someone on my heels, so I let this couple go past, giving them a cheery 'hello' as I did so. They mumbled a greeting back but appeared a little frosty in mood. I temporarily forgot about them as I delighted in the final darkly forested approach to Harrop Tarn. It is strange how one's mind can conjure up a picture of a person or a thing before one sees it for the first time. How many of us have spoken to someone on the telephone and created an image of that person's face, only to find that upon meeting the person they look nothing like the image we created? The same can also be said of natural features. I had imagined Harrop Tarn to be small and surrounded by dense woodland. In reality it was much larger than I had anticipated and largely clear of tree cover. However, it is a grand place, with its backdrop of Tarn Crags and a distinct feeling of peace and tranquillity. This secluded feeling was borne out when I saw a young deer on the far side of the tarn. The moody couple I had met earlier were just a few yards away from me and I did not know whether they had spotted the solitary deer, as it was a small object in a massive setting. So in my enthusiasm I wandered over to them and pointed out the deer on the opposite shore of the tarn. The man simply replied in a very sarcastic voice 'We know'. Maybe I had found someone that craves solitude even more than I do, but this was unnecessarily curt. I don't seek out people in the fells, in fact I would probably rather meet no-one, but I believe that whether we desire our own company or not, there is no reason to shun people or be rude if we meet other walkers and they exchange conversation with us.

Reclining in the depths of some natural trees beside the shore path, I regained peace and equilibrium. Looking directly up I was entranced by the sunlight making vibrant green colours of the canopy of leaves above me. I went unnoticed as the sullen couple passed by and as I never saw them again that day; I guess that Harrop Tarn was their sole objective. Just past Harrop Tarn, Mosshause Gill emerges and, on a warm day, its clear waters were too tempting to resist. There is nothing better when you are overheated than cold mountain water on the back of your neck. A lovely path now continues through the forest in an area whose solitude and atmosphere felt far removed from popular Lakeland. In fact, I could almost

Magical Harrop Tarn

imagine myself wandering through some vast forest in the Canadian Rockies! Eventually I saw the opening in the trees that would signal my emergence from the forest meaning that, for the rest of the day, I would have the fierce June sun on my back. I did of course have high factor sun cream with me, but the thought of hours in the baking heat was still a little unsettling. I hoped that higher up there might be a cooling breeze. There is a bit of leg work before the path joins the fence that will act as your guide for the lonely, boggy miles of the Central Spine. There are three rather insipid pools of water here, not worthy of the description 'tarn', certainly when compared to the also visible and much more admirably proportioned, Blea Tarn.

For now though I had a slight detour to the first and highest summit of the day, Ullscarf. The path winds around the imposing Standing Crag before joining a fence which leads to the summit plateau and then, in ruined form, to the summit itself. Sitting amidst the very Anglicised fell names of High Raise, High Seat and High Tove, Ullscarf speaks of a foreign influence. *Ulfr* is the Old Norse word for a wolf (think also Ulverston) and *Scarf* is the Old Norse word for a pass (think Scarth Gap near Haystacks). So Ullscarf means Wolf Pass, perhaps from a time when wolves roamed these fells, before man, acting in typical fashion, wiped them all out! The Norse invaders came and settled in Cumbria in the tenth century AD, and the Lake District is full of names derived from Old Norse. Indeed many of the names for basic features associated with the Lake District derive from the Norse. 'Beck' for a stream, 'force' for a waterfall, 'dale' for a valley and even 'fell' for a mountain, all derive from the Norse and show the extent of their influence. So although Ullscarf may not be big on drama and excitement, it does boast an interesting name. Another fell in the Central Fells starting with the word 'high' really would have been too much.

Ullscarf, along with perhaps Caw Fell, must be among the least visited of the Lake District's two thousand feet fells. It spans a huge and mainly boggy area, lacking in features of interest, which mainly explains its lack of popularity. However, sitting up there alone, with just enough of a summer breeze to cool me and with the sound of a lark chorus above, more than compensated for the general lack of summit features and interest. The view from here is probably the stand-out feature, displaying a magnificent panorama of the Northern and North Western Fells, an ever present delight on the Central Spine. It is an easy angled descent from the summit; just make sure you detour to Standing Crag, although be careful not to blithely follow the fence further, as it ends abruptly here, before resuming at the foot of the crag! Ahead of me lay a vast expanse of featureless upland wilderness. A nearly three mile tramp to the next Wainwright of High Tove with the promise of copious heather wading and bog trudging in between. My mood was high and I thought 'bring it on'. Before continuing into the bog, I made another very small detour to Blea Tarn's shoreline. There were a couple of reasons for this. Firstly, Blea Tarn was just about the only sizeable Lakeland tarn that I had not yet visited. Secondly, it was my planned idea for a way to cool off on a hot day on the Central Spine. Yes, the author was going for a swim.

To be honest it is a bit boggy going down to the shore of Blea Tarn, but it was worth the effort. I found a tiny beach of grey shingle and donned my swimming gear, checking of course that no-one was around to recoil in horror at the spectacle. There is nothing better for chilling the body than to have a dip in mountain water. Immersed in the tarn I looked round to see thousands of sparkling jewels of light on the water, fleeting wonders that shifted and changed with the sun and the gentle lapping of the tarn's surface. Blea Tarn is not the grandest of tarns. It is shy and retiring. But I can safely say that I would not have had a glorious sun drenched swim had the tarn been swarming with people. Celebrity status of scenery does not necessarily provide the most enjoyable experience.

Much refreshed in body and soul after my swim, I was eager to tackle the lonely miles to High Tove. The Central Spine is described by Wainwright as boggy and 'not to be undertaken for pleasure'. Fortunately I was doing the walk in June, after a dry period and the bogs were nowhere near as bad as I had anticipated from reading the Wainwright guide. In fact the section from Ullscarf to High Tove was nothing more than glorious solitary tramping on heather and with just the occasional bog pool to negotiate. Navigation is simplified by following the line of a fence all the way to High Tove. I would not say there is no path, more that the path is sketchy. Where the ground is dry a path can be followed, winding through the heather. When the ground is squelchy the path vanishes. If you follow the fence though, you will soon return to a thread of path. It is so unusual in the Lake District to have a high ridge to yourself, acres of space in front of you and a genuine feeling of isolation. On a wild and wet day it could be frightening up here. On a warm summer day it is a solo walker's dream. I would like to say that I met no-one on the long tramp to High Tove, but I did in fact meet just one person. This was a middle aged lady, traversing the spine from north to south. We exchanged a few words and then marched off back into our reclusive worlds. They say that talking to yourself is the first sign of madness. If so then I must be ready for sectioning, because when I am alone in the wild, I incessantly talk to myself. Sometimes I reminisce, sometimes

I mull over problems or achievements, sometimes I encourage myself onward, sometimes I just burble about nothing in particular. At the start of the day it is all excited talk about what is ahead, at the end of the day it is talk about where I am going to eat that night. It is above all very cathartic.

High Tove was my first ever Wainwright fell. For that reason it will always be special to me. General consensus though is that it is one of the least appealing of the 214 Wainwright Fells. But on a day of blue sky and warmth, mixed with delicate cooling zephyrs, it was a great place to just soak up the peace. From here onwards the distance between the fell summits is much less than between Ullscarf and High Tove. It is a mile to High Seat and another mile or so to Bleaberry Fell. There was a bit of bog between High Tove and High Seat, but again not as much as I had expected. There is in fact a decent path from the depression between High Tove and the summit of High Seat. I had only been on High Seat once before, but its memory was still a vividly fond one. Wainwright calls the summit a 'welcome dry oasis'. High Seat is also a very fine summit, a little rocky platform rising above the vast heather and swamp clad moorlands. It has an Ordnance Survey column, which always adds interest and makes a good foreground for a photo. It is a favourite place of mine, with the little rocky summit ridge gaining enough

The fence that is your guide on the vast Central Spine

elevation to provide a surprisingly good view, particularly of the Newlands and Coledale Fells and towards Derwent Water and Bassenthwaite, which appeared a wonderful deep blue in the late afternoon light.

It was between High Seat and High Tove that I encountered the worst of the bog that day. Here is a confused landscape of heathery tussocks and hillocks. Bleaberry Fell is in view ahead but seems to take an age to get to. Detours are made from one area of bog only to find another. The fence cannot reasonably be followed without sinking into deep stagnant water. Someone had placed a token couple of wooden boards in places, but they seemed insufficient and precarious for my large frame. The previous summits of the day had been a joy to reach, whereas the summit of Bleaberry Fell was more of a relief. Bleaberry Fell was considered a worthy enough viewpoint by Wainwright for him to devote two and a half pages to every detail of the panorama. So on reaching the top it was not more than a few seconds before my relief turned into the more familiar summit feelings of wonder at the view. As Bleaberry Fell drops away quite steeply from its summit the view north is unobstructed, with Skiddaw, Bassenthwaite Lake and the Coledale Fells being particularly well displayed. There is something about Bleaberry Fell that even at the end of a long day's walking commands a stop. It is a neat summit with a big cairn, although it does in my experience tend to attract any wind that is going spare. It was half past five in the afternoon when I reached Bleaberry Fell and, not surprisingly, I had the place to myself. I still had some way to go back to Keswick, but was aided in my descent by a well constructed path, which after negotiating the initial steep descent becomes a joy to tread for a good half a mile or so. It is the sort of path that is so good to the feet that one can look around at the scenery without risk of a fall or twisted ankle. Tired as my legs now were, with the colours of the landscape changing to an early evening hue, this stretch of path was a tonic and a direct contrast with most of the terrain I had so far covered. This heavenly course continues as far as a sheepfold with an outcrop of rock above it, before becoming grassier then subsequently boggier, just when you thought it was safe to tread without fear of water seeping into your boots.

I recalled my first climb of Bleaberry Fell back in 1993, when I had come up over Walla Crag from Keswick, with my girlfriend, later to be my wife, Jenny. We had known each other for less than a year and our relationship was still at that stage where I was trying to impress her. It was an enterprise that failed. As we walked the boggy stretch from Walla Crag towards Bleaberry Fell, which I am sure was boggier in those days, I was so absorbed in speaking to my new found love that I neglected to look where my feet were going. One minute Jenny had her six foot boyfriend next to her, the next minute he had disappeared into an unholy pool of sphagnum moss. This was more than just bog. It was something hellish that wanted to drag me down into its slimy depths. That day, Jenny, my "knight in shining armour" came to the rescue of this damsel in distress. I'm not proud! These days she just accepts that I am clumsy.

The summit of Walla Crag, with its rocky platform and plunging view down to Derwent Water, provided a fitting finale to a great linear excursion over the Central Spine. The wild moorland was now behind me and was replaced with a scene of stereotypical Lakeland beauty. Here I met another couple, the fourth and fifth people I had seen that day. Between Harrop Tarn and here on Walla Crag, there had been miles of undisturbed walking, broken only by the lady I had met on the wilds of the Central Spine. In nearly ten hours of solitary tramping, I had become familiar with the absence of people and the immersion in my own company. The two people on Walla Crag and the view of Keswick town below brought me starkly back to reality. The couple were friendly enough, although the man was less interested in conversation and more interested in spiking litter on the summit with his walking pole. I can only commend any walkers who take the time to clear up other folks' litter. This shows a true love of the fells. I believe that just as one cannot love a person and do them harm, so one cannot love a landscape if one harms or defiles it by leaving litter behind.

It is a lovely descent from Walla Crag back to Keswick; for the most part smooth grassy paths can be followed on the way. By the time I hit the tarmac of Keswick's streets, my legs were tired and on auto-pilot. The frequent thought enters my head at this stage of the day of a fantastical nightmare where I am placed back at the start of the walk and have to do it all over again. Fortunately the reality was a cold can from the local Spar, a hot bath and a great curry at the local Bangladeshi restaurant. With these thoughts a fantastic day in the fells came to an end. There are many wild, lonely walks in the secret Lakeland list, but few can match the Central Spine for isolation or challenge.

Here seems as good a place as any to mention an alternative ascent route onto the Central Spine. This route does not, unfortunately, provide the advantage of a full traverse of the ridge, but was too interesting and redolent of secret Lakeland to be left out. It starts from Dale Bottom, a tiny collection of houses on the busy A591 road, which could by no stretch of the imagination be considered a popular starting point. It climbs from Dale Bottom to Bleaberry Fell, via Goat Crags.

It was the first day of a break, having arrived in Keswick at about 3pm. I knew that if I dumped my suitcase at the Bed and Breakfast and caught the bus leaving Keswick at 3.40pm, I would have time to complete the ascent of Bleaberry Fell and descend over Walla Crag to arrive back in Keswick at a decent hour. The bus was busy, but once it dropped me off at Dale Bottom and I crossed the road to pass through a gate, I entered a much lonelier world. The narrow grassy path continues level for some way and a hundred feet or so above the busy main road. Before long, trees encroach from the left and the path becomes delightful, as it follows directly beside the rock littered course of Shoulthwaite Gill. The tree topped shape of The Benn, near Raven Crag, looms at the end of a narrow valley. Rising to the right is the wall of Goat Crag, a mixture of scree, crag and vegetation. Between the lower scree and the upper crag, a line of green marks the route of the grass shelf that I would follow beneath Goat Crag. This all looked quite formidable to someone like me, who enjoys a bit of scrambling but easily scares if my life is in danger. Goat Crag is far more often seen than visited, being an easily identified sight on the drive along the A66 from Penrith to Keswick. Wainwright says of the crag that 'if it were in the London green belt no doubt it would be a famous climbing ground'. But in the Lake District, which is crowded with many more dramatic and famous climbing spots, it remains largely unnoticed.

After crossing a dry stone wall the climbing proper begins. There is a vague path upwards, but the wall acts as a good guide to begin with. A large erratic boulder, complete with its own moss and heather hair piece, not only makes a good photo foreground, but also marks the place where you need to leave all vestige of path and make your way up to the grassy shelf beneath Goat Crag. It was a day that threatened rain, with the higher summits decapitated by a uniform line of grey cloud at about 2400 feet. What had appeared to be loose scree from below, turned out to be slippery, boulder strewn scree when under foot, possibly the worst type of ankle endangering terrain a walker can encounter. There were a couple of freshly leaved trees that I used as a rough guide to direction. As luck would have it the rain started coming down as I reached the grassy shelf. I really did not fancy a retreat and descent back over the slippery scree-come-boulder-field. So I carried on along the narrow shelf, knowing that where the crags petered out to my right the route headed up more easily on grass and heather to the summit of Bleaberry Fell. The sense of isolation and drama was acute, even though I was in fact only half a mile away from the busy A591 road. I felt like I was going where no man, other than Wainwright of course, had gone before. All too soon the drama ended and what remained was a confusing, but blissfully wild, ascent of 400 feet over heathery hillocks, before a fence was reached as the unmistakeable knob of Bleaberry Fell and its large cairn came into view.

This time it was blowing a gale on Bleaberry Fell summit as I dived down into the shelter for cover. Although wind is, of all the elements, the number one enemy to the fell walker, there is something perversely wonderful about hunkering down in a summit shelter, protected from the very worst that nature can throw at you. From Bleaberry Fell I took the route described above to Walla Crag, where the wind eased a little and from there took the time honoured path into Keswick. The whole circuit had taken me under three hours, yet there was no doubting that I had come away from this short walk touched by the spirit of the wild places. I had met no-one. I will never travel along the A66 into Keswick again without sparing a glance for Goat Crag and the narrow ribbon of grass, between scree and crag that had provided a seminal moment in my Lakeland experience.

Goat Crag on Bleaberry Fell
(the grassy line between crag and scree is the route!)

Steel and Silver

I am certain that many hill walkers would agree with me that a fair portion of the enjoyment to be had with this hobby is from the planning of a walk. The experience of a day in the fells divides itself, enjoyment wise, between the planning, the execution of the plan and the reminiscence afterwards. The planning starts the excitement, the execution of the plan brings the excitement to a peak, quite literally, and the reminiscence tries to rekindle that excitement, turning the best bits into nostalgic nuggets of gold as the years pass.

Now guidebooks are good for planning and Wainwright's are in my view superior to any, but there is a lot of pleasure sometimes in cobbling together one's own route. This is why for me the idea of being on a guided walk around the fells is anathema, although I can accept that some people may get a lot out of it. If guided, the excitement of the planning belongs to someone else. It is like having the filling and sponge of a cake, without the icing on top. With many thousands of miles of paths in the Lake District there are innumerable routes that can be planned. The time honoured classic routes are just a framework to get started with. So plan a classic of your own and revel in the possibility, albeit a remote one, that you may be the first person ever to have planned that precise route and the first to execute it.

My unusual plan came about through a kind of self-imposed necessity. It had taken me twenty years to complete the Wainwrights and so my first book, *The World of a Wainwright Bagger,* had been twenty years in the making, although only a year in the writing. For my next project, I decided that two years would be a reasonable but challenging time period in which to write this first book in my *Secret Lakeland* trilogy. However, not living in the Lake District, it was going to be a tight agenda to complete all the walks I wanted to do in my spare holiday time, especially as the wife and children expect me, quite rightly, to spend two weeks a year on holiday with them. So when studying my list of secret Lakeland routes, expediency led to seeing if there were ways of combining one route with another, even if it meant climbing two seemingly disparate fells in the same day. The north ridge route up Steel Fell from Thirlmere was one of the secret Lakeland walks and I was looking forward to it. But to just do Steel Fell and come down to Grasmere would occupy no more than a half day. So I started to ponder how I could link Steel Fell with another secret Lakeland route up another fell, with perhaps some beautiful low level paths in between. Then came that wonderful moment when an embryonic plan took its final shape. From Grasmere I could use the minor road round the lake, then the path that leads to Elterwater and through this lower level route, link Steel Feel with none other than Silver How.

Having surveyed and completed the route plan, it was tempting to think it might be my very own creation, that none of the millions of people who walk, and have walked the fells has combined these two fells into one walk. Until such time as I might find out otherwise, I shall indulge myself in the small possibility of having devised a unique plan. In reality I am surely kidding myself.

Once again I was to rely upon the wonderful network of bus routes that thread their way through the Lake District. This time it was the bus that heads through the heart of the area, via the A591, to eventually find itself in far away Lancaster. Now in case you are wondering, I do own a car, albeit a very old run down car, which I quite enjoy driving. However, I am someone who would always rather be driven than drive. I am not a natural driver. I prefer to gaze around at the glories of nature and also, by using the bus, convince myself that I am doing something towards holding back climate change.

A glance at the bus timetable showed me that Wythburn Church was listed as the nearest stop to the Armboth Road junction and my route up Steel Fell. I probably annoy some bus drivers, because I have a kind of paranoia about not missing my stop. The thought of getting up from my seat too late and seeing my walk starting point flash by, fills me with the kind of dread that only fell walkers can understand. This paranoia tends to lead me to walk to the front of the bus and stand by the bus driver at least a mile before really necessary, but to my credit I have never yet missed a stop. Bus drivers in my experience tend to dwell between the extremes of sullen misanthropes, who grunt rather than talk and welcoming, chatty fellows. There is no in-between in my experience. Luckily the Lake District tends to have mostly the welcoming, talkative type and my driver on this day was no exception. We exchanged a few general comments about it being a glorious day, before he suddenly deepened the tone, by telling me how he loved his job because he got to drive through this wonderful landscape every day and each day was different. For a moment fell walker and bus driver revelled in the same awe of nature. Strange how a brief moment, with a man I may never meet again, can remain etched in the memory.

The bus reached the Wythburn Church stop. Two people got off. One was a man who needed to relieve himself and having done so got straight back on the bus and the other was me. I had not been looking forward to the first little section of my walk, which involved walking along the A591 for about a quarter of a mile. Not a long distance, but long enough for me to become a statistic on this treacherous stretch of road. Road walking has its place, if the road is minor and the traffic infrequent and slow moving, although tarmac is the worst surface for the soles and heels of the feet. However, 'A' roads are not for walkers in my view. I know we can be stubborn and say that we have just as much right on them as the cars, but at the end of the day they are just too dangerous for me. I don't enjoy this type of walking, with cars whizzing past a matter of inches away and the constant vigilance for the next ton of metal heading your way. Such walking is purely practical and walking for pleasure should surely never be purely practical. So it was with some annoyance that I reached the Armboth Road junction, only to find out that there was in fact another bus stop here, called unsurprisingly Armboth Road End. I could have met my maker on the A591 for the want of this fact. I now know that not all the stops are listed on the bus timetables and I can only suggest if you are unsure of the best stop, and if your bus driver is of the welcoming, talkative type, that you check with him or her for the nearest stop to your walk starting point.

Now I could finally get into my own stride, as opposed to the flustered, rushing stride on the A591, and immerse myself in my surroundings; the ever so slightly warming sun of a calm March day; the gentlest zephyr of a breeze; the intense clarity; the fells in two layers, one their own skin of brown, green and gold, the other a white coat of snow, decking their highest reaches. I needed a little luck to complete my list of walks in the time I had allowed and here was luck. The perfect fell walking day.

My route branched away from tarmac at West Head farm, where some men were repairing the roof of a farm building and were to prove the only people I saw until I reached the cairn on Steel Fell. At a gate the climbing proper begins on the sort of path feet love, a grassy trod, verdant and even surfaced, ascending to a backdrop of deep blue early morning sky. The path was delicately frosted. Winter still held a grip at Dunmail Raise, but this was not the bitter depths of winter, this was the very first hatchings of spring, struggling for a foot hold. Wainwright calls this walk a trudge, but I consider this early section, in particular, belies such a description. There are worse trudges than this in the Lake District and this one is compensated for by the ever increasing views of Thirlmere, today with a film of wafer thin ice covering the surface. Helvellyn and the elephantine backsides of Nethermost and Dollywagon Pike dominated the scene eastwards, all with seemingly pristine snow above 1600 feet. The lush, grassy path rather loses itself after a second wall, as the steep north ridge dominates the scene ahead. Any thought of trudge, however, was compensated for by my transition into another world, above the snow line. At first it was just a few bits of icy snow, amidst the green, but soon the green was gone and a decent white covering lay beneath my feet, every step I walked defacing this virgin blanket of white.

Here winter still ruled and the higher I climbed the greater sense there was that the world of greens and browns below was left behind. All there was now was the dazzling glare of the snow on the ground and the brilliant blue of the sky above. If time allows – and I tend to make sure it does – a detour can be made from the path to the very edge of the north ridge, where the fell falls away in crags and gullies to the slender ribbon of tarmac of the Dunmail road below. Today however the path was conspicuous by its absence. It lay buried under the snow. However nearing the summit of the fell, one encounters the remains of a fence which makes a beeline for the top. I confidently strode from rusty post to rusty post, not caring that I had no ribbon of path to guide me. After a couple of hundred metres however, I noticed a different texture to the ground beneath me. A firm crunch was replaced by a crunch with a slight skid and the obvious hollow texture of ice beneath my feet. I realised quickly that I was standing on a small tarn and I had a sickening feeling that this tarn would not hold my weight. I did a kind of backwards shuffle as quickly as I could and gave the area around where I supposed the tarn might be a wide berth. Today it was no more than a small alarm, a potential blight on my day that had been avoided. On another day, as described later in this book, my own foolishness resulted in an icy soaking and a day tarnished.

The best routes onto fells save their finest views as a revelation on reaching the very summit and this is true of the north ridge of Steel Fell. At the point where fence post met cairn I was greeted with a scene that smacked me in the face. Revealed in that moment were The Langdale Pikes, Crinkle Crags, the Coniston Fells and a host of other smaller fells, beautifully delineated by the snow, with the crags of every fell above about 1300 feet perfectly highlighted, as black etchings on the white landscape. Wainwright says of this view that 'lateral ridges rise one behind another to the skyline of the Coniston fells, all of them being of striking serrated appearance of Cuillin like quality'. While the reference to the Cuillin on Skye is a forgivable hyperbole, these folds of familiar mountains did seem so much grander and craggier in their winter clothes. To me the true worth of a fell can only be judged when it is given the right conditions. A fell only climbed in poor weather is like viewing a fashion model dressed in rags and wearing no makeup. Twice before I had climbed Steel Fell. The first time in a horseshoe of Wainwright bagging including Gibson Knott and Calf Crag, when low cloud and rain came and went, the second a quick dull weather climb via the south-east ridge. On both occasions there had been a good view, but I sensed that Steel Fell had more to offer. Now I had experienced the fell at its best. There was little improvement that could be made on this perfect day. I would undoubtedly climb Steel Fell again some day, but for now there were other fells that deserved to be seen at their best.

On the summit I encountered a couple in the early years of their retirement. This glorious day was their last day of a three week long holiday in the Lakes. I try not to feel envy in life, but it was hard not to just a little, limited as I was to a week here and there in the fells. Mind you it is hard work to walk fells every day for three weeks and if I am in the Lakes I like to be on the fells, so perhaps a week at a time is long enough for the body.

It was only when I had a little wander around the vicinity of the summit that I realised that the thick and uniform covering of snow on the northern facing slopes of the fells was somewhat patchier on the south facing slopes,

The Southern Fells looking Alpine from Steel Fell

where the bright March sun had got to work. I managed to find a relatively dry patch of grass, above a huge lip of snow, to have a spot of solitary contemplation. It was tempting to linger but I had only done one of the two fells I had set myself that day and Silver How was still some distance away.

For a descent route from Steel Fell or indeed from any fell, there are few more pleasant than the south-east ridge. I have not included this route in my *secret Lakeland* list because it is the most popular route of ascent up Steel Fell, and easily accessible to the Grasmere hoards. However, that is not to detract from the merits of this route. Apart from a short and quite dramatic rocky knobble at about 1200 feet, this is about as luxurious as Lakeland walking gets. Particularly below the knobble, when it has not rained too much and the grass is quite dry, the terrain is not dissimilar to a cricket outfield set at an angle. The massive bulk of Helm Crag, seeming small when viewed from the summit of Steel Fell, loomed a dark shadowed face over me for the last few hundred feet of descent. Its summit rocks stood out black against the vivid blue of the sky. It reminded me of my awkward efforts to touch the summit of the Howitzer, during my Wainwright bagging years. Then fellside merged into pasture and pasture merged into minor road, as I headed past Ghyll Foot, bound for Grasmere. Road walking of the sort I had encountered earlier on the A591, by Thirlmere, is not enjoyable walking, but on minor roads and out of season it can be pleasant enough, although never as pleasant as being on the fells themselves. So I enjoyed the minor road as it threaded its contour hugging course to Grasmere. This day was truly alternating from winter to spring as the invigorating chill of Steel Fell was now replaced by the sensuous, and for many months missed, warmth of early spring. It was only a mile or so to the centre of Grasmere village and did not take long on the tarmac.

Upon arrival at the village I had developed a raging thirst. I had drink in my rucksack but somehow a cold can from the Grasmere newsagent appealed infinitely more. As I sat on a bench, swigging my can, dressed in my tatty old walking clothes and alive with sweat, I couldn't help but observe the contingent of tourists that, even in early March, thronged the village. It was like a fashion parade of top of the range walking gear and yet most of the wearers looked as if they were merely out for a potter around the lake. Nothing wrong with a potter around Grasmere, but it was the looks I got from a few couples and groups as I drank my can, not harming anyone, but of course not dressed to 'standard'. How strange to find snobs in the fells, where we should all feel merely humbled by nature and embrace being unconscious of worldly fashions. I thought of Wainwright walking around with his small rucksack, baggy old coat and hob nailed boots and smiled.

The next short section of my walk was definitely not secret Lakeland, as I followed the minor road around the western shore of Grasmere. It was under a mile and apart from the odd confusion of walkers and cars trying to pass each other, was a pleasant walk beside tree lined banks, interspersed with some very desirable properties. The sun was now brilliant in the sky and it seemed another world from the winter summit of Steel Fell. Before too long a rough, stony track branches off near The Wyke and this was my route back into secret Lakeland. There was a young couple walking the same route ahead of me, hand in hand and going very slowly. I know I should have tried not to be, but I was irritated by them. I had the unrealistic expectation that once I left the road I would be alone; I wanted my solitude back. My irritation was compounded by the way this couple walked with arms stretched out and holding hands at a distance, so that in the confines of the walled track it was almost impossible to pass them. I found myself either having to stop every few yards and wait for them to go on some distance, or uncomfortably close to them, so that both their and my personal space seemed invaded. An overtake seemed risky. I spotted something though that boded well. The couple were both wearing light trainers and seemed unlikely to be heading far. Sure enough after a couple of hundred metres more of playing tag and tail with me the couple abruptly turned around. Then they noticed me up their backsides for the first time, gave me a look as if I had been snooping on their bliss and headed back down the track. I was alone at last.

I found a beautiful dry spot under the trees, a gentle toying breeze caressing my face as I peered down at Grasmere through the leafless branches. I stared up into the immaculate blue sky above, my mind bereft of all concern. Carrying on, the route soon came out of the trees and, with the rather imposing block of Huntingstile Crag to one side and glorious retrospective views of Grasmere and Seat Sandal, the beautiful path was a fine and quiet place to be. I had in mind the climb of Silver How from Elterwater. Although I must confess that it made no sense to follow the route all the way from Elterwater village, so I began my ascent just above the narrow road to Chapel Stile. It was now that I played my game of hunt the obscure features from the Wainwright guide – Stan wasn't with me so I could really indulge myself! I suppose this is a form of trivia bagging for someone who has already bagged the 214 Wainwrights, but it is also about treading where the great man trod and using the map and a little navigation to hunt out these features. The first was a water substation, found while still descending to the start of the route proper but part of Silver How page 5 nonetheless. It was easy to locate although not very interesting. Then on the climb proper, which begins with a narrow rising shelf of a path above Ashleygarth Crag, I found myself hunting for the tiny tarn that Wainwright mentions. This involved a slight detour from the grassy path. The tarn was found in a nice enough setting, with a backdrop of rising broken crag. It was indeed rather a tiddler, but some tiny tarns can be very photogenic. This one was not in that category, being little more than a reed strewn puddle. Wainwright comments that the tarn has the unique feature of issuing at both ends after heavy rain, but this does little to heighten the appeal. I took a photo for the records and the outcome spoke more for the crag behind and a couple of small trees, than for the tarn itself. Here the camera did not lie. Still it was worth finding and had I not found it there would have been a tiny part of my favourite Lake District that I had failed to locate and that would have gnawed away at me. One does wonder though how many times Wainwright had to visit this tiny tarn to find it in heavy rain and issuing at both ends. Perhaps it was just the once in bad weather, but as he had to define every feature of the walk for his guides, no doubt this master of detail even visited this reedy puddle on a few occasions.

As I continued, the views to the head of Langdale were increasingly impressive. The Langdale Pikes themselves are always impressive, but even more so, because it carried a huge amount of snow and appeared simply as a white wedge, was Bowfell. The path rises easily and blissfully and the few people I met were coming down, as it was already after four in the afternoon. One way of increasing solitude on your chosen fell for the day is to either start early or finish late. The majority of walkers, me included sometimes, have the habit of starting a walk at about 9.30 in the morning, after a hearty breakfast and finishing about 5 in the afternoon for a pint, pub meal or cup of tea. Nothing wrong with that; I am loath to miss my bacon and eggs in the morning, but if you want the fells to yourself, you have to use a little lateral thought and make a few sacrifices sometimes.

The top of Dow Bank was a wonderful place to linger, with its little rocky top and glorious view down to Grasmere and Rydal Water and with the fells now beginning to take on their evening colours. From Dow Bank, Silver How shows its most imposing side, replete with growth like protrusions of crag. Moving on, the path enters the hollow of Walthwaite Bottom and a crossroads of paths bound for Grasmere, Langdale and Silver How itself. From this crossroads until the end of my walk, I did not see another soul. The final pull onto Silver How is sporting, with the path following in heady fashion the line of the crags and yes, I did look out for the holly tree Wainwright mentions. I had expected my time on Silver How's summit to be an evening of relaxation and contemplation after a wonderful day on the fells. However, this day of changing seasons had another surprise. On reaching the top I was greeted by a bitter wind, the kind that puts an immediate halt to thoughts of a long stop. The view of the snow clad Bowfell and the snow spattered crags of the Langdales was mightily impressive. So was the foreground of bumps and knobbles on the ridge to Blea Rigg, alternately coloured green, where the grass showed through, and white, where the snow lingered. Dark evening shadows contrasted with the golden sunlit browns of the lower fells. It would have been magical without that damned wind.

Descending into the scree gully that forms the usual route of ascent up Silver How from Grasmere, winter had one final surprise for me. The wind of past days had obviously played games with the snow and channelled it into this narrow confined space. There still lay a good two feet of snow in places, and my boots and those of others before me, made massive holes in this snow field. It was not the easiest ground to descend, but as soon as I was out of the gully, the lush green grass resumed all the way back to Grasmere. It was glorious to have this popular route all to myself in the magical colours of a fine March evening, with beautiful vistas ahead of a near perfect landscape of scattered trees, lake, mountain and sky. The MP3 player came on again and I hummed to and conducted Richard Strauss' *Alpine Symphony*, fairly confident that no-one was around to witness or be annoyed by this spectacle. My only minor concern was in making sure I did not miss the last bus from Grasmere back to Keswick. When catching buses at the end of a day, I always work on the generous side of time, figuring that it is better to get there early and wait for a few minutes, than to frantically find oneself running in vain, for a bus that pulls away when you are a hundred yards away, leaving you in despair, ruining a great day. I had figured it would take a leisurely hour from the summit of Silver How to reach the bus stop in the heart of Grasmere. I then added ten minutes to this figure, just to err on the ultra safe side and allow for a few minutes contemplative stop in descent, if needed. Sure enough I arrived in Grasmere with about 15 minutes to spare and sat on a bench in the little green square, looking even more bedraggled than on my earlier visit to Grasmere that day. I was still no doubt attracting the attention of the fashion conscious, but cared even less than before. I had lived the fells, known the joys of solitude and most importantly made it in time for the last bus. As the execution of my plan came to fruition, it was still tempting to fantasise that I might have been the first person to link together Steel Fell and Silver How in one long walk. Such delusions of grandeur will always be part of the joy of fell walking.

An Exploration of Grange Fell

The Jaws of Borrowdale are a familiar sight to the many pilgrims who walk around Derwent Water, or who look down on them from Skiddaw Little Man. The Jaws are formed by two peaks, one being the lowest of all the Wainwrights, Castle Crag, and the other being a prominent and popular satellite of Grange Fell, known as King's How. As King's How is over 200 feet higher than Castle Crag, the jaws they form are in fact rather uneven. One can imagine they are those of some deformed monster, for the landscape here has something primeval and fantastical about it. With its thick, jungle-like covering of trees one can almost picture an enormous wooden gate slung between The Jaws, with King Kong lurking somewhere behind.

Grange Fell, the slightly unromantically named main summit of the jaw of King's How, is likewise a popular destination. Yet a search through the Grange Fell chapter in the *Central Fells Guide*, reveals that Grange Fell covers a large area, has several routes to its summit and an area of almost untrodden wildness that is within easy reach of the summit, but in spirit seems a thousand miles away. This is the East Ridge, tucked away in the *Central Fells Guide* without a picture or a map to accompany it. Just a few words of text, almost as if Wainwright wanted to avoid drawing attention to it and perhaps keep it for himself.

My exploration would start from Rosthwaite, cover an ascent of King's How and Grange Fell and then continue to the extremity of the East Ridge. I had only climbed Grange Fell once before, on a hot August day via the popular Grange ascent route. This hazy day was memorable for only two things: some of the worst midges I have encountered in the Lake District and also the only time I have encountered someone in a bikini on a summit. Being also the last fell I climbed before my first child Timothy was born, my mind was filled with thoughts of smelly nappies, sleepless nights and stymied hill walking ambitions. Fortunately, due to an ever understanding wife this has not proved the case. So having done the popular route up Grange Fell, at a popular time of year and in some of the worst conditions a fell walker could encounter, I now longed to give the fell its due. I had touched its summit before but felt that I still barely had more than a quick, shake of the hand, acquaintance with Grange Fell.

I had chosen for my second climb of Grange Fell the ascent from Rosthwaite, hoping that this would prove to be secret Lakeland terrain which for the main, did prove to be the case. It was a late May climb, on a sunny and warm Sunday, a good indicator of the popularity of this ascent, being the sort of day when people were bound to head for the fells. The route from Rosthwaite starts urbanely enough along a walled lane with the lovely Hazel Bank Hotel over the wall to the right. Someone was mowing the lawn in the hotel grounds, a noise I always associate with lazy summer days. At first the route follows the time honoured track to Watendlath, but at a junction of two walls a new path is joined, heading across the lower flanks of Grange Fell and through Frith Wood. Here the popular path to Watendlath is left behind and secret Lakeland is regained. The path continues above the wall with lush banks of grass beneath some overhanging trees. It is the sort of place for a walker who takes his or her time (i.e. me), that calls for a stop. The view over Castle Crag to the Newlands Fells was cast in a pale Mediterranean summer light; the blues of the skies and the greens of the fells spoke of summer tones, like an Impressionist painting. It was tempting, on this lonely path that leads simply across the fellside, to retreat from the world of self-imposed grind. Yet, somehow the fulfilment of the plan ultimately takes precedence and soon I was heading down through the delightful Frith Wood, whose foliage still had the vibrant fresh green of spring, the soft droning of bees an ever-present aural accompaniment to my passage. This route eventually reaches a small car park. This would also be a convenient starting point to climb Grange Fell and a lot quicker than my route. Indeed I was actually no further up the fell in height than I was when I started the walk. However, a fell walk should if possible be about more than simply finding the shortest route to the summit. It is about an exploration, finding those hidden places, making a full and rounded walk and just revelling in the joy of putting one foot in front of another in the glorious landscape of the Lake District.

At the car park the climb proper begins. There seem to be a number of small tracks heading up Grange Fell from here. I found one that seemed slightly wider and more certain of its destination than the others. Having avidly studied my Wainwright guide beforehand, I knew that after a wall at about 700 feet, this route zig-zagged up through deciduous woodland. Having sampled this type of tree lined ascent on many other Lakeland Fells, I knew I was in for a treat. I was not to be disappointed. The narrow path winds steeply up through boulders and tree roots with the odd magical grassy ledge, like a miniature Alpine pasture, to recline upon. It is just a shame that this section lasts for only a couple of hundred feet of climbing, soon emerging onto open, heather clad moorland. From here it is a short pull up onto the summit of King's How. Since I had left the Watendlath path

I had met no-one, but on the summit of King's How my solitude was rudely interrupted. Its small summit, with a bird's eye view of Derwent Water and Skiddaw, is a popular place, although it seems to be far more often climbed from Grange than from Rosthwaite. I said a few 'hellos', took a couple of photos and then headed on to Brund Fell, the highest point of Grange Fell. As I threaded my way through a complex topography of paths, crags and heather, I left the King's How day-trippers far behind. Mind you this is the sort of confined terrain where one could easily think oneself alone, only to find a party of people round the next twist of the path.

There were a couple of people on the true summit of Brund Fell, so I stopped on a slightly lower subsidiary top, which in some ways was a finer place than the actual summit. For here I could stare across at a remarkable tor like rock, square in shape and an ideal subject for the foreground of a photo, with Derwent Water as a backdrop. This was a perfect set piece of glacial gardening. Until this point the walk had been secret Lakeland in patches, but the next sizeable leg of the walk was to reveal one of Lakeland's most forgotten corners. This is the east ridge of Grange Fell. Its description

A glacial boulder on Grange Fell, perfectly placed for a photo

is easily missed within the pages of the *Central Fells Guide*. Not being a route of ascent it has no map to indicate the route and no pen and ink drawing to illustrate its delights. It is instead squeezed into half a page of Wainwright's fanatically justified text. One could almost be forgiven for thinking that Wainwright did not want to draw attention to this quiet sanctuary.

By no stretch of the imagination could the East Ridge be called a wilderness. It is nowhere more than a third of a mile from the Watendlath road, or two thirds of a mile from the Borrowdale road. However it is undeniably wild. It is a precious, rough and uncompromising area and, as I was to discover, a haven for wildlife. I'll make a pact with you, dear reader, that if I reveal this secret, you will take my earlier advice to go alone and go quietly. This advice was never more relevant than on the East Ridge of Grange Fell.

It is odd to find such an uncultivated, yet beautiful corner of Lakeland joined to the hip with one of the area's more popular fells. It is perhaps the seemingly uninspiring half mile between Brund Fell and Ether Knott that puts most people off. The ridge proper begins at the curiously shaped and even more curiously named Jopplety How. This again turns out to be a glacial remnant and its upthrust from the otherwise flat moorland around is noticeable from places several miles away, including, in miniature, from the summit of Skiddaw Little Man. From here a fence provides a guide to the grassy knobble of Ether Knott. Apart from the fence and a modest track, there is nothing but short heather and patches of bog. This area shares the characteristics of the great Central Spine of Lakeland, albeit diminutive in comparison. Likewise here there is nothing but space and silence, nothing glamorous, but in its own unobtrusive way, still soothing of the mind. Just before Ether Knott the fence rises to join another fence which has a small stile for a crossing. This marks a change in scenery. There is now a much more pronounced essence of neglect and disarray; although it is far removed in meaning from those words in an urban context. It is simply the way nature has grown completely unfettered by mankind. Ether Knott itself requires a slight deviation from the track – the short climb to its summit is steep and covered with coarse grass and heather. The small detour is, however, more than worthwhile, for the summit is luxuriantly grassed and sufficiently elevated to provide a wonderful stopping place. Although this summit is only a short distance from the tourist honey pot of Watendlath, it could not be further removed in character. I have seldom visited a place in Lakeland that had such a feeling of peace. It is a wonder, but a gratifying wonder, that Ether Knott has escaped the crowds. Long may it remain that way.

Lonely, empty space from Ether Knott on Grange Fell's east ridge

Back on the East Ridge track, the fence that had been the guide morphs into a rather more aesthetically pleasing dry stone wall. The intense quiet here was interrupted by one of those fleeting glories that define one's memories in the fells. To the other side of the dry stone wall there was a herd of deer, in amongst a chaos of bracken, crags and small trees. Although I did not consider I was making any noise, the sound of my shuffling feet was enough to send the deer scattering every which way. I felt a little guilty at having disturbed their peaceful grazing. This was their place and I was an intruder. Within a few brief moments they had disappeared from view.

The dry stone wall is a lovely guide on the fifteen minute tramp from Ether Knott to Brown Dodd. The track that runs alongside is sometimes obvious, sometimes just a thin ribbon through coarse grass. At one point a craggy outcrop meets the wall, calling for about five feet of ungainly scrambling; the kind of obstacle that initially leads one to look for a way round, before realising that in such an uncompromising place as this, there is no alternative route – hands, feet and other available parts of the

Looking down the South West Arete of Skiddaw Little Man

Heading into Barkbethdale

The view from the flanks of Carrock Fell

Looking into Doddick Gill

Thirlmere from Steel Fell's north ridge

Dollywagon Pike and Seat Sandal from Steel Fell

Heading towards the ravine beneath Whitegill Crag

The view from Harrison Stickle

Wainwright's favourite fell Haystacks, with its inverted reflection in Buttermere

Above High Snab Bank on Robinson

Stan gazing into the valley of Scope Beck'

Approaching Hopegill Head summit

The sweeping panorama from above Addacomb Hole on Wandope

Stan descending the Lad Hows ridge of Grasmoor on the final walk in this book

anatomy would be called upon to surmount this obstacle. Still, there is unlikely to be anyone here to witness this graceless spectacle!

Just before the summit of Brown Dodd, I rounded a natural corner and came across two more deer. This time they were closer at hand but did not immediately dash for cover. Instead they froze, rooted to the spot, unsure of this thing that walked on two legs and the danger or otherwise it posed. With their heads and ears cocked, they presented an ideal photo opportunity. For such circumstances, I always keep my camera in a pocket of my fleece, so that I can call upon it at a moment's notice. I moved my hand towards my pocket as slowly as I could, however this seemingly subtle movement was too much for them as they darted off into the undergrowth. Humans thankfully no longer need an ability to detect the slightest noise or movement as potential danger. We have lost the keenness of sense we must have once had. It was no surprise therefore that what seemed like subtle movements to me, were ringing alarm bells to the deer.

The wall ends in dramatic fashion, perched at a junction of crag and rock just before the rise to Brown Dodd. There is no doubt that at this point the wall should be left behind and a pathless, but simple, ascent made onto Brown Dodd. One can only wonder at both the skill and bravery of the men who built this wall. Not contenting themselves with cutting corners, they followed the natural line of the landscape to the very edge of a plunging downfall. Brown Dodd is a real prize for the lover of solitude. The only two ways of getting to it are an arduous, pathless ascent or the long detour from established ways that is the East Ridge. Brown Dodd, as well as its prized solitude, also has a fine view of Derwent Water. It is otherwise an unassuming place, but nonetheless a place where the spirit can soar in quiet reverie.

At this point I have a confession to make. For days before this walk I had considered the 'sporting crossing of very steep ground', that Wainwright describes as the descent route from Brown Dodd. He also describes a rough gully and pathless bracken covered ground. Although this sounded like challenging terrain, it was nothing I had not negotiated dozens of times on other fells and mountains. The problem lay in the fact that I was dependant on a bus timetable. I was due to catch the last bus as it was and had to make my way to the stop by the Borrowdale Hotel. The dilemma was whether to tackle the unknown of this route down from Brown Dodd, which might end up floundering around trying to find the way to a decent path, and so waste precious time, or simply to head back along the East Ridge and then contour down to Watendlath and the certainty of a road and path network that led to the Borrowdale Road. I had decided the night before the walk that I would survey the route down from above, before making a last minute choice. The trouble with doing this was that unless the route is a sheer and uniform slope down, one can only see so much of the terrain to be crossed. I had just under two hours to get back to the bus stop. It was only a half a mile distant as the crow flies, if I took the direct route down from Brown Dodd, but possibly a lot more than that if I got lost or met some overgrown terrain. The alternative, via Watendlath, would be about 3 miles, but I knew I could guarantee meeting the bus that way. I have deliberately set out not to make the secret Lakeland list too rule bound, hence my suggestion that the routes can be done in ascent or descent. I decided at this point that the essence of this walk was in the East Ridge, in the solitude I had on Ether Knott and Brown Dodd and in the splendour of seeing deer in their natural habitat. However, I determined that I would have to come back and ascend Brown Dodd from the Lodore side before I could say that I had completed all the secret Lakeland walks.

If the bagger (and author) in me was somewhat depressed at this timetable induced technicality, the walker in me could not have cared less, for not only would I have the chance to retrace the East Ridge, but I would also have the delights of Watendlath and the popular route down to Lodore. Any deer on my way out to Brown Dodd, had obviously fled to lower ground for my return journey. Still the peace was glorious. I simply did not expect to meet anyone here and how often can one say that in the Lake District. I decided to contour down from Ether Knott on what seemed to be a track over rather boggy ground, but turned out to be a red herring and necessitated the ungainly crossing of a dry stone wall, decorated with barbed wire, to reach the usual route from Grange Fell down to Watendlath.

I had not visited Watendlath for over 20 years. The last time had been in September 1989, when I descended to the hamlet, having unknowingly completed my first Wainwright, High Tove. Now here I was again, twice as old, greying hair and an ever harder to remove spare tyre around my midriff. I had changed, but I was gladdened to find that Watendlath had not. Despite a few tourists taking photos of the tarn and the small cluster of houses, the place has still managed to retain its charm, nestled away at the terminus of a minor road, inured into the landscape surrounding it. This was the place where Hugh Walpole's fictional character, Judith Paris, sought refuge from the troubles of her life. Here amid the turmoil of life's short existence she could be grounded for a while, amongst the eternity of the fells. One could almost imagine this small but feisty daughter of a rogue and a gipsy, standing in poised reflection by the waters of the tarn and longing for her untrustworthy and often absent husband, Georges Paris, to return. All fiction of course, but written by Walpole with such a convincing thread and eye for detail of character, that one cannot visit the Lakeland places mentioned in it without an odd feeling that the events surely did occur.

Coming out of Watendlath, I had the choice of the path beside Watendlath Beck or the quiet road on the opposite side of the beck. Towards the end of my day it was the smooth surface of the road that appealed to me. Here I could look around at the beautiful valley, with its walls of crag on either side. But I had not quite abandoned adventure for the day – before the road descends towards Ashness, I took to a path, which crossed over Watendlath Beck, via a lovely bridge. An idyllic spot in the late spring weather. The path then enters a wooded area above Gowder Crag and Shepherd's Crag. There are a number of different paths here, but as long as you don't cross over the beck you should end up at High Lodore. The path hugs to the contours of the land, winding its way between trees and their roots. Somewhere around here the route down from Brown Dodd would have joined this route, but I never saw it.

In due course the path ended at the busy Borrowdale Road. It was another thirty minutes till the last bus back to Keswick. I had been too cautious time-wise. Now there are places where half an hour of waiting could be drudgery at the end of a day's walk, but this was thankfully not such a place. Here the half an hour provided just enough time for me to have a pint in The Borrowdale Hotel. The receptionist that greeted me was as polite to the dishevelled entity that presented itself to her, as I'm sure she would have been to the better dressed residents she was accustomed to. I was shown in the direction of the bar and found myself wandering down a quiet corridor, feeling out of place as I trod the lush carpets in my old boots. The bar was duly located and although I had to wait a few minutes for the barman, I had the whole bar area to myself, which made me feel a lot less self-conscious about my scruffy appearance. I could see residents sunning themselves on the hotel terrace outside, but I'd had enough of the sun and was quite happy to just find a comfy chair in the corner of the bar area and drink my pint undisturbed. I contemplated that Ether Knott and Brown Dodd were both less than a mile from where I sat in the bar. Indeed the roots of Brown Dodd lay beneath the very hotel I was sat in. Perhaps one of the glories of exploring the secret places of the Lake District is that in this small corner of the world it is never very far from a place of utter solitude to a place of creature comforts. On the open topped bus alongside Derwent Water, and with the wind fanning my sun reddened face, I reflected on another seemingly small area on the map that had opened up its age old secrets of solitude and peace to me and left my heart the gladder.

The Traverse of High Rigg

High Rigg is not a fell one would label dull. It is too rough in nature, too often climbed, too beautiful in its surrounds, to be cast as a lesser light. However, the time honoured route to the top is a rather staid bagging route that does no justice to the fell. Most ascenders, including myself on my first three occasions, take the route of least resistance straight up from the Church of St John's in the Vale. It's a 20 minute climb and the summit is bagged and the view seen. Although anyone who has driven down the A591 past High Rigg, will get a sense that there is something more to this fell than can be experienced by the traditional short climb. The answer is in the Wainwright guides, for those that care to look. The great man has a little paragraph in his High Rigg chapter headed 'The Traverse of the Ridge'. It's just a few lines, not even a separate ascent page in itself, but when coupled with a study of his detailed map of the fell, it is as if the door has opened to a secret passage and the key to an intimate knowledge of what I consider one of the finest lower Lakeland fells is discovered. On the right type of day this walk is classic Lakeland, a microcosm of everything that millions love and have loved about this small corner of the World.

Now as time passes and my outlook on the fells slowly and subtly changes from what it was a decade before, I have found myself less and less wanting to plan walks that start from a car parked at the very foot of the fell and more and more to look upon a fell as the high point of a long, self sufficient walk without transport. From Keswick, my preferred mountain base, there are a plethora of these types of 'legs only' outings. Whatever the Superpowers decide about climate change, it would be good to say we each individually did what we could. Routes without the need for a car, or perhaps planned using a bus shared with 30 other people, are a small way of contributing to the cutting of harmful emissions. Such self reliant walks are also highly satisfying. In any case, parking outside the bed and breakfast that I stay in is something of a lottery. If you find a space within a couple of hundred yards of your lodging place, it's best if at all possible to keep the car parked there and use the legs. High Rigg from Keswick may seem a very long outing, but it is not quite as long as may be thought.

Not that any lack of parking has ever put me off staying in bed and breakfasts. To me posh and overpriced hotels are not what I require for a walking holiday. I want a place that will welcome me, without a look of disdain, if I arrive soaked to the skin and with mud half way up my trousers. The right bed and breakfast is a crucial element in the enjoyment of a walking holiday. It is a real shame when you find a great B&B with friendly owners, only for them to retire or close a few years later. At the opposite end of the scale, I have stayed in B&Bs from Hell. For example, places where there were flies hovering over the breakfast table, en-suites the size of a broom cupboard, where you needed to have the dexterity of Harry Houdini to use the toilet, televisions – in this digital age – that could not even pick up the BBC without a fuzzy reception, and owners who were so fond of their new decor and wallpaper, that you felt like you were walking through Buckingham Palace when you discretely tip-toed up the stairs at the end of a long walk. For those that stay in B&Bs and love long walks on the fells, it cannot be emphasised strongly enough how important a B&B is. It is the place you arrive at, cold, knackered and hungry, having dreamt of its warmth and that lovely hot shower and cup of tea, for the last five miles of a rain lashed walk. It is the place you sometimes call your home for a week or more. So it must feel relaxed, like home. It is the place that provides you with a filling breakfast that can keep you going for several hours into your walk. It is the place where, when you are walking solo, can provide you with a few friendly words of company in the morning or evening. Luckily for the last three years I have been staying in a B&B that combines great breakfast, with comfortable rooms and very importantly two great owners. These people work hard almost every day of the year and so it is with pleasure that I can heartily recommend Sandon Guest House, Southey Street, Keswick and its proprietors Margaret and Stephen.

It was from this home from home that I set out one March morning to climb High Rigg. It was a day of sunshine and wintry showers, the showers intense and enveloping, the sunshine lighting up every crag and contour, field and tree, in a dazzlingly fresh and luminescent blaze. The Railway Path out of Keswick formed the first three or so miles of my walk and it was here that the first snow shower came over. Until now the Railway Path had been as urbane and friendly a stretch of walking as one could encounter. Suddenly visibility dropped to barely a few feet, as a ground level blizzard swept over me. It was an exhilarating cocoon to be within. On Sharp Edge it would have been terrifying, but on the benign Railway Path it was a thing of intoxication that came and went, leaving the soul cleansed. In just a few minutes the Railway Path and its surrounds were decked in a layer of fresh snow. The blizzard quickly blew onwards and revealed once again the flanks of Blease Fell on Blencathra, now dusted with white that was tinged with blue.

Eventually the Railway Path is left for a narrow rising path that dives under the concrete span of the A66, emerging on a minor road beyond. My apologies in advance, for here this walk involves about three quarters of a mile of road walking, although the road is not that busy and there are striking views behind to the East Face of Lonscale Fell and ahead to the objective High Rigg, the Helvellyn Range lurking behind. Road walking ends where a rather boggy path leads over a couple of fields to Tewit Tarn.

Now Tewit Tarn is one of those stretches of water that is, I imagine, more often viewed from a distance than from its shore. It is a familiar speck of blue in the view from the summit of Blencathra and also from the Cumbria Way path beneath the flanks of Lonscale Fell. The tarn though has a reticent charm and feels further away from the throng of the A66 than it actually is. It presents a fine photo opportunity, with a good backdrop of the Coledale

A fell pony near Tewit Tarn, with the Coledale giants behind

Fells and has a solitary twisted tree near its shore, which provided a momentary shelter from the bitter March wind that day. The path now skirts Low Rigg and alternates between luxuriant grass and boggy patches, all the way to the minor road by the Church of St John's. Here starts the traditional whistle stop route up High Rigg and also the much finer traverse route.

It seems rather an odd and inaccessible place to have a church. However this is based upon our modern pre-conception of accessible being a place near to a Motorway or an 'A' road. When the church was built in 1544, the 'minor road' past it was actually part of a major route from Matterdale to Wanthwaite. Its tiny tower, almost model village in proportion, still manages to hold a bell. This is perhaps my favourite of Lakeland's churches, unassuming as it is, almost a part of the landscape. For those that pray, to whoever or whatever, the inside or outside of this church is a perfect place. Best not to pray for too long though, for what is in my view one of Lakeland's finest low level paths awaits. From where the church wall meets the minor road, the traverse path starts and in an instant one is transported away from popular and into secret Lakeland. The path is broad and a delight to walk upon, as it constantly dips and falls, twists and turns, with the massive bulk of Wanthwaite Crags opposite for brooding companionship. Some ruined stone farm buildings along the way seem to be organically mouldering back into the land. Half an hour before I had been frozen to the marrow whilst having the briefest of stops by Tewit Tarn. Now in a blaze of sun and the lee of the wind, March became more lamb than lion and I had one of those first sun drenched stops of the year, glorifying in this harbinger of the coming spring.

Soon the path levelled out and I unexpectedly came across a small children's nature trail, followed by a sign saying something like 'refreshments available'. The sign pointed down some steps that led into the back garden of an old farm cottage. I have always been someone who drinks copious volumes of liquid on walks and as the sun had surprisingly heated me up, I followed the sign. No-one was in the small garden, so I knocked at the back door and poked my head round, with an 'anybody there' thrown in for good measure. I hoped the sign was accurate and I was not about to encounter some homicidal lunatic.

A short while later a portly gentleman of retirement age appeared and provided me with a little menu of drinks. Now here was another advantage to not having brought a car on the walk, as I indulged in a cold pint without fear of the consequences. The man went to get my drink and I sat down on a metal bench outside. I was suddenly struck by the amount of birds gathered around a nut feeder on a nearby tree. With the quaint old cottage and a host of blue tits, chaffinches, sparrows and even the odd wren gathered about me, I felt that it would not have been entirely surprising if Snow White suddenly appeared carrying my drink and with birds singing around her shoulders. Instead, and perhaps slightly to the disappointment of my fancy, the man returned with my beverage. For a while he talked about the dozens of bird species that visited his garden and about how many locals and farmers were now having to make a little money by opening their farms up for selling refreshments, nature trails and such like. The farms and farming make Lakeland what it is, especially its beauty below the open fell side, and it would be tragic if traditional farming practices continue to die out as they currently are. After a while the man popped back inside and I was left finishing my pint, while staring towards the majestic Castle Rock of Triermain, looking every bit like the 'mighty keep and tower' description Sir Walter Scott gave it, with its every feature picked out by the bright sunshine and clear air.

As the path continues its course, gradually trending towards St John's Beck and the butt end of High Rigg, it traverses dramatically above the beck (not a good place for vertigo sufferers), becoming narrow and shelf like, as it weaves amongst some fine natural trees beneath the aptly named Wren Crag. This is the start of a truly magical section of the walk, as the route now climbs the unfamiliar southern end of High Rigg. After a short rise there appears ahead a piece of hidden Lakeland heaven, a little stretch of walk that invites you to run, childlike, into its embrace. The broad, grassy and easy path now rises among some gloriously twisted pine trees. With the dazzling March blue above me and the ground and trees coloured in various radiant shades of green and brown, surely even Heaven could not have delivered much better. It was not a question of my needing to stop beneath these trees. It was more the place suggesting itself as a place to have to stop. For here there is sufficient height and depth of scene for a truly fine view. Most compelling that day was the intimate view of the Helvellyn range, sinking and rising inexorably to its crowning glory, the dark crags of the ridge standing bold against the pure white of the freshly fallen snow. Opposite and beyond a bird's eye view of the A591, rose the impressive tree plastered Great How (a hill outcast from any tick list) and beneath this Thirlmere and its dam. This for me is the finest view High Rigg has to offer and yet I was all alone and aside from the man who had served me the pint, had met just one person since the Church of St John's.

It is strange how one can follow a course, just a few hundred metres removed in distance and height from that trodden earlier in the day and yet feel in a totally different world. But that is how it is following the ridge back

A little piece of heaven on the traverse of High Rigg

over High Rigg. All is now open skies, short cropped, tufty grass and a smattering of small but idyllic tarns. High Rigg's tarns are elusive. After heavy rain there may be a number of small tarns, but only one is a permanent resident. The ridge has something of Loughrigg Fell about its immediate terrain, although there the similarity with that other wonderful island fell ends. For those seeking quiet contemplation, the ridge of High Rigg is ideal. When the summit is finally attained one has the strange feeling of having climbed some different fell to the one previously climbed from St John's, but that somehow happens to share the same name. There is also a real sense of having earned the summit and done justice to High Rigg by a full exploration, instead of giving it a rough and ready half hour, on a poor day. By the time I reached the summit the best of the day was over. Snow showers were packing densely into longer periods of snow in the direction of a glowering Coledale Round and there was a steadily increasing wind chill. The lion of March was returning. This had been one of those fell walking experiences that are not defined by the summit, but by the quiet nooks and crannies, the delightful turns of the path and the joys of personal exploration.

Awkward Moments
on the Langdale Pikes

The car park at the New Dungeon Ghyll Hotel was almost packed by the time Stan and I pulled into one of the few remaining spaces in the grassy field. It was a sunny Sunday in July and therefore crowds on the celebrated Langdale Pikes were guaranteed. An army of walkers were putting on their boots and donning their sun cream in synchronised motions. Normally you would not see me walking in July in the fells for love nor money; too hot, too crowded and too many insects. However, I had been nominated for the Lakeland Book of The Year Award, which is held annually in July and it seemed a bit of a rush to just drive up to the Lake District, attend the awards and then scuttle back down to Kent. The awards were on a Tuesday, so we decided to travel up on the Sunday before and sneak in a couple of days of hopefully secret Lakeland walking. At this time of year, and in this particular showpiece area of the Lake District, it was going to be hard work. We had a plan though that would hopefully manage to avoid the crowds in the main, but would not avoid them altogether. This was to be the only walk in this book that would include three secret Lakeland routes in one day, two in ascent and one in descent.

From the crowded car park we could already see our first objective of the day, the towering cliffs of Whitegill Crag, a looming, seemingly impregnable bastion of solitude. In the clear morning light it looked stunning and more than a little intimidating. However, Wainwright assured us that there was a route that avoided the difficulties.

Straightaway we shunned the popular routes up towards Stickle Tarn, which ninety per cent of the walkers were taking, instead heading about a quarter of a mile along the Great Langdale Road, in the direction of Chapel Stile. From a gate at the roadside, we made our way into a lush green meadow with an old barn, behind which a large contingent of sheep were sheltering from the scorching morning sun, before then crossing another wall into a typically (for south Lakeland) chaotic area of rocks and giant boulders. The path climbs steeply up the side of a little rock cliff, whose flat topped rocky top was a nice place for a short stop and to survey the already expanding prospect away down Great Langdale. Over another stile the path branched, with a right hand fork a little climber's path heading for the impressive Scout Crag, whose walls already accommodated several climbers, with the left hand fork – the one we followed – heading towards a plantation of larch trees. The beautiful path here is not followed for long, before a stony and parched stream bed is crossed. One half longs to carry on along the path through the larches, but you've guessed it, this being secret Lakeland we were heading straight up the rocky stream bed. Here there was no path, just a chaos of boulders and a small stream. Still with the walls of Whitegill Crag now dominating to the right, this was an impressive place to be. Several more climbers were in various positions of self-imposed lunacy, some splayed in a kind of sacrificial stance against the rock face, looking for handholds, others at the top of an absurd flake of rock calling down to their comrades below. Along the gill bed though there was nobody but myself and Stan. Only climbers seemed to come this way.

We had a stop to duck our heads into a little rocky pool and at the same time decide which of the two routes Wainwright describes we should take. There was a choice of a rocky scramble up loose stones and scree to the top of Whitegill Crag, or a grassy but steep route past Swine Knott. The Swine Knott route was suggested as the best place to view the crags and the climbers from, so we decided to take that. As we looked up at this flank of grass and loose gravel, I remember Stan commenting that it

The bouldery bed of the gill beneath Whitegill Crag

did not look very inviting with me just dismissing it with mindless optimism, remarking that it would be fine. Five minutes later, I found myself wishing I had heeded Stan's warning as we found ourselves on a very steep slope, made very awkward by dry loose gravel. Every inch of ascent was punishment as we fought our way upwards with the ever-present unpleasant prospect of sliding back down to the gill bed below should we slip. Higher up, thick bracken and nettles made progress even more unbearable, the sweat pouring from our brows, stinging our eyes in the mid July heat. At one point Stan seemed to slightly lose his balance and my heart leapt into my throat as I pictured him tumbling back to the gill. Luckily he held on, just. All thoughts of stopping and taking in the grand view of Whitegill Crag and the climbers were extinguished. This was not the sort of terrain conducive to sightseeing! When eventually the path levelled off at about 1500 feet, we were panting for breath. My legs, which were bare because I was wearing shorts, had been badly grazed and cut. I would not recommend this route, which is up there with Doddick Gill as the most awkward in this book. We took a long rest now on firmer and flatter ground and finally got our chance to look across at the climbers on Whitegill Crag. Perhaps more of interest to us now, was the alternative scree gully route that we had spurned. This looked none too pleasant either, but certainly shorter and perhaps a little surer than the grassy way. I would suggest taking the gully route if you want to come this way. At this stage, having already used up copious supplies of energy, I could not contemplate the fact that we had done about a mile of walking and were less than a quarter of the way through our day.

Spirits began to rise however as we crossed some open moorland to reach the Wainwright summit of Blea Rigg. Blea Rigg is only 1776 feet in height and yet the effort so far expended was akin to a 3000 feet peak. Its top features several little rocky summits and is a fine place. From Blea Rigg it was a rather boggy and featureless trudge down to the banks of Stickle Tarn, although the view ahead to Harrison Stickle and the shattered cliffs of Pavey Ark livened things up, especially in the knowledge that I was about to climb a new route on to the summit of the Ark. Stickle Tarn was about as crowded as one would expect on a Sunday in July. I doubt Hyde Park would have been much less popular. Huge parties of walkers were picnicking by the banks of the tarn and there was a hubbub of noisy activity that grated in this place of supposed tranquillity. Stan and I found a little grassy bank by the tarn and joined the throng for a few moments. Secret Lakeland had been left behind, but I recalled a January day, when Stan and I had started a walk to Stickle Tarn in the dark and watched the first rays of dawn light up the snow covered face of Pavey Ark in pink and orange hues. That day there had been no-one at Stickle Tarn and even we had to leave soon after, chased back to the car by a swirling blizzard.

Those of a nervous disposition may decide to miss out the next section of the walk up Easy Gully on Pavey Ark. The alternatives could either be the usual North Rake on to Pavey Ark, or even to bypass Pavey Ark altogether and take the usual route on to Harrison Stickle. Those with a head for heights and desirous of a little more solitude please read on. It had been fifteen years since I had climbed Jack's Rake in my mid twenties and had on the same day sworn that I would never do it again. Now I found myself on the initial scree slope, not this time headed for Jack's Rake, but for its supposedly easier companion, accordingly named Easy Gully. Here we were to learn that the term 'easy' on the climbing ground of Pavey Ark, is a relative term. Wainwright describes the early section of this climb as 'mainly a steep walk on grass and sliding scree'. This is reasonably accurate, although I could not see much of the grass while there was an awful lot of the sliding scree, along with a littering of boulders which the great man did not mention. Stan commented that this section resembled Lord's Rake on Scafell, although I would have to take his word for this, as this is one Lakeland scramble that he has done about five times and I have done zero times (this may change for the next volume of *Secret Lakeland!*). As height is gained, you get the feeling that you would rather not go back down the way you came. So it is a horrible conundrum when the way ahead suddenly becomes blocked by several huge boulders. It is a moment of decided pique and surging adrenalin when a walker realises that neither the prospects forward or backward are desirable but that one or other has to be negotiated. Wainwright mentions climbing for 50 feet over the boulders, with 'one awkward obstacle'. I will kid you not. These boulders were very awkward and not a little terrifying. Indeed there are a few places where a slip could have serious consequences. One tends to imagine boulders as being round in shape. These boulders might more correctly be called slabs of rocks, with hard edges, set at a slanting angle and just to be extra awkward, placed one on top of the other, so that the next boulder is constantly impeding progress over the previous one. Ungainly positions and use of arms, knees and any other part of the anatomy available are all necessary. It was with great relief that these boulders were left behind, a short climb leading on to North Rake and thence to the summit of Pavey Ark. Comparing them in retrospect, Easy Gully is in my view slightly easier than Jack's Rake. I may even do it again sometime. It is however certainly not 'easy', but it was at least very quiet.

Pavey Ark, with its high mountain feel and sweeping view along Great Langdale to Windermere, is a wonderful place to be on most days. Not so, however, when the summit is occupied by a family including two screaming and shouting brats. I would rather have shared this summit with 100 respectful and quiet walkers, than with this noisy and disrespectful family, where the parents seemed to have no control or desire to control the Neanderthal antics of their children. As a result, it was a short stop on the summit of Pavey Ark that day; thankfully the noise gradually faded as we marched off towards Harrison Stickle. After a difficult day, with little in the way of relaxing stops to speak of, the final section of this walk was an utter tonic. Harrison Stickle has always been a favourite summit of mine, not only for the outstanding view, but also for the high platform, dropping away on all sides, that forms the little summit ridge. There were a few walkers sharing this great place, but they were all of the unobtrusive, respectful type. Stan and I were able to find a beautiful perch, at the south top of the fell, with a glorious plunge down to Pike Howe and the dog-leg of the Langdale valley below. As I have said, July is not a favourite month of mine to walk. However today, this time of year lent a quality to the valley floor that I had seldom seen. The fields, instead of being deep green in colour, were either a light green, or a sandy brown where they had been harvested. There seemed to be a fete going on in Elterwater, judging from the large marquee and the sun glinting off the innumerable vehicles parked nearby. It was a glorious summer scene with no fear of blizzards, no chill wind or rain and no deadline for descent to avoid darkness.

Our route of descent from Harrison Stickle was to be as glorious as any route used in descent in this book. To begin with head for Pike o'Stickle and Loft Crag, but before either of these Wainwright summits, a slender path heads down towards a ravine at the base of Thorn Crag. The ravine is a spectacular sight, its walls sheer and its bottom littered with scree and boulders. Above this a delightful path traverses the fell side, quite dramatically in places and with wonderful views ahead. Before long the rocky path is replaced with lush grass, on the route to Pike Howe. A very short pull leads to the final summit of the day. Pike Howe is not a Wainwright fell, but it is a fine top and viewpoint to spend a few minutes on a balmy summer evening, with Side Pike and the Coniston range forming a high backdrop. The route slightly deteriorates in quality from Pike Howe onwards, but it is not far to the valley floor. By the time we arrived at the New Dungeon Ghyll Hotel, our throats were dry and our stomachs empty so it was an easy decision to stop for refreshment. Once again I found myself relishing the joys of a summer walk, sitting in the evening sunshine replenishing our energy with burgers and beers whilst looking back up at Pike Howe and the impossibly high Harrison Stickle. It was good enough to win me round to the idea of some more summer walks. Well almost.

The Reluctant King

If there was a quiz for fell walkers and they were asked to name the highest fells in each of the seven *Pictorial Guides*, almost all would get Scafell Pike for the Southern Fells, Skiddaw for the Northern Fells and Helvellyn for the Eastern Fells. When asked for the highest point in the Central Fells though, more than a few might say Harrison Stickle, whose towering form dominates Langdale. How many though would guess correctly that it was High Raise? At 2500 feet, this King of the Central Fells does not exactly display his wares for all to see. He is a shy king, content to let his lower but more splendid subjects bask in the glory that should be his. From a distance High Raise is quite difficult to pick out, being merely a slightly pointed dome. Closer acquaintance with the summit, however, reveals a worthy highest point, with a commanding view and a true mountain feel. A fine summit and a fine viewpoint, but what about a fine climb? Many, me included, pick off High Raise as a detour out and back from Sergeant Man or Harrison Stickle. Nonetheless, I wanted to include High Raise in this book as a fell climbed for its own sake. It would be a shame to write a section about the Central Fells and neglect the highest of them. For a while nothing really suggested itself as an interesting and possibly secretive route. Then I hit upon a climb that is in my view the finest way to the summit of High Raise and contains some thrilling and dramatic moments. This is the climb of High Raise via Eagle Crag and Sergeant's Crag.

This route begins at the charming hamlet of Stonethwaite, tucked away from civilization at the end of a minor road. Cross a bridge over Stonethwaite Beck to join the familiar path that leads to Greenup Edge. Straight ahead, Eagle Crag dominates. It seems impregnable but Wainwright reveals that there is one chink in the armour of these crags and that is the way Stan and I were heading. In the early stages of this walk, Stonethwaite Beck cascades alongside the path, the sound of surging water dominating the senses. Before long Sergeant's Crag also comes into view – the profile of this fell from here, along with the neighbouring Eagle Crag, rather resembling the profile of mighty Suilven in the Far North of Scotland. Sometimes a scrambling prospect, such as Eagle Crag, will cause me a little panic in the approach, but here my feelings were only of excitement at the prospect, the Wainwright guide reassuring me that the climb was fairly straightforward.

Eagle Crag and Sergeant's Crag resembling Suilven in the author's opinion

The route leaves the Greenup Edge path at a junction and heads over a lovely footbridge, spanning a particularly delightful part of Stonethwaite Beck. We stopped for a while by the banks of the beck to indulge in a childlike, but wonderfully relaxing game of 'hit a particular rock in the middle of the beck with a pebble'. The footbridge forms part of another popular highway, being the start of the route down Langstrath, over Stake Pass – also a section of the Cumbria Way. Directly after the footbridge though, we left popular paths for quieter ones. Yes it was time to wade through heather, bog and bracken. Wainwright marks just two possible ascent routes to the summit of Eagle Crag, called prosaically routes A and B. Route B he calls a 'back door' route to the summit and is best used in descent. Route A is a totally different and finer experience, although as we floundered through the undergrowth on the pathless side of Stonethwaite Beck this did not at first seem very 'fine'. We were very surprised to see a walker ahead of us and seemingly going the same way, although we never saw him going up the steep flanks of Eagle Crag, which he clearly would have done had he gone that way. Perhaps he was a climber, heading for an even lonelier and even more dramatic situation than we were.

After the crossing of a second wall the climb proper begins; it is a joy to find a steep, grassy path heading up alongside an equally steep section of dry stone wall. At the top of this initial section of steepness begins the upper section of Route A, to which Wainwright devotes almost a whole page of his guide. The wall ends abruptly beneath a large crag and here is found one of the more unusually situated stiles in the district. Instead of a room with a view, this is a stile with a view looking as it does back along the Stonethwaite valley with Dale Head and High Spy beyond. The walk continues along the base of the crag on easy ground, but it is clear that somewhere there is going to be some steep climbing if upward progress is to be made. There is one route only between the crags, a short rocky gully, calling for a little mild scrambling. Above this gully the exposure increases as the path makes a raking line above the fierce plunge of Heron Crag. Just when you start to wonder again about the route onward, a faint path heads up a series of heather terraces and ledges. These reminded me somewhat of the terraces of a rice paddy field. Some of them need to be scrambled up, but they provide great places to sit and admire the spacious drops into Langstrath and other than the sense of exposure and height, there is nothing to cause alarm here. Indeed it is in such places that the finest of secret Lakeland can be found. It is not far to the rocky summit cairn of Eagle Crag, which is set on an angled slab of rock providing a wonderful airy perch for viewing the Stonethwaite Valley, although the surrounding higher fells conspire to prevent a good all round view.

Two other walkers were in the immediate vicinity of the summit and its cairn, so Stan and I (being anti-social) chose to head slightly down from the summit towards the edge of Eagle Crag. It was to our chagrin therefore when these two walkers followed us and chose a spot about five feet away from us to have their rest. Is it a little churlish of me to have found this irritating? Perhaps it is, but I can only judge by my own yardstick and where there is space on a summit, I like to give myself and other people their space. The exception perhaps being the summit of Sgurr nan Gillean on the Isle of Skye, where there is only space for about three people to stand! There was no wind on the summit of Eagle Crag that day and no need to shelter away from the summit, so having left the summit for these two men to enjoy and seek out a lower refuge, why did they have to follow us like lemmings to the cliff?

The half mile route from Eagle Crag to neighbouring Sergeant's Crag is a simple walk, although there is one small 'granny stopper' beneath the summit of Eagle Crag, where a wall is joined. The summit of Sergeant's Crag is sufficiently rocky to merit interest. The view is not as fine or dramatic as that from Eagle Crag, but there is a good prospect to Bowfell and Esk Pike, with the Langstrath valley far below. Wainwright describes the one and a half mile ridge route from Sergeant's Crag to High Raise as 'an easy, tedious climb on grass'. I would disagree with this on two counts. Firstly, this climb is altogether longer and less easy than expected and, secondly, I rather enjoyed this climb. Here is a giant flank of fell side, a huge grassy acreage that is largely pathless and a place where a person feels dwarfed by the immensity of the surroundings. I guess again that when Wainwright was writing his guides there were less people on the fells generally and so perhaps he did not appreciate the solitude of this ridge route as much as the modern walker might.

I had been on the summit of High Raise half a dozen times, but it was odd to approach it from a different angle and to suddenly appear on the ridge just a few yards away from the summit cairn. Today there was a considerable wind chill on the summit and the clouds had begun to obscure the higher fells, but it was still a wonderful prospect towards Skiddaw and Bassenthwaite Lake, while Eagle Crag, which had seemed so high and unattainable at the start of the day, had now become a mere minion to the King of the Central Fells, its lofty summit now seen some 850 feet below. Wainwright devoted four pages of guide book to a 360 degree detailed panorama from High Raise and on a day of fine weather it is easy to see why, as over 75 Wainwright Fells can be spotted from the summit. We were not so lucky today however, as the morning sunshine we experienced climbing Eagle Crag had given way to gloom and threatening rain. Our escape route followed the fence posts down to Greenup Edge and from there down into the Stonethwaite Valley. The top of Lining Crag is worth a detour for its airy little summit. After Lining Crag one of the finest and most extensive areas of glacial moraines can be seen, the little humpy hillocks reminding me of the Teletubbies' landscaped garden. Heavy rain now accompanied us from here all the way back to Stonethwaite and the car, although the wonderful views earlier in the day remained firmly in the mind's eye.

opposite: *The reservoir at the head of Scope Beck*

The North Western Fells

'There are many corners rarely visited, many excellent routes rarely trodden, many interesting pastures rarely seen.'
Alfred Wainwright, *Pictorial Guide to the North Western Fells*
Some Personal Notes in Conclusion

What an endorsement from the great man for a walker wanting to find secret Lakeland. In many ways the North Western Fells are the ideal terrain for a lover of hill walking. Glorious outlines give promise of wonderful expeditions. The Coledale and Newlands Rounds are magnets for the crowds and for Wainwright baggers desirous of knocking off half a dozen summits in a single day. My first time walking these high ridges will stay in the memory banks for ever. Yet I knew that there was more to this area than could be gained from merely linking one fell to another via a high ridge. Wandope is a case in point. I had summited this fell three or four times, but always as a detour from Eel Crag or a gentle, grassy stroll from Thirdgill Head Man. I had never climbed Wandope for its own sake. Now, on Wandope's flanks, I was to find two of the steepest, yet wonderfully situated, walks in this book. The same handshake acquaintance had hitherto been made with Grasmoor, Eel Crag, Whiteside and Hopegill Head. Even Grisedale Pike had only been climbed via the familiar route from Braithwaite over Kinn. Now I was longing to explore the 'many excellent routes rarely trodden' that Wainwright so beautifully catalogues in his guides. Here I was to discover a number of classic routes of ascent, by and large devoid of people. The situational drama of the Shelf Route on Tower Ridge; the wonderful Dove Crags and Lad Hows routes on Grasmoor; the quiet north-east ridge of Grisedale Pike and the dramatic descent of Hopegill Head, via Ladyside Pike. All these were 'as good as anything else in Lakeland', as Wainwright describes them. All of them proved that Coledale is about so much more than high level ridge walking. The joy of all of these alternative routes was that once up on the high ridge, several summits could easily be bolted on to a secret Lakeland classic, so combining lonely routes with high level ridge tramping, in some unforgettable days.

The fells of the Newlands Round also yielded some memorable new routes, although not as many or perhaps as varied as those found on the Coledale Fells. High Spy, which had hitherto been just a summit cairn with a great view, was given character and stature on a beautiful and lonely climb from Grange. Robinson, so often bagged as an out and back exercise from the Newlands Round proper, yielded three new routes of ascent, two of which are as fine and varied as anything in this book. Great pleasure was had in turning Robinson from an acquaintance into a wonderful new friend. A couple of straightforward new descent routes from Dale Head proved excellent tonics at the end of long days. Indeed the descent from Dale Head to the Honister Slate Mine can be recommended for those who wish to see the rare sight of a winter sunset from a high fell and still have time for a safe and quick descent.

Wainwright divides the North Western Fells into three distinct areas, cut into three slices by high road passes. The Newlands Hause road separates the Coledale and Newlands Fells, while the Whinlatter Pass road separates the Coledale Fells from what one might call the Whinlatter Fells. Many will look at these Whinlatter Fells and think of them as the smallest and least desirable of the three slices. However, here are also found some hidden gems. Two routes onto Graystones are as charming, pastoral and quiet as one could wish for. Routes on easy ground – the odd patch of bog excluded – where time will be on your side, where you can relax and allow it to pass unnoticed for a few hours. For a lover of solitude the Wythop Moss must be visited. It has a curious atmosphere and, in the right conditions, a certain charm that one would not expect from what is essentially a flat piece of moorland. Sale Fell, via the Wythop Wood, although not described by Wainwright as a route of ascent, provides a beautiful contrast between dark and dense forest and glorious, pastoral fell side. This less celebrated portion of the North Western Fells can also boast one of the toughest little scrambles in the area. The ascent of Barf direct from Thornthwaite was a prospect that sent pangs of adrenalin whizzing round my stomach, but an accomplishment that gave a great sense of achievement. For the sheer variety of scenery, drama and beauty, I consider the North Western Fells just won out over the other two fell areas described in this book, although I accept that such comparisons are by and large meaningless and arbitrary. Suffice it to conclude that in these fells can be found everything a lover of secret Lakeland could possibly want.

Secret Newlands

The fells of Newlands are to my mind some of the most graceful in the British Isles. They are not as dramatic as some, not as craggy or high as others, but they make up for this in their wonderful sleek lines and contours. Catbells with its familiar humps and knobbles, the soaring pyramid of Hindscarth, the rounded arc of Robinson. Within their valleys one feels enfolded, comforted, at ease. Their summits can be as wild as any, yet in the memory they are forever beautiful and homely friends. It is no wonder that Hugh Walpole's fictional characters Vanessa Paris and Benjie Herris would choose to seclude themselves, away from their troubles in the welcoming embrace of the Newlands Valley.

It is in part because of their beauty and in part because of the wonderful fell walking round they offer that the Newlands Fells are justifiably popular. Catbells in particular must lay claim to be the most often climbed fell in the Lake District. So I knew that I was going to have my work cut out to find the secrets of Newlands, those routes away from the crowds. However, a study of Wainwright's *North Western Fells Guide* showed me that amongst this relatively small cluster of fells and away from the time honoured round, there were a number of routes that were not only seldom used, but also climbed and threaded their way amidst some spectacular surroundings.

Robinson is the outlier of the Newlands circuit. The other Newlands Fells look after themselves on the round, but it takes a little bit of extra effort and a walk there and back along the Littledale Edge to take in Robinson as well. For many fell walkers, that may be their only experience of Robinson. Indeed for a very long time I fell into that category. However, in recent times I have come to realise, or perhaps discover might be a better word, that this massive fell with its roots in different valleys, has a lot more to offer and is a very worthy climb in itself. Here I offer three alternative ascents of Robinson, as well as a different and very quiet route off the fell. They all come highly recommended.

The climb of Robinson from Buttermere village provides the greatest amount of ascent of any route onto Robinson. I was a little concerned with the inclusion of this route in a book entitled *Secret Lakeland*, due to the fact that Wainwright calls it a 'popular climb'. However, I figured that the times change and that it was worth climbing this route in 2010, to see whether it merited inclusion in this book. As the walk was to be a proper round, rather than just an ascent and descent by the same route, Stan and I decided that the best place to park the car and start the walk from was in one of the lay-bys roughly midway between Gatesgarth farm and Honister Pass. This would mean we could walk down Buttermere in the early spring morning light and also avoid a long and potentially dispiriting road walk at the end of the day.

Buttermere had never looked finer than it did on that spring morning. The lake was as calm and still as the proverbial mill pond with the huge buttresses of the High Crag and High Stile perfectly mirrored in its glassy waters. A cluster of trees at the Gatesgarth end of the lake, with shaggy Haystacks as a backdrop, found a temporary twin on the lake's surface. Such a scene is rare and fleeting and the more magical for being so. For it only takes a breath of wind to cause the slightest of ripples, that then works its way insidiously across the lake surface dashing the mirror to pieces. The lakeside path was busy even in early spring, but the scene was so breathtaking and such a privilege that we almost became one awestruck entity. Not even the most metronomic of hearts could have failed to miss a beat here. So focused was everybody on the lake, on taking his or her photographic memento, that we all quite lost ourselves.

The perfect reflection lasted perhaps twenty minutes, before a small zephyr of wind drifted down the lake and broke the spell. The reflection became distorted and twisted as in a Hall of Mirrors. The people on the path lost their oneness and became individual groups once more with their own thoughts and agendas. We marched on down Buttermere, suddenly conscious of the passage of time again, whereas before time had stood as still as the lake's reflection.

The tiny church of St. James, on the road to Newlands and immediately above Buttermere village is worthy of a visit. It seems as much a part of the landscape as the fells themselves and yet surprisingly only dates back to the 1840s. It is perhaps these days most often visited in homage to Wainwright. Here a small but dignified plaque sits beneath one of the church windows, through which the crag girt outline of Haystacks 'his favourite place', can be seen.

Starts to walks can be magical as civilization is left behind and an ancient world entered. However, the ascent of Robinson from Buttermere, starts not with a bang, but a whimper although pleasant enough whimper all the same. Tarmac road simply merges with a lush verdant grassy path. There is no wall, no gate and no passage through trees to reach the open fell side. It's road one second and bare fell side the next. It was about now that I began to have doubts as to whether this ascent would appear in a book entitled *Secret Lakeland*. For ahead of us was a group of three, two ladies and a man, heading up the ice encrusted path with no more than trainers on their feet and no sign of jackets and coats that would no doubt be needed as the air cooled higher up. The man was in a mood of bravado, as he raced up the wide grass path like a rabbit. The ladies seemed more reluctant and hung some way behind him, common sense tugging at their conscience. The man kept turning to beckon and shout for the ladies to come on and eventually the ladies would follow. It was the classic recipe for a fell walking disaster. Rules of clothing, footwear and the time honoured rule of going at the pace and willingness of the slowest member of the party were abandoned. They were the only people ahead, but the attitude of the man as he cajoled the ladies onward in a loud voice irritated me in the extreme.

Not that I, in all honesty, was as well prepared that day as I should have been. I had come up by train from my home in Kent, and my suitcase was so crammed that I figured that I could get by without the awkward encumbrance of crampons and ice axe for a few days fell walking in mid-March. I could hardly carry the ice axe around with me through the centre of London and on to a train, so when it could not squeeze into the suitcase without risk of puncturing it, I left it behind. A decision I was to regret.

The wide green path merges into an old sled road, one of a number in the district using for carrying peat off the fell. Ahead of us we could see the man and two ladies making a very awkward and somewhat reluctant traverse of the rocky passage at the head of Near Broken Gill. When we caught up with them we realised why they had been so reluctant. This narrow passage, sitting above a nasty plunge down the gill, was covered in a thick layer of sheet ice. It was only a few feet of late winter spite to cross, before giving way once more to spring grass, but even though I was wearing thick tread winter boots, I could have done with the reassurance of crampons here. I gingerly stepped across, leaning into the fell side and away from the ravine, happily making it across without a slip. Stan followed, not bothering with his crampons for the short distance, but with his axe to keep him steady. At this point the party of three ahead, disappeared over the horizon onto Buttermere Moss, and we never saw them again that day. I am certain they could not have made it onto the final snow covered slopes of Robinson and can only assume that put off by the featureless expanse of Buttermere Moss, they made their escape via Moss Force and Newlands Hause. Either that or maybe they became consumed by the peat bog of the Moss and will be discovered five thousand years from now, by an advanced technological society that has lost its soul and wonders why on Earth people ever climbed fells, especially in trainers!

Although not strictly part of the ascent route, it would be selling this climb short not to make the short detour to the summit of High Snockrigg. For this is one of those defined little summits, with its sense of depth, plunging away over crags to Buttermere, that leaves one wondering why it is not a Wainwright fell. It certainly has more merit than Sallows, Little Mell Fell and half a dozen other genuine Wainwrights. It can be an advantage though to be a summit that lacks classification. You are less likely to be visited.

Down by the lake, Spring had seemed upon us, but up at 1700 feet on High Snockrigg, the view spoke of winter on the high fells. The giant buttress of High Stile and High Crag were laced with snow from about 2000 feet upwards, the darkness of the crags a conspicuous contrast. Higher still, Pillar was a dome of white, its summit just poking above High Crag. Great Gable and Kirk Fell's whitened flanks overtopped the snowless black walls of Haystacks. By contrast, the smooth grassy outline of Rannerdale Knotts perfectly bisected Crummock Water. This is more than just a detour. It is a place to linger if time permits.

Buttermere Moss was very different from my last visit twelve years before. That day it had been a squelchy early summer heat trap. This time in March, a lot of the bog was still frozen into corrugated rivulets, which made for much firmer walking than the sponge encountered in summer. The final pull from Buttermere Moss to the summit of Robinson is normally easy enough. Today, however, it was covered in a thick layer of old, crusty snow. This was not the firm, powdery freshly laid stuff, but compacted snow and ice and without an ice axe it made for very uncertain and difficult climbing. This final pull has no sizeable crags, no massive plunging drops, and yet I cursed myself for having left the axe at home, as my feet struggled to gain any sort of purchase on the slippery surface. Occasional rocky snowless sections became an oasis of respite from the struggle. On several occasions I found myself performing a kind of comedy walking motion that actually, if anything, ended up propelling me backwards rather than forwards. Had I tumbled back down the snow slope, I would at the very least have suffered a fatal blow to my resilience for the day, if not the odd broken bone as well. I started cursing loudly as my energy became sapped in vainly trying to struggle upwards. Stan could easily have laughed at this sorry effort, but instead proved why he is my best mate of 30 years and my ideal hill walking companion. He simply held out the end of his axe for me to grab on to and hauled me up to the next

Heading from Robinson towards Dale Head

bare path amidst the snow and by repeating this a dozen times the last couple of hundred feet of Robinson were at last tamed. This is the last time I will forget the axe in the winter months, even if it does end up poking through my suitcase on the train up!

The summit of Robinson should have been a place for celebration, the vast snow topped panorama taking in everything from Wetherlam in the south to Binsey in the north with Great Gable, Kirk Fell and Scafell particularly finely displayed. But we had only been there for a few seconds, not even enough to get our breath back, when we both had one of the more unpleasant encounters we have had on the fells. A man of about 60 years old came up from the Littledale Edge direction and joined us on the summit. Now I'm not one to seek out company on the fells as you know. I'd rather be alone or perhaps with one or two other favourite companions. However, I will at least make an effort to talk to the people I meet on summits and by doing so have had conversations that ranged from the amusing, to the entertaining and informative, and yes occasionally the downright dull or annoying. It's in my nature to be sociable when I need to be or when it is polite to be. So I greeted the man with a friendly 'hello' and one of the standard phrases for meeting someone of the summit such as 'great view' or 'which way have you come up' or 'glorious day', I can't recall which. In return I got a look I can only describe as hatred, as if instead of just politely greeting him, I had just committed some heinous crime against humanity. I like solitude, as did Wainwright, but this man's attitude was Wainwright's philosophy on steroids. As he walked a few paces away from us to find his own summit seat we both muttered under our breaths something to the effect of 'why did we bother'. However the smell of that bad attitude made the whole summit experience stink. Just the knowledge that such a bad tempered specimen of humanity sat a few feet away from us, made it impossible to enjoy the view. Surely fell walking should if anything make us more human. How can we take that deep inner peace from the fells and not use it to radiate some kindness and care back to others. The experience has reaffirmed to me that while I remain a lover of solitude, I will always continue to be polite and try to be engaging to those I do happen to bump into in the wild spaces.

We took the joint decision to leave the summit of Robinson to the curmudgeon. In any case the afternoon was drawing on and as well as practical reasons, we had another more spiritual reason to get a move on before the sunset. The Littledale Edge we descended was more or less free from snow, but the subsequent ascent onto Dale Head with its narrowing ridge towards the summit was still covered in thick snow. Viewed from a distance this looked like it might be a little tricky and dangerous for a man who had forgotten his ice axe and who had as a result struggled embarrassingly up the relatively bland snowy face of Robinson. However, the ridge, on closer inspection was not as narrow as it had appeared from distance, a clear line of boot prints marking the route onward through the thick snow. I was lucky. This section was merely enjoyable, as it wound its way between and over some minor rock excrescences. In the winter fells though, one should never trust to luck.

It was not long before the familiar and beautiful pillar of a cairn that marks the summit of Dale Head sitting dramatically on the edge of an abyss came into view. The scene was now set for one of the most precious and privileged scenes that a fell walker can witness. In my previous 20 or so years of fell walking, I had witnessed the sunset from lower fells such as Scope End and Shipman Knotts. There had then been time to dash down to low level before darkness descended. However, in more recent years the advent of a head torch meant that, within reason, a sunset could now be fully enjoyed from the grandstand position of a high Lakeland summit. I had sought this experience out for a few years, but somehow it had never come. Either it became cloudy late in the day, or the distance back to the car was just too long to hang around, or in summer the sunset too late to wait for and unlikely to be as fine as a winter sunset. Now at last everything was perfectly set up. Of all the Lakeland summits above 2000 feet, Dale Head is probably the most convenient choice for witnessing the sunset. The descent of 1300 feet down to Honister Pass is both short, easy and in the main follows fence posts. Its ease allows just enough time to view the full drama of the sunset and dash down in fading light. But of course one's position on a mountain is nothing if the weather does not conspire to deliver the goods. It had been a day of sun and cloud, so there always remained the possibility that a bank of cloud on the horizon might obscure the orb of the setting sun. However, today things were perfectly balanced for a classic sunset. Although there was a fair amount of cloud cover above and some fearsome grimacing black snow clouds towards Helvellyn in the east, a great swathe of the horizon to the west was still clear. This area, behind the massive darkening wall of High Stile, now burnt golden while the clouds immediately above, far from detracting from the scene, enhanced it by lighting up in waves and folds ranging in colour from bright orange through to deep red and purple. In the far distance the Isle of Man sat on the horizon, lit up like some fleeting fantasy creation from another world.

We were alone. The last visitor had probably left half an hour or so before our arrival on Dale Head. Here was another sort of secret Lakeland. It was one that was not dictated by having to find the right route of ascent or descent, but by thinking outside of the normal constraints of a day on the fells. It is a secret that all can share in given a little planning and preparedness. Having whooped with the joy of the experience, Stan and I then gave each other some space and on came the MP3 players. For me watching the ever changing colour spectacle of the sunset from a high vantage point in my beloved Lakeland and at the same time listening to *Sunset* from Richard Strauss' *Alpine Symphony* – in my view the finest musical accompaniment to such a scene – was an unforgettable experience. It was an emotional juxtaposition of nature and music coming together in perfect synchronicity. I admit that tears of joy streamed down my face. Perhaps I am just a soppy, heart-on-sleeve sort of guy. However, working in an office environment, one is taught to rein in the emotions, to go with the team dynamic, whatever that is, and to treat the angry customer with a calm air of understanding. So why, when the modern world seems to constrict our emotions so much, should a man or woman not let it all flow out for such a scene? I like to imagine that old AW would have experienced similar washes of emotion on the fells. He was after all in love with these fells and his writings were a self-confessed 'love letter' to them.

As the sun dipped below High Stile and the spectacle seemed to have passed its apex, we reluctantly left the summit. But every few steps on the descent we found ourselves looking up from our boots and becoming again entranced in the scene. Blow the constraints of time, this was too good for us to simply carry on. We found a curious dip in the land, which the snows of winter had filled to a depth of a few feet, but which had compacted and provided a lovely shelter. And there we witnessed one the finest moments I have ever seen in the hills. Finer perhaps, although much briefer, than the sunset from Dale Head, because this was so fleeting, so unexpected, so magical. In the deepening purple, a final ray of the setting sun lit up the summit ridge of Pillar in the most strangely beautiful crescent of pearlescent crimson. This fleeting vision lasted for only a few seconds, but is an image forever burned into my subconscious. Such magic cannot be planned for. It just happens and one is privileged and grateful to be in the right place at the right time. There are great all round days in the fells and days which are not in themselves great but contain perhaps one great moment. It is sometimes the unexpected that provides the most memorable experience. For such moments all the hours of trudge, bog, rain, blizzards, cold and sweat are worthwhile.

So was the climb of Robinson from Buttermere a walk worthy of *Secret Lakeland?* Despite Wainwright's assertion that this is a popular climb, Stan and I only met the three poorly shod walkers on the way up, plus one grumpy man on the summit. Yes on a May Bank Holiday this route might be quite popular, but certainly outside of the peak season it appears to see little traffic.

The remaining two routes onto Robinson definitely caused no doubts in my mind as to whether they merit inclusion in this book. Not only were they quiet, one of them even on a busy Bank Holiday week, but they also both rank amongst the finest walks in this volume in terms of scenery and drama. Approximately half way along Buttermere lake lies Hassness House, often just referred to as Hassness and here begins a 1900 feet climb to the summit of Robinson. It was the identical weekend, only a year later, to the climb of Robinson described above, but while the time of year was the same, there were some significant differences. We parked between Honister and Gatesgarth again, but today the lake was not a mirror and the fell tops held no snow. Nonetheless it was a bright and cheery enough day and there were to be delights of a different kind to maintain our interest.

A kissing gate and a sign for Robinson mark the start of the ascent. Almost immediately the busy world of Buttermere and the road seem far away as you enter a little copse of natural woodland called Kirk Close. The early stages of this walk combine the beauty of the trees, with the sound and sight of water running over rocks in the form of Hassnesshow Beck. It is typical lower Lakeland scenery but no less arresting or beautiful for being so. The path, at first closely tracking a drystone wall, soon breaks free of the tree cover as an emerging Goat Crag ahead commands attention. The crag and ravine of Goats Gill, dominate the scene. Here, a chaos of savage rock, intermingled with brown heather, casts a gloomy face of impregnability. It is classic Lakeland drama, yet without the crowds and seemingly neglected. You can gain some impression of Goat Crag from the road, but to get a real sense of the place you have to make the climb. Some solitary trees hug the edge of a sizeable drop into the ravine and make nice subjects for photography.

It was at a large step stile crossing another wall that we looked up as a fox dashed across the path and away towards Gatesgarth. It appeared startled. Foxes are not uncommon and indeed they are often and with justification, regarded as pests. I must admit I soon put the fox to the back of my mind until a few minutes later we heard a loud barking noise as a couple of fell hounds came into view coming down the route towards us. We thought that there must be some kind of hunt going on and expected to see people following close behind the dogs, but no people appeared. We figured that the dogs must be part of a fell pack set loose to track a fox or some foxes. This is often an activity that accompanies the lambing season, when the last thing a farmer wants is to lose new born lambs. The reason there were no people following is that they cannot keep up with the pace of these lithe and supple animals. Indeed we had no expectation of what was to happen next. For rather than pursuing the fox we had seen in the direction of Gatesgarth, the hounds appeared to have found another scent as first one hound and then the other made a perilous descent into Goats Gill, a route that would have tested the best of human scramblers and probably merited taking a rope. I must admit that I was slightly concerned for the dogs as a slip would have proved fatal. My concern was unfounded however, as first one hound and then its companion not only emerged safe from the ravine, but started climbing straight up the seemingly impossible ledges of Goat Crag. Concern turned to admiration as we watched the ease with which these dogs romped over rock and round boulder, where a person would have needed to pause over every move. There was no sense of fear in the dogs, just one of purpose and enjoyment. Before long they had disappeared above the crags and onto the plateau of Buttermere Moss. It seemed that the spectacle that had left us spellbound and a little concerned, was just a normal jaunt for these fell hounds. However, it would appear that the fox got away.

The next 500 feet or so of the climb follows a fence rather than a wall. This part of the climb is among the steeper climbs in the district and there are one or two places that call for some mild scrambly moves. It is tempting at times to use the fence to haul oneself up, but it is both a little rusty and in places not very well secured to the ground. The slog is compensated for by the odd rest (if you can find a flat place) to look at the ever increasing drama of High Stile and the beauty of Buttermere and Crummock spread below you. There is also of course 'Wainwright's Rowan'. The story behind this little tree is that when Wainwright was preparing the *North Western Fells Guide* he came across a young rowan tree eking out an existence on a small crag. He duly noted this in the guide and asked his readers to contact him with progress reports on the well-being of the tree. And so a rather humble little specimen of a rowan tree got a spot in the limelight and became 'Wainwright's Rowan'. As at March

The wonderful climb of Robinson from Hassness

2011 it is still there, twenty years after its namesake died, still clinging inconspicuously to a little patch of vegetation on a bit of crag. For the lover of Wainwright's guides finding this tree is an almost mystical experience; a sort of Holy Grail. I accept, however, that for some it will just be a rather puny little rowan tree and not exactly something to get the juices flowing. I must admit that in nearly 50 years of existence it has not exactly broken records for its growth rate.

If you are not excited by 'Wainwright's Rowan' it is likely that you will also find the climb from the rowan onwards rather uninspiring. Gone are the crags and the gorge to be replaced by the upland grass on the edges of the Buttermere Moss. Still, the lower reaches of the climb are exquisite and having come this far you might as well get to the summit of Robinson.

Robinson is one of very few fells that are named after a person. But who was Robinson? For a long time I had assumed that he must be John Wilson Robinson, a pioneering rock climber and founding member of the Fell and Rock Climbing Club, after whom Robinson's Cairn next to the famous climbing ground of Pillar Rock is named. It seemed a fairly safe assumption, but I wanted to be sure and here, as many times before Alfred Wainwright put me straight. A little footnote on the first page of his Robinson chapter states that the Robinson in question was a Richard Robinson, an estate owner whose land included this fell. The truth was not quite so romantic as the fell being named after a great climber, but as Wainwright points out at least the estate owner was not called 'Smith' or we might have a Smith fell.

Previously on the summit of Robinson I had encountered an archetype grumpy man as described earlier. This time there was another annoyance. A man, probably in his early thirties, was just aside from the summit cairn doing an odd collection of exercises, such a touching his toes, stretching from side to side and hip rotations. All very strange and to me it was completely unnecessary. I have noticed that there are times when certain men have to show their manliness on the fells in the human equivalent of a peacock display. Presumably the remaining male fell walkers at this point are supposed to scatter at the sight of such a display, leaving the gyrating man with a selection of female fell walkers as mates to choose from.

Gyrating narcissist behind us, we left Robinson and made for a new secret Lakeland route. As I have stated, some of the routes in this book recommend themselves as routes of ascent and others as routes of descent – if based in Gatesgarth or along the road to Honister, the huge flank from the Littledale Edge sweeping down to the road makes an ideal descent route. It is not easy to locate and there are crags on this side as well.

However the best guide is a junction of fences, in the dip between Robinson and Dale Head. From here a narrow trod crosses scree in a delightful isolated situation, before a pleasant descent over the type of grass that is neither too wet and slippery nor too riddled with potholes. In its lower reaches all traces of a path vanish but just make for the obvious road bridge over Gatesgarthdale Beck and you can't go wrong. Before long you will be back on tarmac with the car hopefully conveniently nearby.

I have saved the grandest and best of Robinson's quiet ascents for the last. The ascent from Newlands Church to Robinson is arguably one of the finest and most beautiful of any ascent routes in the Lake District. Yet even on Bank Holiday week in late May I did not find it to be at all popular. Although the described route in the guide starts from Newlands Church, for those with a car it is easier to park at the National Trust car park, which is found in a dip in the road between the hamlet of Little Town and Newlands Beck. A lovely little stone bridge crosses the beck with Newlands Church a minute or two's walk further on. One of the delights of the Lake District is the many small and sometimes tiny churches to be found tucked away in the folds of valleys. The brilliantly whitewashed Newlands Church is one the finest and most beautifully situated examples in the area. Indeed the famous Lakeland poet Wordsworth was so impressed by the church when he was on a walk in 1826, that he wrote a poem about the church and its surrounds entitled *To May*. Early May is indeed a beautiful time of year. The fresh leaves are a luminous green when caught by the sun's rays. Like many of the finest wonders in nature the green of the new leaves is a fleeting event. Around three weeks after the leaves unfold, they lose that fresh, vibrant tone and adopt a deeper green mantle for the rest of the summer. Walking at this time of the year is like being spiritually reborn.

The minor road becomes a rough lane then a path, as civilization gives way to wildness. At the end of the wooded lane, just before the track emerges onto open fell side, stands a lovely cottage, called rather oddly Low High Snab, flanked by bluebells and at the time of writing boasting one of the friendliest cats I have encountered in the Lake District. The animal would have happily let me stroke its chest all day as it rolled over on the path and must have wondered at this peculiar creature's seemingly aimless wandering, when the easier pastimes of rest, relaxation and basking in the Spring sunshine were vastly more attractive propositions.

Until this point the walk had been little more than a lazy stroll. A flat start to a mountain walk invariably means that there will be a steep section coming up somewhere – the haul up onto the ridge of High Snab Bank justifies the theory. It's a short haul though, of 400 feet, before the path levels off on a narrowing ridge as the exhilaration builds at the prospect of the high level promenade ahead. Wainwright mentions three rocks steps that have to be negotiated on the climb, each around 20 to 30 feet high. I'm alright as a scrambler, but am notoriously clumsy and, therefore, the mention of any scrambling on a route I am planning always provokes an instinctive rising of the blood pressure. The first rock step proved very easy, the second one a little trickier with one or two awkward grooves where Stan and I had to search for handholds. The third was easier than the second step but harder than the first. The last two involve a little scrambling, but they are short lived and anyone who has done Striding Edge, let alone Sharp Edge will find them easy enough. They are however one of the thrilling features that adds to the joy of this climb. Once above the rock steps, the path curves round to join the edge of Robinson Crags. There is another little rocky step, which is trivial compared to the earlier ones and after this the path literally hugs the edge of a near vertical abyss above the crags. This is Robinson's finest face, that which gives it distinction when viewed from a distance. To stand on the very edge of these crags and look straight down 1500 feet to the slender steel blue meanders of Keskadale Beck is to know something of what it is like to be a soaring bird of prey. It is not a place to stand if you have vertigo and also best avoided in mist or high winds. I have a reasonable head for heights, as long as I am in a safe situation. However, I could still feel a sense of floating away, like some part of my essence was not grounded to the fell.

In such thrilling places the actual effort of climbing is forgotten, although on this climb it is as well to remember that the large cairn seen up ahead is not the summit, which lies a flattish few hundred yards further on. Having had the summit disturbed by a curmudgeon and a gyrating narcissist on my previous two visits, I figured I deserved an altogether finer experience. Just one person accompanied Stan and I on the summit and he was the type of walker one does not mind meeting. We exchanged a few words about how fine the view was and where we were heading and that is all that was really needed. We had our summit stop a few feet away from the main cairn, where the ground slopes away to reveal two segments of Crummock Water, split by the bold outline of little Rannerdale Knotts, backed by shaggy Mellbreak and lovely Loweswater. The grey whalebacks of Grasmoor and Eel Crag loomed above the pointed summit of Wandope. Solway and Southern Scotland could clearly be seen on the distant horizon.

The summit of Robinson is a great springboard to tackle the other fells of the Newlands Round. A longish circuit over Dale Head, High Spy, Maiden

Pausing above the dramatic Robinson Crags on the climb from Newlands Church

Moor and Catbells can be done before dropping back down to Little Town. However, for us, today was all about Robinson alone. With an onerous agenda ahead to complete all the secret Lakeland walks, it might be four or five years before I could visit Robinson again. Only right, therefore, that this worthy mountain should dominate the day, rather than being a prelude to other things. In addition, although I had now crawled all over Robinson and felt that I truly knew the fell, there was still one route that I wanted to explore and one place that I wanted to visit. From the summit we retraced our steps along the edge of Robinson Crags as far as the highest of the rock steps and then began to veer away to the right of the route up. The Wainwright guide refers to this route as a former path. Former proved to be an accurate description as we searched in vain for a shred of path, finding red herrings in dried up stream beds and patches of loose stone. The simple fact is that there is no longer a path down, so in light of this keep to the grassy slopes as much as possible rather than heading too near to Blea Crags to the left, which would prove awkward to negotiate. As you contour down the grassy slopes of Robinson, the pyramid ahead, banded in green and grey slopes, is Hindscarth. Eventually you will pick up a faint grassy path heading in a roughly northerly direction, which soon becomes rocky and calls for a little care as you descend into a narrow gorge between Blea Crags and High Crags, before arriving at a diminutive jewel-like sheet of water. This is the reservoir at the head of Scope Beck. You may have noticed it when climbing the rocky steps on the way up Robinson, where it appeared as a dark green emerald below. Although I am not generally a great fan of reservoirs, there is something delightful and special about this place. Sometimes reservoir dams are dirty grey stone edifices. Here a grassy bank dams the reservoir, a delightful place to sit and admire the emerald green of the water and the precipitous vegetated cliffs behind. The reservoir is part of Lakelands former industrial past. Once used for mining work, it now sits lonely and peaceful. It is seldom visited and even more seldom spoken of and yet although it does not quite have the charm of Lakeland's finest natural tarns, it does make a very good effort for something man-made.

The final stretch of the route back to Newlands Church is about as easy and pleasant as hill walking gets, as the path becomes grassy before becoming a gentle track. That day the lower reaches of High Snab bank were covered in flowering gorse. In the fresh spring air the yellow flowers stood out dazzlingly. Gorse bushes are lovely to look at from a distance when in flower but absolute purgatory to try and walk through.

In summary Robinson both has the most secret Lakeland walks of the Newlands fells and also the finest. It is undoubtedly a fine mountain in its own right and does not really deserve to be ticked off via a 'there and back' from Dale Head or Hindscarth, or sold short by a climb from Newlands Hause. My agenda for writing this series of books inevitably means that I have to say goodbye for a while to some old favourites as I pursue secret walks in different areas, and to a tight schedule. I will miss Robinson, but like someone torn from his lover's arms I have made a promise with the fell that I shall return as soon as I can.

In a similar vein I have promised a return to the Nitting Haws drove road, a place whose memory can still bring a wash of calm and serenity over me, as I sit at my office desk working out the complexity of some redress calculation. How does one define a classic ascent route? A classic must have variety of scenery; some running water or cascading becks; a little drama but not too much to ever make the route ahead unclear or overly difficult; perhaps a wild upper section that ends close to a neat summit cairn, with plunging cliffs nearby and dramatic views that are revealed only in the final few steps to the top. High Spy from Grange fits the bill.

The early May day started cloudy, but with the promise of it brightening through the morning and being positively warm and sunny by the afternoon. I took the little bus from Keswick to Grange enticed by the prospect of the climb that awaited me and the improving forecast. The bus was more packed than would perhaps be legally permitted. With a carefree, beckoning gesture the bus driver kept letting more and more folk onto his bus, as if the vehicle would magically increase in size to accommodate them. Was this an attempt to break the world record for the number of people squeezed onto a small bus? Unofficially I think we did. I have had less crowded journeys on a rush hour tube from London Bridge to Canary Wharf. I think I actually released constricted breath that had been held in my lungs for twenty minutes when I escaped the bus at Grange. I deserved a secret and wild walk as reward for the confines of my journey.

Having done a little walking through the delightful village of Grange, a gate leads into the embrace of Peace How, a lowly but beautiful eminence of interspersed trees. Already the slanting line of the Nitting Haws drove road can be seen looking dramatic but inviting on the face of High Spy. It's a little early in the walk for a stop on the stone seat hereabouts, so carry on to the next gate and then by a wall. The water tank mentioned by Wainwright was duly located – surprise, it was nothing to write home about! After a little boggy section the path leads up a delightful grassy strip, with rushing water heard but not seen. I took a little detour path to find the weir over Ellers Beck, worthwhile to see into the dark vegetated crevice at the base of the waterfalls. Higher up I took a stop beneath some trees decked with vibrant green leaves that had appeared to have unfolded from their buds just a day or two before. From here I could just about see the upper cataract of the waterfalls, not wishing to venture any further towards the sheer slimy banks. Here were found the simple pleasures of a cooling breeze on my face, the sound of water cavorting over rocks and the view across Borrowdale to the forested flanks of Kings How. The sun suddenly, but with an air of permanence, breached the morning cloud and cast its warming rays onto my face. This immersion in the simple acts of nature is perhaps the essence of what I love about fell walking. Mozart's piano music is sometimes judged simple when the notes are viewed on a score and yet it is perhaps some of the most profoundly beautiful and difficult music to master when played. It is similar with the simple pleasure of a lonely stop in the fells, no show-stopping events or spectacular occurrences, but surely as profound as anything in life. To witness the random beauty of nature is surely a special privilege.

A little further and higher, the path crosses a little tributary of Ellers Beck from which Wainwright offers two route choices: one heading towards Cockley How, the other heading towards the bracken and grass of Greenup. Both routes will end on the familiar Newlands Round path, but having done both there is no doubt which is the superior. The Greenup route is a pathless thousand feet haul through heather, grass and bracken and is exactly as Wainwright describes 'vastly more extensive than it appears from below'. It is among the least accommodating climbs I have done. By contrast the route via Cockley How and the Nitting Haws drove road is a joy that touches the essence of the craggy mountain drama of High Spy. The square boulder on Cockley How, its perpendicular shape somehow at odds with the seemingly random processes of nature, was still a fine foreground subject for a photograph looking down to Derwent Water. It defies explanation that this otherwise unremarkable piece of the Earth's crust, formed many millions of years ago, should warrant special attention. However at this moment, on this day, it somehow captured my imagination as I pictured the forces and time that shaped its form and passage.

At a sheep fold there is again another route choice. High White Rake makes a fine scrambly course, but who can resist the lure of the drove road, slanting across the face of the crag, its easy and well constructed path seemingly so at odds with this lonely place. The purpose for contriving such a path here, was not for the likes of fell walkers such as you and I, but as a means of driving sheep down from the massive moorland pastures above. Its line forms the only chink in the armour of Blea Crag and Nitting Haws. As a walker one can only be thankful for such a beautifully inviting route. The drove road peters out at a cairn perched neatly on a precipice. Ahead lies a vast acreage of moorland, which Wainwright dubs an amphitheatre. It is indeed true that one has no idea of the vastness of this area from either above on the Newlands ridge, or from below on the Grange Road. Now the sun was warm, this place of peace beckoned me to rest. The morning sun glistened in the heavy dew revealing innumerable shimmering water-laced cobwebs, a spectrum of colour on the water droplets, sparkling like precious stones. It was a magical and slightly sensuous spot, where I could have easily dozed for an hour or so under the spell of Morpheus. High Spy though had just a little more pulling power than the God of sleep and I carried on, past Minum Crag to my left and via a short section of the Newlands motorway to the summit of High Spy.

There were a number of people at the summit of High Spy, but it could not detract either from the loneliness of my walk to the summit, or from the impressive mountain prospect in front of me. It is in fact pretty much a 360 degree panorama from here, with large sections of the North-Western, Northern, Eastern, Central and Southern Fells being in view. However most impressive here were the sheer cliffs of Gable Crag on neighbouring Dale Head, with every feature lit up by the intense but clear May sunshine. I moved a few feet away from the summit cairn and found a spot at the edge of some precipitous crags, which provided both a little seclusion from the summit throng and also an even better and deeper view into the Newlands valley and across to the shattered crags and scree of Dale Head. Dale Head still had a little cap of cloud on its highest few feet which spurred me to carry on, in the hope of some spectacular clearance at the summit. It was a false hope though, for by the time I had made a rather dispiriting and considerably crowded descent to Dalehead Tarn, any mist had cleared. It was by now 2.30pm and I had noticed that most of the people I was encountering seemed to be doing the Newlands round heading for an ending on Catbells, rather than starting with Catbells. Thoughts of mist on the summit of Dale Head were replaced with thoughts that I might just be lucky enough to have its wonderful summit to myself. I knew though that I needed to give it a little more time, as I could still see several people heading towards the summit. Down by Dalehead Tarn, I was alone. The crowds for the day seemed to be either heading on towards Maiden Moor, or on towards Dale Head. Here at the rough mid-point of the Newlands Round, there was no-one. To ensure the passage of time, and because this mountain col was something of a heat trap, I decided I would test the waters of Newlands Beck and Dalehead Tarn. This was not to be the kind of all out swim you will have read about earlier at Blea Tarn, just a trousers rolled up paddle. It was though magically cooling and balming. Nearly an hour passed at this spot and gradually the crowds faded and I was left wondering whether they had ever really been here. I just had a sixth sense that there would be no-one on Dale Head and, when I reached it, I was glad to be proved right. I got there just in time to see the last couple of people heading onwards to Hindscarth at the end of their round. For the second time in three months, I had this wonderful summit, with its beautifully built cairn and awe inspiring drop to Newlands to myself.

My route off the fells was again the easy descent down to the Honister Mine and from there to Seatoller. I had unlocked the secrets of the Newlands Round and now I was to unlock the secret of getting a seat on the bus back to Keswick. Make sure you arrive early at the Seatoller bus terminus! If you want to continue to Grange and make a full round of the walk you do of course have the freedom to do so. However if you do catch the bus back from Grange, abandon all hope of comfort.

Shadows in the Mist

In my book *The World of a Wainwright Bagger*, I made the bold and perhaps slightly controversial statement that there are no dull fells. I would also add to this that sometimes a fell that may seem dull on a first acquaintance, may yield an altogether different experience if explored in different circumstances. Sometimes the weather may make the experience of a dull hill interesting. On Sallows for example, a contender for dullest Wainwright, I was witness to a remarkable display of sun shafts piercing a steely grey sky, each one casting a UFO like beam of focused colour and brightness, on an otherwise monochrome landscape. Not the fell's doing, but it made Sallows memorable to a degree.

Another way of eking the best out of the lesser lights of Lakeland is to take a different route of ascent. Because these fells are deemed somehow unworthy of Lakeland celebrity, they are often climbed in an unworthy manner. Those who care to bag all the Wainwrights, myself included, often bag the dullest ones by the quickest, most convenient route, or tagged on to a round, just to get it done. One such fell is Graystones, once just a rather unmemorable outlier of the North Western Fells, now a firm favourite. The first time I climbed Graystones, as part of my round of the Wainwrights, I did the normal thing and tagged it on, as a bit of an out and back exercise from Broom Fell and Lord's Seat. It was not an altogether unenjoyable experience. I got my first view of the drab expanse of Wythop Moss and some rather special shower strewn views towards Mellbreak. I was also given a surprise by my best friend Stan, who I had thought was climbing another fell, but who had at the last moment decided to climb Graystones. I still remember the shock and feeling of misplacement that I had when first Stan's voice and then his figure appeared from a hollow, where he had been hiding and watching me as I ascended from Widow Hause. It was also Stan's first climb of Graystones and he had taken the quickest and most direct way to the summit, a nice little 1000 feet leg warmer straight up from Scawgill Bridge.

Neither my route nor Stan's really did any justice to Graystones, although Stan's at least did the fell the honour of climbing it, as opposed to merely linking by ridge. For most fellow walkers, one or other of these two methods of getting to the top of Graystones will be the route of choice. A further glance at the Graystones chapter, in Wainwright's *North Western Fells Guide*, is worth making, because here lies a route to

Graystones that does the fell justice and, at the same time, definitely classes as secret Lakeland. This is Graystones from Armaside.

Armaside is nothing more than a farm and a couple of cottages. Tucked out of sight and out of mind from the busy road down Lorton Vale to Buttermere, it is a secret start to a secret walk. The narrow road that leads to the starting point at Harrot Hill Farm is quite rough, with a healthy grass strip growing down its middle, to testify to how much in Lakeland's backwater this is. It's not easy to find a parking place here if you come by car, but then I suppose large car parks are not the hallmark of a solitary walk. However, I only needed dropping off and picking up and was lucky that Stan was slightly the worse for wear from several pints the night before, not feeling up to a walk, on what was not in any case the best of weather days. I felt a little forlorn being dropped off on a drizzly day, in the middle of nowhere and with a walk which was an unknown quantity in front of me. Still as I headed up the wide metalled lane that begins this walk, I reminded myself I was at least alone.

This was not to be an out and out poor weather day though – as lane gave way to path, a rather watery transient sun poked through the murk serving to lift my spirits. A detour to Harrot was recommended by the great man and I have never found his recommendations to be wanting. Harrot, sounding more like a vegetable than a fell ('eat up your Harrots!'), is one of those unclassified hills, such as Rowling End, Scope End and Knock Murton that prove that ticks on a list are not necessarily a symbol of worthiness. Harrot became one of the delights of my post Wainwright bagging era, a place to savour because it spoke of the unbridled freedom I now yearned for in the fells.

It's a very simple climb to the top of Harrot, which although little more than a grassy mound, has enough elevation to have a striking view south towards Mellbreak and west towards the Fellbarrow Group. Harrot would be an ideal place for a warm summer's day, a place to rest for an hour or two, without an agenda or the constraints of time. This was March though and warmth was in very short supply. The scene around had all the ominous signs of weather turning for the worse that any experienced fell walker easily recognises. The brief flirting sunshine on Harrot was quickly being replaced by an advancing monochrome bank of grey, uniform stratus clouds which had cut down the massive hulk of Grasmoor to half its normal height. This was to be the end of panoramic views for the day.

My spirits were high though, this was but a short and easy walk. Let the weather do its worst, I didn't care. On taking a different line to descend Harrot, I came across a curious and roughly circular rash of stones, on an otherwise flat, grassy area. I half fancied it might be the remains of some ancient tumulus, but I expect only the most ardent ancient historian (or regular climbers of Harrot – if there are any?), know the truth. Yet again, a fell was half the reality before me and perhaps half an interpretation of sights, sounds and feelings.

The path wound lazily upwards, without any real sense of urgency as the monochrome grey mass above me shed its first drops of rain. Ahead rose the flanks of Graystones, the mist skirting the summit and threatening to engulf the fell. It had become a somewhat bleak scene, but the long grassy slopes that I climbed, using a wall for a time as a handrail, seemed to be anything but dull for the plethora of sheep that were grazing them. In fact if these sheep could talk they would have told me that they would rather graze the ocean of grass on Graystones, than scavenge for scant pickings on the likes of Bowfell. I have always found an adventurous, mysterious quality accompanies ascents into the mist and this was no exception. As I crossed the wall (higher up than I should have), I came across the cairn on Lakeland's other forgotten Kirk Fell. This again would have been a good point for a stop on a sunny clear day, but at that precise moment the mist thickened and blotted out the last remnants of the view towards Grasmoor. The page for this walk in my Wainwright guide, which was now becoming rather wet with the fine drizzle that accompanies this more permanent kind of mist, showed that it was just a short grassy pull up to the summit of Graystones, a few unattractive contours on the Ordnance Survey Map. But this had now become a world of eerie shapes looming out of the mist. Nothing was as it seemed. I knew there was a little rocky outcrop beneath the utmost top of Graystones and thought I had spotted it, spectral and shadowed in the mist. But when I got closer, I realised that what had appeared a high, summit like mound in the mist, was just a little raised area of a few feet in height. The mist was creating illusory giants everywhere.

It was at this stage that the bagger within me reared its ugly head again. Although I had bagged all the Wainwrights, I now realised that locating the exact high point of a fell still meant almost as much as it had before. I have to also confess that there was another reason for wanting to get to the summit, a reason that my freedom having completed the Wainwrights is constantly at odds with. The 'trainspotter with altitude' database of the Wainwrights that I lovingly maintained, was able to tell me not just that I had climbed all the Wainwrights, but also how many times I had done each one. By now there were nearly 100 that I had climbed twice or more. So while the esoteric in me was joyous at uncovering secret Lakeland,

Wainwright summit or not, the trainspotter in me could not help thinking that I was well on the way to completing my second round of the Wainwright fells. So you will understand it was of some importance that I did find the summit of Graystones, regardless of any view! It was now that I longed for a hand held GPS unit, for this walk was done before I had acquired one.

I met another couple who had also been on their own search for Graystones' high point. They thought they had found it, but could not be certain and, as the weather was now closing in and the wind was whipping up, they were content with that. Five minutes later I came across a little pile of stones, doing its best to be a cairn. A top of sorts but it did not seem like the summit I remembered from before, and nor did it have the familiar little escarpment dropping from it. Suddenly, cocooned in this elemental world, where nothing except the uppermost part of Graystones existed, I received a jolt to my senses – a text on my mobile phone from Stan. I read the text with a growing sense of surprise. For once again Stan had decided to climb Graystones, having convinced me that he was not going to. Only this time he had reached the summit and not found me. His text also told me that he was still in the general summit area but was about to head off. Despite possibly being just a hundred yards from each other, I never saw Stan on the summit area, such was the limited visibility.

By the time I had finally located the summit, the weather was beginning to drop some heavy hints to leave. Having satisfied the summit collector in me and paused for about 10 seconds in a gale to take an approximate compass bearing, I headed off. Moments later a small and final hole appeared in the mist, revealing for the briefest of moments the dreary expanse of the Wythop Moss to my right, its apparent utter bleakness tailor-made for the prevailing conditions. It seemed to me that I was bearing too far towards the general direction of Wythop, so without bothering to check my bearing again, I headed further left. After several hundred yards of descent I was given a lesson in taking ill-considered short cutting as, dropping beneath the mist, I realised that I was now descending too far towards Lorton and into a narrow valley formed by the flanks of Kirk Fell. There was a bit of awkward contouring, with rain pelting in my face, before I found myself back in the familiar grassy sheep pasture from earlier in the day.

This was not, however, quite the end of the day's adventure, for what happened next was one of the more extraordinary occurrences I have had on the fells. As I crossed the sheep's feeding ground, I was conscious of becoming the objective of a kind of mass sheep pincer movement. Sheep to the left and sheep to the right closed in on me. Sheep behind me nudged me up the backside. Sheep ahead of me ran to join the throng. Surrounded by a close pack of about a hundred sheep, I resembled some Biblical character tending his flock. For a while I moved with the herd, so tightly hemmed in that I felt part of this heaving entity! Perhaps they thought I was a shepherd who would lead them to shelter or perhaps I was on the menu and would be taken down by the pack! They were to be sadly disappointed when I proved unfit either as a shepherd or as main course as they soon dispersed back to their damp and blustery home, leaving me to tramp unhindered the last mile back to the waiting car and Stan. Graystones is no Great Gable and never will be, but I'd had a memorable time and no longer considered Graystones a dull fell. It is perhaps therefore true that if we take the view that a fell is dull and therefore seek a dull way of bagging it, then the outcome can only be dull. It's very much a question of one's own outlook rather than the hill itself. As Hamish Brown (mountaineer and author) once said 'no hill is dull between the sunset and the sea'.

Sale Fell sits on the far Northern perimeter of the Lake District. It is another place where Lakeland ends and the high ground recedes in lower and lower undulations towards the plains of Solway. The fell is most popularly 'bagged' from Wythop Mill. Although not linked by any ridge to its neighbour Ling Fell, the two can easily be climbed as a pair in a half day's outing. Ling Fell is truly one of the lesser lights of the 214 Wainwrights. If the Wainwright Fells were the cast and crew of a movie, and Scafell or Great Gable was the leading man or lady, then Ling Fell would be Key Grip Number 3. Having climbed Ling Fell once, you will know just about as much about the fell as one would ever need to know. There are no hidden secret routes on Ling Fell, except perhaps for the sheep that roam it. Some would regard Sale Fell in the same fashion. For others though, myself included, Sale Fell has something altogether superior about it. It also has a choice of routes to the summit and one of these is a little corner of secret Lakeland. Technically the ascent from Beck Wythop is not strictly a route of ascent for Sale Fell. I guess that's why this is one of the few routes in my secret Lakeland list that is not a Wainwright route of ascent in the guides. However, for those wanting an element of contrast, and to savour Sale Fell by making a decent round walk of it, this is perhaps the ideal choice.

The tucked away car park, just off the A66 at Beck Wythop, has managed to escape the Pay and Display bandwagon. It was a day of nonstop drizzle, which occasionally broke into heavy rain, occasionally relenting for a few minutes. The undulating route through Wythop Wood begins as a proper footpath, resplendent with dark, dank pine forest covering and an assortment of twisted roots to try and avoid tripping over. This path snakes just a couple of hundred feet above the busy 'A' road and yet here is an illusion of solitude. Wainwright comments that Roe deer are present in Wythop Wood and a couple of times we thought we heard the cracking of twigs in the dense wood that might signal a deer running away from our plodding course. All too soon the footpath meets a wide forest road and the next half mile or so are relatively uneventful. The forest road eventually bends back upon itself and begins to climb in some pleasant zig-zags as the forest cover thickens again. At one bend a further footpath beckons the walker out of the forest and this is the route onto the slopes of Sale Fell.

Now just as I enjoy the emersion in the depth and darkness of such pine forests, I have also found that the emergence from this dark underworld, into the light of day, is a special moment. Perhaps it calls to a primal sense of our own birth into the light of the world, or even a prequel of our exit into the light of the hereafter. Even on a rather dull and wet day, emerging onto the shoulder of Lowthwaite, with its gentle flanks skirted with twisted and gnarled trees, is a special moment. This path could be followed down into the Wythop Valley, but there is a fell to be climbed and any of the various paths and tracks that lead up the side of Lowthwaite can now be taken.

Lowthwaite itself is merely a grassy eminence, but with a certain quiet charm and an abundance of cushioned ground to recline on, when blessed with a dry day. From here it is a pleasant grassy promenade to the summit of Sale Fell. This particular day it was not a place that recommended itself for a long stay. In spite of the relative darkness and drabness of the scene, the Wythop Valley retained its customary charm. Most striking in the view was the high outline of Grisedale Pike and Hopegill Head, overtopping the nearer ridge of Broom Fell and bedecked in a late winter covering of snow, of a curiously yellow tinge that day. Being typically me I wanted to recline on the rather wet ground and soak in the atmosphere of a Wainwright reached in the company of my best mate. Stan and I usually share a like-minded attitude to such matters. We are both not averse to a few minutes of rain soaked summit experience. However, a kind of second sense told me that Stan was not exactly keen on hanging around on Sale Fell. Not one for dramatics, it gradually emerged that Stan was feeling the early throes of flu symptoms. The fact of the matter is that although the fells can give us many soul enriching experiences, the experience is generally much richer if you are feeling well. Whereas I was enjoying the rain and the cold, fully fit, Stan was longing for central heating and bed. On another brighter and drier day we had traversed the ridge of Sale Fell further over Dodd Crag, in what is an expansive and smooth high level tramp, the kind of walking where hands can be placed in pockets and you can look around you as you walk, without the worry of twisting your ankle. To one side of this promenade views stretch to Solway and if you are lucky the Galloway and Borders hills. For a fell of lowly height, an outpost of Lakeland, Sale Fell has a surprisingly expansive feel to its summit ridge.

Today we had to imagine the expansive views from the ridge, as the persistent drizzle and Stan's developing flu sent us straight down from the fell into Wythop Valley. This valley oozes secret Lakeland. It is just a short distance from the busy hubbub of the A66 and yet nothing can be sensed here of modern society's constant rush and stress. Hidden here is a place where time has stopped, a reminder of a Lakeland before it opened its welcoming, natural riches to the millions. This time warp to a Lakeland past is not the only illusion in the Wythop Valley. There is also the false impression that some huge forgotten mountain dominates the head of the valley. However, when sense prevails, it becomes clear that this is only dear old Skiddaw, the sizeable trench holding Bass Lake unseen, like a trap door on a stage. As we headed back towards the Wythop Wood the sham gradually revealed itself, as we could clearly see where the upper part of the wood dropped away down to Bassenthwaite. Wythop and its illusions were left behind, as the path re-entered the wood, before falling steeply down reaching, after a short while, familiar ground near Beck Wythop. This is a memorable half day's outing, with the contrasts of dense wood, expansive fell and beautiful valley. To cap it all we had the whole walk to ourselves that day.

After 20 odd years in the fells and with the achievement of the 214 summits now fading into the realms of memory, I have recently become more conscious of two concurrent yet separate streams to my life and I sense that a lot of hill walkers must feel this too. On the one hand there is the non-hills life, a life enveloped in daily routines and hassles, but also in my case filled with the riches, joys (and occasional stresses) of spending time with my wife and three young children. Separate from this is another life. This is the life spent in the hills. It is a life spent removed from all the supposed difficulties and worries, a life where self becomes unimportant, a mere speck amidst the vast flanks and folds of the mountains. Sometimes in a world where targets, money and status fool you into believing they are important, it is well to be reminded that one is but a fleeting nothing, crawling on these unfathomably old landscapes. Some might find it frightening to contemplate their own existence, their joys, achievements, stresses and sadness, as insignificant. I find it rather comforting. To this end one trip to the hills seems very much to be merely an extension of the last trip and the routine time between, which seems to drag in endless five day weeks of work, is almost forgotten. Did that life really exist? If so does it really matter? Of course family and friends do, but so little else really does.

When the car pulled into the car park at Newlands Hause, I felt this sense of time not in fact being a straight line. Suddenly this was merely an extension of other days at Newlands Hause, of the day I first walked to the Hause with my brother more than 20 years ago, before descending to Buttermere, of another day we took the car to the Hause only to find the steep route down to Buttermere made perilous and impassable by sheet ice on the narrow road, and of a time when I walked over Ard Crags and Knott Rigg before descending to a crowded Newlands Hause, only to escape the crowds by heading onto Buttermere Moss. The past crowded into the present. The chosen fell for the day – Knott Rigg – had last been climbed nearly a decade ago, but rather than repeat the route of last time by romping up from the Hause to the summit and back again, I wanted to do something different, to distinguish this Knott Rigg from the last time, so that in the mind and memory they did not just merge into one and the same experience. And I guess this is why exploring secret Lakeland has proved such a vibrant experience. In the other non-hills life I tread the same treadmill week upon week, so why, when living the precious hills life, should I and others wish to repeat the same routes up our favourite hills. The hills should never become stale.

There are only two routes onto Knott Rigg, unless you want to invent some masochistic line of punishment straight up the side of the fell. The one from Newlands Hause is popular and better in descent and the one from Keskadale is secret and very seldom used. There is about a mile of road walking from Newlands Hause to the start of the ascent proper, but gain comfort by the fact that at the end of the day you will just have a simple romp off Knott Rigg back to a car at 1096 feet! The sharply curving bend of road at Keskadale Farm does not seem a very promising place for a route to begin, but on the opposing bank of the road to the farm, a walker can make out the sign of a track to a stile, that those driving past in a car would be hard pressed to spot. Hereabouts there used to be a curious purple coloured house by the roadside. It was a bit of an eyesore to be honest, but it was a familiar and hence much loved eyesore. Now it has been pulled down and replaced with a more modern dwelling and a little piece of Lakeland memorabilia has gone. Slightly nostalgic for those that knew the purple house, but those new to fell walking this area will wonder what the fuss was about.

Shortly after the crossing of two stiles, there is a choice of route, the old A or B thing again. The grassy drove road route 'A' is easy but inferior to route 'B', which is a proper and rather splendid little ridge route. It follows a fence and also the line of crags above Ill Gill. The valley this ridge looks down into is one of the more secluded in the district and on its opposing side are Keskadale Oakwood (a Site of Special Scientific Interest) and also a delightful bower of native trees. The ridge is sporting without requiring any scrambling moves. This is definitely Knott Rigg's shyer side, but equally as delightful as the familiar route. Those among you who have read my previous book, *The World of a Wainwright Bagger*, may recall my

The author exhibits fanatical delight on locating another fenced boghole

twisted obsession in finding some fenced bogholes that Wainwright mentioned on Hen Comb. Well low and behold, here were some more to locate on the route up Knott Rigg! Stan shook his head, the look saying more than words could, but at least this time there was no need to make a detour to find these swampy specimens. Perhaps if I run out of ideas for a future book, I could write *The World of a Fenced Boghole Bagger*, although I don't think it would attain bestseller status (too right, readership of one, the author – Ed).

The summit of Knott Rigg is just short cropped grass and a few stones heaped into an abortive cairn. It's a grand little place to linger a while though, with a good sense of height and a delightful prospect down Newlands Valley towards the huge backs of Wandope, Eel Crag and Sail. Unless the weather really turns against you, or you have something pressing to attend like a job interview, the glorious ridge walk should be made to Ard Crags. You will have to retrace your steps, but your reward will be a delightful little Wainwright summit and who really minds retracing steps in such grand surrounds. So once more to the familiar descent from Knott Rigg to Newlands Hause, a magnificent path with a sweeping plunge to left and right of it and a mere twenty minutes back to the car at the Hause. How long would it be before the seamless extension of time spent in the fells would bring me here again?

When Secret Lakeland Went Wrong

Planning is undoubtedly one of the joys of the pastime of fell walking, although sometimes a plan can go awry. When the germ of the idea for *Secret Lakeland* came to me, I eagerly scoured every page of the Wainwright guides and listed all the potential walks. I am glad to say that in the majority of cases, the walks planned did turn out to be worthy of the description 'Secret Lakeland'. There was, however, one very notable exception.

My two previous climbs of Castle Crag had been from the Rosthwaite approach. This is the smallest of all the Wainwright fells, and the only fell under 1000 feet to make it into the seven main guides. Despite that, even this small fell, with a very modest surface area, has a choice of two routes. I had heard that the route from Grange was very beautiful and that a detour to some caves was possible. I figured that it might just be feasible to find some secret areas on Castle Crag. Admittedly the day that I had earmarked for the walk did not give it the best chance of being quiet. It was a warm Bank Holiday weekend in May. My friend Kev dropped me off in the village of Grange, by then packed with walkers and tourists, where I had arranged to meet him two hours later. Directly opposite the church in Grange is a narrow minor road, leading to the Hollows Farm campsite. This leafy walk has bundles of Lakeland charm and in one place a fine vista towards Castle Crag. Today, however, it was very popular. No sooner had I greeted one party of walkers than another party came round the corner. I hoped that these might just be people from the campsite and that things might get quieter after the site. The site was indeed packed, but there was no relief to be had once I had walked through it. Instead I encountered a steady stream of families and children in swimming attire. The path trends down to the River Derwent, a beautiful river, but today occupied by dozens of swimmers, people in wet suits and canoeists. I can't blame them, as I quite fancied a dip myself. Beautiful as the walk was, this was not secret Lakeland. In fact it occurred to me that I would struggle to find anywhere less secret.

There was some hope when, having left the river behind the people seemed to thin out slightly. The next section of the walk is through a wonderful natural defile that separates Castle Crag from High Spy. All around is craggy scenery and on a hot, sunny day the landscape, with its littering of boulders, had something of the Wild West about it. Where a stream crosses the ravine path, the route branches off up Castle Crag. For a little while I had the route to myself. I found the seat mentioned in the Wainwright guide, a lovely shady wooden bench with a stone plaque behind it. This short detour of about twenty yards from the main route up Castle Crag, was about as secret as my day got. A secret Lakeland bench perhaps? Beyond the bench the path heads steeply upwards towards a high step stile over a fence, where the zig-zags up the slate spoil heap that sits just below the summit begin.

A few moments of solitude on the climb of Castle Crag from Grange

At the top of the spoil heap there is a lovely view down to Rosthwaite, backed by Eagle Crag. Normally my thoughts would have been solely occupied by this heavenly vista but today there was a distraction in the form of loud pop music. Now, although I am an obsessive fan of classical music, I don't mind pop music. Music of any type has a place. Unless you are at a concert, where everyone goes to hear the same music, I believe that music should be a private experience and that, especially in the countryside, it is impolite to expect others to share in your music. I listen to mine on headphones as do ninety-nine per cent of other music loving fell walkers. Today I encountered the one per cent. The music was not just audible, it was loud. It cut through the charm and atmosphere of the place like a road drill at a church service. The culprits turned out to be two young foreign lads with spiky bleached hair. Not that I have anything against young or foreign people, a lot of whom come to the fells and treat them with respect. I am just stating the facts. Clearly these two had no appreciation of the fells or care for the enjoyment of those around them. To them it was the same as the local park. I had a mind to say something but what good would it be. Soon enough they would be gone and Castle Crag would remain for another, quieter day.

Just a little further up the fell and directly below the summit is a small circular quarry. This quarry is littered with slate remains, some of which have been placed upright to create something resembling a druid site of worship. On a windy day the wind whistles eerily through the slate. I sought this quarry out as a place of refuge, only to find myself again thwarted by a couple who appeared to also have sought out the quarry for other purposes. They appeared to be welded to each other's faces in the early stages of who knows what. I began to think that I would have more chance of finding solitude and decorum in Amsterdam's Red Light District.

In spite of all this, the top still had to be visited and it actually was less busy than I feared, with perhaps half a dozen people clustered around the massive block of rock that is the summit. I placed myself on the edge of the summit, with the drop and the picture postcard view towards Derwentwater and Skiddaw at my feet with my MP3 player on and for a few minutes managing to at least create an illusion of solitude. My route back was the same as that I had taken up, but with a slight detour planned. I wanted to see if I could find Millican Dalton's cave. For those unfamiliar with the story of Millican Dalton, he was born in 1867. His life was unremarkable, working as an insurance clerk, until he started gradually to forsake everyday existence and society and spend longer and longer periods of his life living out of doors. This culminated in the 1920s into his taking permanent residence in a cave on Castle Crag. He named this, with tongue in cheek, The Cave Hotel and it became his home for a number of years, with only a weekly trip by bicycle to Keswick for some provisions and his favourite coffee and woodbine cigarettes, taking him away from his life of wildness. He also acted as a cheerful guide to the fells and was much admired for this, although people remarked that due to his lack of hygiene it was best to stand up wind from him. He eventually died at the age of 80, having contracted pneumonia whilst sleeping rough, during the harsh winter of 1947. Millican Dalton had long fascinated me for his total abandonment of the material life, of status, money and luxury, to pursue a simple life in the fells. Each of us dedicated fell walkers has something of Millican Dalton in them. He is known for a number of quotes, the most famous of which he inscribed at the entrance to his sleeping area called the 'Attic' and which reads, 'Don't waste words, jump to conclusions'. My own personal favourite quote though, because it echoes my beliefs, is 'You can't feel lonely with nature as your companion.' I was now desperately short of time. Kev was due to pick me up from Grange in less than thirty minutes and I did not want him waiting for me in the crowded village, where he might have to find a very inconvenient parking place, or not at all. I started doing a kind of walking trotting motion, hot and sweaty beneath the strong May sunshine. I never reached the cave. Time got the better of me and it got to the stage where I had to head back from Grange and quickly. I figured there was little point in rushing such a pilgrimage and that I would come back and explore Millican's cave another day, perhaps in March when there were less people about. Knowing my luck, if I had found the cave that day, it would have been host to something resembling the Glastonbury Festival!

Heading back at high speed (for me anyway), I came to a place above the River Derwent where there was a gate and a wooden stile crossing a wall. I decided to use the gate and noticing that there were two walkers a few feet behind me, I did the polite thing and held the gate open for them. I was astonished when one of them said in an irritated and sharp tone, 'No, we'll use the stile!' What kind of human being takes objection to having a gate held open for them? I had no time to do anything more than close the gate abruptly, shake my head a little and march on back to Grange. The walk had by now become a prototype for everything I dislike about humanity on the fells. Everyone has the right to roam, that is a fundamental principle and the majority of fell walkers respect their fellow walkers. Today I was just unfortunate. So this turned out to be the one walk in this book that did not make it into the list of secret Lakeland walks as shown at the back of this book. I think I was expecting too much of Castle Crag. I am determined though that I shall return one day and hopefully find at least a little solitude.

A Different View of Coledale

The horseshoe of the Coledale Round is justifiably popular. The Wainwright Fells that form this round will see visitors on all but the very worst weather days during any year. When I first did the Coledale Round, back in 1991, it was easy to see why it was so popular. Once height is gained, either by climbing Causey Pike or Grisedale Pike depending on your starting point, the remainder of the walk is ridge walking at its finest. The view from Eel Crag, the hub of the round, is one of the greatest in the Lake District for depth and distance. Add to this the fact that five Wainwrights can be bagged in the horseshoe, with an optional four further Wainwrights for those prepared to detour out and back and Coledale amounts to a must do pilgrimage for fell walking enthusiasts.

However, having climbed Causey Pike or Grisedale Pike at the start of the day, or having detoured from Coledale Hause to Grasmoor, or Hopegill Head, can a walker really say that they have gained an intimate knowledge of those fells? The view from those fells perhaps, but not their complexity or hidden corners and well defined ridges. In this chapter I want to take you on an exploration of a totally different Coledale, one that eschews the crowds; one that at times might as well be a million miles away from these propular places.

Grisedale Pike is an iconic fell and, as with many of the fells of the North Western group, is a thing of beauty. As a mountain lover you never forget your first view of Grisedale Pike. With its soaring, slender outlines, tapering to a neat and defined summit, it is just asking to be climbed. Although broad paths and erosion are never a good thing, the fact that one can see the course of the popular ascent path, from so many places in and around the Vale of Keswick, adds to the magnetic lure of this fell. For a way of descent from Grisedale Pike, or a way up it, the route from Braithwaite has a lot to commend it. However, there is an alternative, that is both quieter, no less varied and in places dramatic. This is the ascent from Thornthwaite, or from the Whinlatter visitor centre, depending on your preference. I had previously taken the delightful wooded walk from Thornthwaite to the visitor centre, a walk that greatly benefitted from the shade on what was a hot and sunny day in June. Now it was late February. A pristine covering of thick snow had fallen on the fells overnight. Both Stan and I wanted to dispense with a couple of miles of walk in from Thornthwaite and use the Whinlatter visitor centre as a high vantage point to get onto the fells.

It seemed that we might live to regret this choice, as the car struggled to negotiate the patches of ice and snow on the road from Braithwaite to the visitor centre. Having just about managed this and with the car parked up, we knew we had chosen correctly. The visitor centre, not normally a place that I would rave about, had become a magical winter scene. Our car was the only one there and we the only people there to witness the brilliant white of the snow covered pines, the sparkle of colours created by the shafts of morning sunlight on the snow crystals and the invigorating morning air. One half expected Santa and his elves to emerge from the wooden building of the visitor centre, or a talking badger from winter Narnia to appear out of the fake badger's set. The route up Grisedale Pike crosses the road and follows a wooded path to the delightful Comb Bridge. Here a forest road is joined and followed for another half mile, taking care to branch left over another bridge. It was at this second bridge that we met our first and only people on the route up. They were preceded by two friendly Labrador dogs, excitable but unthreatening, one of the nicest breeds one can meet on a walk. In general as a walker I am not a great lover of dogs, or more precisely of dog owners.

To illustrate this, here are three incidents from my walking career that stand out among quite a few others. The first was a bite on the calf from a Jack Russell, which left teeth marks and nasty bruising. My crime to deserve such punishment was simply to be out walking on a public footpath. I had some angry words with the male owner about keeping his dog on a lead if it could not behave itself and was promptly sworn at. The second incident is perhaps slightly more amusing, but also indicative of the state of mind of some dog owners. Again I was innocently minding my own business on a footpath, when an intimidating Alsatian came bounding up to me and started jumping up at me and barking. Now you do hear stories of people getting badly mauled by such dogs and so my mood on the walk had now changed from relaxed reflection to one resembling terror. After a few seconds the owner appeared, called the dog away and then said, 'Don't worry, he won't hurt you.' To my astonishment she was not saying this to me, but to her dog! As if in some deluded way she thought I was the one posing the threat! It is as if some dog owners are so bound to their dogs that they cannot see how intimidating they can be to others. To them the dog has become more important than the person being intimidated or molested. My final incident was equally bizarre. This time I was walking through a wood, thinking peaceful thoughts, when a couple of Alaskan Husky dogs came running up to me and then jumped up and barked threateningly at me. I called to the owner to get them off, and after what seemed like an age he managed to do so. This was the most recent of the incidents I am relating, and I had frankly had enough by this time. I gave the male owner a lecture on how I did not expect to be molested by dogs when I was doing nothing more than enjoying a walk. I was staggered when in reply he said, 'Well, I don't expect to meet strange men when I go on a walk.' He was not in the least bit apologetic and had just thrown back an insult. So I told him that he was both an idiot and also a lot stranger than me.

I would add that the majority of dog owners and dogs pass you peacefully by, or are simply friendly. However, it seems to me that incidents of threatening dog behaviour are becoming more and more frequent. It is a human right to walk on our beautiful islands and so long as we stick to rights of way, to not feel intimidated or threatened. Walking has become a great human stress reliever in modern times. Walkers don't harm anyone or anything and we should be free to pursue our interest without such threats. Having said this, the dogs that I have met up on the fells have generally been of the friendly kind and likewise their owners and I have often marvelled at how these dogs, some of which, such as the terriers, have very short legs, can gallivant up the fells. Some people say that we merely interpret animal's emotions by projecting our own human emotions on to them. But I have too often seen the look of boundless enthusiasm on a dog's face, when it is climbing a fell, to come to any other conclusion that in their own way these dogs enjoy the fells as much as we humans do.

Shortly after the second bridge, a path signposted for Grisedale Pike, diverts from the forest road and emerging from the forest, climbs free from the tree cover. This is the start of the North-East Ridge proper and it was here that the snow suddenly thickened to a uniform depth of about a foot. Ahead, as the eyes trended upwards, was a wonderful combination of pure virgin snow, with the deepest winter blue sky above. Behind though, towards the direction of Skiddaw, loomed a crop of snow showers, casting their whitened fingers over Skiddaw and towards Solway. Through some meteorological fluke the showers avoided the Coledale area for most of the day, and merely provided an atmospheric backdrop to our walk. Trudging uphill through thick snow is hard work and energy sapping, but in such conditions the rewards around you more than compensate for the bit of extra effort. As we climbed, the Helvellyn range came magnificently into view, with every gully on its long whaleback making a perfect crease in the uniform snow. Behind us Skiddaw and Blencathra were like large wedding cakes and Latrigg's bald, white summit was surrounded by the green of its woods. The North-East Ridge is not quite as well defined as the closing stages of the popular East Ridge from Braithwaite, but it does have a grandstand view of that ridge. Today, plastered in snow, the steep last few hundred feet of the East Ridge looked beautifully delineated against a backdrop of sunshine and cloud, and the ants that were people climbing the East Ridge assumed the stature of hardened mountaineers. The North-East Ridge had its own highlights not seen by those on the East Ridge – its curving course above the plunge of Grisedale Gill, the dramatic revelation of Hopegill Head with every protruding outcrop on Hobcarton Crag displayed as a perfect black and white etching. The sheer vastness of the pristine snow flank of Ladyside Pike brought into perspective the majesty and scale of these fells.

After what had seemed a very short time, we reached the slender summit of Grisedale Pike, covered in a slippery mixture of hard snow and ice. Its legendary view across the Vale of Keswick and out towards the Pennines was as clear as one could want it. Hopegill Head was a slender spire, soaring gracefully into the heavens, while Eel Crag and Grasmoor were massive white domes. We had met no-one on the North-East Ridge, but now up on the main Coledale ridge route there were a smattering of battle hardened winter walkers. The ridge down from Grisedale Pike and along Hobcarton Crag was a joy to walk. Winter walking has always brought out the child in Stan and I, and we delighted first in snowballing each other and then in moulding a rugby ball shaped piece of snow and passing it back and forth between ourselves.

The uniform slopes of Sand Hill were hard work, treading at times knee deep in snow, but the reward was the wonderful final approach to the summit of Hopegill Head, whose corniced summit area had something of a smaller scale version of the summit of Everest about it. From here Mellbreak cast its darkly iced crags over Loweswater while Hope Gill wound dramatically below our feet, to the point where the snow line ceased and was replaced by the more familiar Lakeland scene of patchwork green fields towards Cockermouth. As summits go, Hopegill Head is a fine perch, although as with many fells its dramatic crags are one sided, with Sand Hill here forming the less inspiring tail.

We had intended to go on to Eel Crag and even Grasmoor that day, but the plans made in the B&B and finalised in the car that morning, were quelled by the painful reality of muscles tired from incessant wading through deep snow and the limited daylight hours of February. It is always best, especially when winter walking, to have a backup plan or escape route. We decided to take a route down from Hobcarton End and via Black Crag that would eventually merge with the forest roads from our approach route. However, first we wanted another look at the view from Grisedale Pike, now

Enjoying a snow plastered Coledale Round before losing a tussle with an icy puddle

in evening colours. It was at the col between Sand Hill and the pull back onto Grisedale Pike that we came across a small frozen pool, about three feet square. It was here that my twenty odd years' experience in the fells was set aside in one moment of mindless madness. No defence can be given for my impulsive action, unless I can claim the poor judgement of a weary mind, although in truth I have been wearier on walks and not done something this stupid. A test on the pool with my walking pole seemed to tell me that the ice was thick and rock hard. Perhaps the pool was totally solid, although tests with light walking poles are not really suitable as a precursor for a test with a fifteen stone human body. As soon as my right leg put my full weight onto the pool, I knew I was in trouble. My entire right leg burst through the ice and half of me submerged up to my nether regions in icy water. Luckily Stan grabbed on to the other half of me and between us the fifteen stone idiot was hauled clear. Unfortunately a Satanic offspring of the ice pool now filled my right boot and my right trouser leg was soaked with icy water. Whereas the first time on Grisedale Pike that day had been a time of joy and thrill, the second time was one of frozen moodiness. I did not care for the view, I just wanted to get back to the car and get my frozen trousers off.

Especially in winter, one's mood depends on how comfortable one feels. I was getting seriously cold and was keen to avoid going from uncomfortably cold to a state of hypothermia. I informed Stan that I would rather not take a different route down via Hobcarton Crag. I wanted the surety of a route that I knew and where I could know exactly how far it was back to the car. Stan, being ever supportive of his sometimes wayward friend, was happy to oblige. It did not help matters that the snow showers, which had merely provided a dramatic backdrop on the way up, had now clumped together and were releasing their frozen pellets at us. After what seemed an age of seeping cold, the car was finally reached and it was not too long before I was able to joke about my fall through the ice, in front of a nice warm fire. Despite my self-inflicted incident I can thoroughly recommend the North-East Ridge of Grisedale Pike.

I did not really do justice to Wandope the first time I bagged it. From Eel Crag it is so easy to walk the fifteen minute ridge route down to Wandope, via the rim of Addacomb Hole and claim another Wainwright summit. Many fell baggers will similarly be tempted to detour from the main Coledale Round and come away from their day with an extra tick. There is nothing wrong with that, in fact such is the freedom of the fells. However, it does serve to illustrate how bagging all the Wainwrights is only part of a full exploration of the Lake District. Bagging summits and views (if the weather is kind) is all very well but does not necessarily allow for an intimate knowledge of the fell to be gained. The second time I climbed Wandope, it was somewhat better served by climbing from Buttermere, via Whiteless Pike on a linear route that then continued on over Eel Crag and Causey Pike. Even then, Wandope was a grassy detour from Thirdgill Head Man. I felt that Wandope had more to offer than just a stunning view. A thumb through the *North Western Fells Guide*, showed me that there were two other routes up Wandope from Buttermere, purist routes where the summit alone was the objective.

The first of these two routes was the ascent via the Addacomb Ridge. It was a late May day of outstanding clarity and clean spring colours; sunny and warm in spite of ranks of high cirrus clouds filtering the sun's rays. Just beside Sail Beck and across the way from the famous Fish Hotel, a path makes a lovely course through a patch of woodland by the beck. So many Lakeland walks start with the combination of wood and beck, but it never fails to be an enticing combination. It is not far until a fence and wall are crossed and the trees are left behind for the rest of the day. Here the drama of the High Stile ridge comes into view, but the route turns its back to this spectacle and makes a gently rising line above Sail Beck. The purpose of this path is not to climb Wandope, or indeed any fell, but to provide a low level walkers' pass between the Buttermere and Newlands valleys. I had often looked down on this path from the high ridges of Coledale, or from Ard Crags, but it was strange to be on the route itself with the giants of Coledale on one side and Knott Rigg on the other. Indeed Knott Rigg's massive, creased flanks looked quite imposing. This is the angle Knott Rigg would like to be seen from. The path detours a little way into the gully containing Third Gill, with the crags of Saddle Gate towering above. It then levels off onto a grassy shelf at about 1200 feet, a lovely piece of walking amongst grand surroundings. However, although it is now less than a half mile to the summit of Wandope, there is still over 1300 feet of climbing to be done.

From here it is a case of pathless scrambling all the way to the summit. If you can identify the two dry grooves mentioned in the Wainwright guide, then head up just after the second of these. You will know you have carried on too far if you get to Addacomb Beck. The wall of heather and grass above you is topped mostly by loose crag and scree, but a rockier, defined ridge can be seen at the Addacomb Hole end of this mountain wall and it is this that you need to head for. Once you have chosen your line to get to the ridge proper, the next 600 feet is hard climbing through very steep heather and grass. For those comfortable with space beneath their feet, look behind you (whilst clinging onto a clump of heather) to survey ridge upon ridge into the distance, a feature typical of views from this part of the Coledale massif.

Eventually rock starts to protrude through heather and grass and the Addacomb Ridge becomes more clearly defined ahead. The remaining 600 or so feet to the summit is fine, airy ridge walking, with little danger, but lots of drama and solitude. As an added bonus the superb hanging valley of Addacomb Hole now appears and this is undoubtedly the best place from which to view its fine architecture. Grassy at the bottom, the hole then rears up in a steep semicircle of scree and crag – the handiwork of millions of tons of ice, one of nature's most effective sculptors. The airy ridge now makes a beeline for the summit of Wandope to complete a true purist climb of this fell. Only now did I feel that Wandope had been given its due, that I really knew what it meant to climb Wandope.

The summit, although grassy in itself, is close enough to the edge of the fell to provide a view of both depth and distance. Most striking to me has

The view from Wandope

always been the series of ridges, six in total, stretching like great whalebacks to Helvellyn and the shapely summit of Catstycam. However, High Stile, Pillar, Great Gable and the mighty Scafells are also well profiled, and the glimpse of Buttermere provides a sense of the height you have gained. Through a combination of a later breakfast and some post breakfast dithering, Stan and I had made a late start that day and the plan had been about Wandope and Wandope alone. However, with the view clear out to Solway and the Isle of Man with plenty of daylight to play with in May, it was impossible to resist the lure of Eel Crag and its enormous panorama. It was interesting to contour around the rim of Addacomb Hole from above, where the sheer scale of the hole is foreshortened. As usual Eel Crag did not disappoint, although unlike Wandope it was not sheltered from a stiff breeze, meriting the donning of woolly hats and coats. It was by now after four o'clock in the afternoon and we had the rare experience of having the summit of Eel Crag to ourselves. Nestled down in a shelter near to the summit, the time honoured debate continued as to whether the view from Eel Crag is the finest in the Lake District. Such choices are matters of personal opinion. In my view, for what it's worth, the summits of Eel Crag and Skiddaw have among the greatest sense of panoramic distance as viewpoints, although whether that makes them better views than say Swirl How, with its view into mountains from a position perched over an abyss, is not for me to decide.

It did not do Wandope justice to revisit it in descent so we headed over short cropped grass to Thirdgill Head Man and from there along a delectable little ridge to Whiteless Pike. Whiteless Pike is a superb airy summit with a classic sylvan view down to Crummock Water, backed by the dark walls of Mellbreak with pastoral fields leading to Loweswater and the Fellbarrow Group. It is often the case, and quite natural, that having visited the last summit of a day in the fells, the enthusiasm diminishes. Limbs start to ache, the mind is not as fresh as at the start of the day and thoughts turn to evening meals, a pint and a comfy bed. Occasionally however, when light and landscape conspire, the final stages of a walk can be so special as to overwhelm the jaded senses and enable body and soul to be uplifted in a way quite contradictory to the norm. Such was the case this day on the descent from Whiteless Pike. The view in descent towards the High Stile range and lower down towards Buttermere is one of drama and classic beauty. The path, which is mostly smooth and carpet like, is a joy to tread. However, it was the utmost clarity and freshness of a spring evening that made the descent such a joy that day, with the landscape as colourful and vibrant as it could possibly be. Food and creature comforts could wait. This was too fine to be abandoned in haste.

The enormous sweeping flank of Wandope that encompasses the Addacomb Ridge climb, also holds another secret Lakeland route. This is the ascent via Third Gill and not surprisingly follows the same approach as the Addacomb Ridge route until the narrow confines of Third Gill are crossed. A steep and grassy sward marks the start of this climb. Any attempt to look for a path will be futile, this climb has no compromise and without even a reference in the Wainwright guide I doubt anyone would even look twice at climbing it. The initial section is a tough and leg burning slog up the grass slope. Aim for the rocky ridge set perpendicular to the steep grass slope you are climbing. On reaching this ridge, heather and rock replaces grass, but the angle of ascent becomes even more vertically challenging. At one point I found myself scrambling up heather of such steepness that my head was looking in between my legs at a vertigo inducing four hundred feet of sweeping fell side beneath me. It felt like if any of the clumps of heather I was using for handholds pulled away from the soil, I would make a dramatic and very rapid descent whose momentum might only be arrested by the waters of Sail Beck far below. Was there anything to commend this climb, I hear you ask? Well oddly enough although this type of situation and exposure may not be everyone's cup of tea, I found it quite exciting. This route seemed about as off the beaten track as one could wish for and in retrospect I'm glad I did it. Also, once the rocky pinnacle is reached, there is a delectable grassy shelf to sit and appraise the craggy and wild terminus of Third Gill. Here again secret Lakeland sat within a stone's throw, or perhaps a wild coomb's width, of popular Lakeland. Across the yawning chasm Whiteless Pike looked imposing with a number of miniature figures traipsing their way along the popular path over Whiteless Pike and on to Wandope and Eel Crag. From the pinnacle the steepness gradually relents as you wind your way through the heather and rock to a final grassy section and thence to the summit of Wandope. The remnants of heather

Looking into Third Gill (the ascent route is up the steep grassy flank to the right)

and grass on my clothes and in my fingernails bore witness to the fact that I had now fully paid my dues to Wandope, a fell which deserves so much more than a quick detour from Eel Crag.

One of the great joys of using a map is to be had in making up your own route. To slavishly follow a guide book or a book of walks is to limit the spirit of freedom. With a little bit of thought and imagination, there are simply thousands of walks and routes that can be linked together into one long expedition. Towards the end of my research for this book, I began to realise the number of days that holiday would allow in the fells was dwindling rapidly, in proportion with the number of walks I still needed to complete for this book. At times like that I longed to live in the Lake District, or within spitting distance, so that on any given weekend I could just pack a little rucksack, take a bus or train and head for the hills. This cannot be done due to the fact that I live in Kent, have a full time job, three children and a wife. I am indeed lucky and owe a debt of gratitude to my family that they let me go away as many times to the Lake District as I do. Kent has some hills and is not called the Garden of England for nothing, but its lure is pale when compared to the Lake District. Kent's hills are mere bumps. Although living in or near the Lake District would solve the problem of days needed versus walks to do, it would deny me the long winter nights of planning, far away from my beloved hills. On one such evening, a study of the map showed what I had thought would need to be two separate walks on the Coledale range, could in fact be combined into one long fell walk that was mouth-watering in anticipation. The long dark nights of winter gave way to the promise of spring as Stan and I found ourselves back in the Lake District, living out the plan. This is perhaps the finest secret Lakeland walk in the North Western Fells. Other walks may have moments of greater beauty or drama, but for a sustained high quality experience, with a bit of everything a great walk should have, this cannot be beaten.

I like occasionally to walk into the valley of Coledale, rather than survey it from the surrounding peaks of the Coledale Round. It is also one of the easiest starts to any walk in the district. The small but very busy car park just outside of Braithwaite not only marks the start of the Coledale Valley track, but also the start of the Coledale Round for those who prefer to tackle Grisedale Pike first. So get here early! The first two and a quarter miles are along the mine road, which provides one of the smoothest and most level walks into the heart of the fells anywhere in the District. This part of the walk is invariably popular, but don't worry, as you are headed for a place where few people dare to tread. On this April day of Mediterranean light and warm sunshine, with the gorse in brilliant yellow bloom and the crags ahead looking clear and imposing, it did not matter that we shared the walk in with a few walkers, as well as a party of workers with a digger, repairing the track. Most of them are volunteers, and without their work many of our favourite walks would be spoiled by erosion. You could argue that well maintained tracks are themselves a scar of civilisation, but due to the popularity of the Lakeland Fells they are a necessity and by far the lesser of the evils. The valley head gradually encloses around you and after fifty minutes of tramping you cross Coledale Beck; having had a virtually level walk so far, the climbing proper now begins. This is still the quite popular route to Coledale Hause, although it is more often used in descent from the fells. It's not long now though to secret Lakeland, so relax and admire the towering and vertiginous Force Crag to your right. A massive vertical gouge at the valley head, a huge glacial bite out of the mountainside, nature in the raw.

It is just after a higher crossing of the now infant Coledale Beck that the route takes a turn away from popular Lakeland into much quieter places. A little causeway is marked on the Wainwright guide, but don't expect anything fancy. It is just a little bridge of moss, grass and a few buried stones. The next part of the climb is a little tiresome and boggy, although the wall of Eel Crag now towers above. An old sheep fold marks a quiet spot to rest for a while, before a final mossy push takes you to the start of the drama. Now at around 2000 feet, a large rocky amphitheatre is ahead. A wild and secret coomb and part of Eel Crag that few people are privileged to see. Here there is a choice of two routes, the Shelf Route or Tower Ridge. Tower Ridge appears from here as an imposing, rocky arête, making a straight but perilous looking course towards the summit ridge. The Shelf Route on the other hand takes a more slanting rake across the face of the mountain. I would stress that in winter conditions either route would be a major undertaking requiring crampons and ice axe. The choice of two equally thrilling routes, both of which were undoubtedly secret Lakeland in essence, presented a dilemma to the author. This walk was completed towards the end of the list of walks needed for this book, when my publisher's deadline was looming and time was running out. I simply did not have enough available days to spend one day climbing Eel Crag via the Shelf Route and another climbing Eel Crag via Tower Ridge. Luckily my trusty companion Stan was available and for the one and only time in this book, I sent someone else to do one of the chosen secret Lakeland routes. Of course I felt a tinge of guilt and annoyance that I had not quite been able to complete my task for this book, but we were only talking about a very small portion of that task. I could in any sense go back and complete the other route on another day. But setting aside the self-imposed necessities of book writing or route bagging, it was an enticing proposition to separate here and have the prospect of meeting Stan later on the summit, with our differing dramas and stories to share. There was also another dilemma. Having decided to split up, who would do which route? Both were dramatic and both of us wanted to do both routes. The only option was to take emotion out of the equation and toss a coin. It was heads for Tower Ridge and tails for the Shelf Route. Stan called heads and so it was decided.

It was not long before we parted company. Stan seemed a little edgy. Twenty years ago, he used to do hard scrambles, such as Jack's Rake, without a care. However age, wisdom and a few scary moments in the past, had quelled his ambitions as a scrambler and heightened his sense of mortality. It is odd how the older we get the more we seem to savour life. One would think it would be the other way round. I said goodbye to him as we both wished each other a safe walk and to take care. I felt a bit of a charlatan, as I saw Stan almost instantly begin his scramble steeply upwards over rock, whereas my route began very gently through grass and a bit of bog. There was, however, a strong feeling of exploration and freedom as I headed for the Shelf Route. There is little in the way of a path here, more a kind of obvious line, leading to the equally obvious rake of the shelf itself. Before long one gets a sense of the ground falling away sharply a few feet away, this sense gradually heightening as progress is made. I kept looking round to see where Stan was on Tower Ridge and to take the odd picture or video of him. He kept popping in and out of view, as his route switched between one side of the ridge and the other. He reached a tiny notch in the ridge about half way up then disappeared from view for good. I put my head down and focused on my own route. Just before the shelf itself is reached the top of a gully is traversed, with dizzying views down towards Coledale Hause and the mine road some 600 feet below – needless to say a slip here could have serious consequences. The shelf itself is the highpoint of this route. There is rock rising steeply on one side and the huge plunge of Eel Crag itself on the other; sandwiched in between, somehow defying the perils, is the slanting rake of grass that is the Shelf. This is quite easy, although the ground is angled steeper than it appears to be on approach and I found it best to make use of hands in places and hug quite closely to the inside rocky face of the Shelf. Here is a place, not far from the time honoured tracks of the Coledale Round and yet in essence a million miles away. If there is a slight sense of disappointment, it is only because the Shelf is quite short and one wishes for longer, more sustained thrills. Where the Shelf Route levels out, there is a tiny, flat plinth of grass, perched above the abyss and this must be one of the finest and most thrilling places to rest in the whole of the Lake District. On came my MP3 player as I found a suitable piece of music to accompany the grandeur. This was *Jupiter* from *The Planets*, by Gustav Holst. The combination of this sensational place and one of the greatest tunes ever written was overwhelming. I got the urge, as I have had before, to stand up and conduct, using my walking pole as a kind of baton. It was almost as though I was conducting nature, for once conquered and seemingly submissive to my commands. I appreciate that such antics may not be everyone's cup of tea, but if there is no-one to see you, then why not? I would certainly never dream of doing such things on the crowded summit of Scafell Pike, or I might get carted off in a straitjacket!

Antics completed, the final climb to the summit of Eel Crag is a singular joy with the path sticking close to the rim of the summit ridge and the enormous views unfolding. It was something of a Stanley and Doctor

Livingstone moment when I met and gave a hug to Stan, who had reached the summit first. We both described our route to each other in detail and here is an account of what Stan had to say.

As he left me Stan was having second thoughts about doing the ridge. He scanned the rock towers above and there did not seem to be any obvious line of ascent. He knew though that if he did not do it, he would regret it.

Staying to the left was the advice from the Wainwright guide. Alongside the ridge was steep grass, which can also be dangerous, with nothing to hold onto in the event of slip. To stay right was to meet oblivion, a vertical, shattered cathedral of tumbling masonry, with no chink in its ancient armour. Within these confines, Stan aimed to plot a central left course, only to find that he became increasingly 'ledged out'. The only solution was for him to take his courage in both hands and stick to the apex of the ridge. Somehow it was more reassuring to climb directly upwards in symmetry, rather than try to shuffle tentatively across the face of the mountain. Stan concentrated on the rock in front of him, an effective way not to be reminded of his precarious position!

After a number of awkward but satisfying moves he was able to reach a vantage point where he could safely take a breather and survey the familiar Lakeland horizons. The Coledale valley, leading onto the bulk of Skiddaw, the Helvellyn Ridge in its entirety, including Calfhow Pikes (a point which can be seen seemingly from almost anywhere in the Lake District), the Scafells sprawling massively to the South. He could also now see across to the Shelf Route where I was standing, on a ledge of eye-watering exposure. Using his camera, Stan was able to zoom in and see that I was waving my arms about like a madman. Knowing that I was a classical music devotee, enthusiastically and demonstratively so, it was clear to him that I was in my element, at peace with my world. Stan was right!

Stan called out to me across the forbidding chasm that lay between us, his voice echoing between the vertical walls of rock, but I was deaf to his entreaty, with my headphones on and in a world of my own. Tower Ridge is a place emphatically not for those that with no head for heights. For those that crave adventure and excitement, assuredly one of the finest spots in the Lake District.

We both headed onwards, Stan realising that my Lakeland overture was done, as I headed out of sight. As Stan climbed further upwards, the ridge became wider, ahead of him merely a grassy sneck meeting the mountain side and the way onwards to the summit plateau.

On reaching the summit and hearing Stan's story, I was quite glad that he had 'won' our coin toss and chosen Tower Ridge, for it sounded like it would have tested my limits. The Shelf Route had been wonderful, with moments of vertigo inducing drama, where a slip could be costly. Tower Ridge though, was more difficult. Being a determined, bagging type, and having come up with this secret Lakeland agenda, I will have to come back and climb Tower Ridge one day. At least I will have Stan's description for a guide.

As I have said earlier, it is a matter for debate as to whether the view from Eel Crag is the finest in the Lake District. It would certainly figure in my top ten views and on a clear day it is as wide ranging a view as any in the district. For its feeling of height above the massive panorama of the Cumbrian plains and the Solway Firth, it shares something in common with the summit of Skiddaw. However, it also has the drama of the plunge from the summit ridge down to the Coledale valley and the fine array to the south and east, where fold after fold of wonderful and familiar mountain shapes and ridges recede into the distance. Only towards Grasmoor, which is some 40 feet or so higher, is the view restricted.

Sometimes I have wished that I had read my Wainwright guide in a little more detail before choosing my way off a mountain. To ascend from Eel Crag towards Coledale Hause, AW gives a choice of the prominent and largely grassy path down the tailing flanks of the fell, or a scree route. In a mood of joy at having done the Shelf Route, I only gave a cursory glance to the route down to the Hause. It was obviously shorter to take the scree route and maintained the drama of having the edge of the summit ridge on one side. It would also pass the exit of the Shelf Route, which I could then show Stan. What I did not take into account was Wainwright's notes in descent about this scree route, which say, 'the bad scree above Coledale Hause ought to be avoided in favour of a direct descent on grass west'. Clearly the old fellow was giving a strong hint here, which, to my regret, I failed to notice. Things began well enough, on ground I had already trodden coming up from the Shelf Route and a path that was clear and decent. However, just after the exit of the Shelf Route, the path began to take a turn for the worse. The scree route, as it now became, looked steep and awkward from above. Stan questioned me as to whether this was a safe route and I just muttered something about it being a proper route of descent or ascent in the Wainwright guide, not having read the caveat given by Wainwright. Scree comes in many different forms and I don't always mind scree in descent. I recall a descent from the ridge of Ben Eighe in Scotland, where Stan and I glided down a smooth scree slope as though on skis managing to get down from 3000 feet in around half an hour! So scree can have its advantages, however the scree on descent from Eel Crag was littered with little rocky ledges. These ledges, although only about five or six feet high at most, still presented the kind of obstacles that a walker would be less than enthused at being faced with. There appeared to be no path through this scree and the best route down through the difficulties was anyone's guess.

Our progress was painful and made doubly so by being able to see the wide smooth Coledale Hause path, just a couple of hundred feet below yet seemingly unattainable. Suddenly and with no warning I found myself sliding down the scree towards one of the mini ledges shouting various profanities as bemused walkers stared upwards at the commotion from the comfort of the Hause below. Thankfully, I managed to brake myself to a stop before going headfirst over the ledge. Stan suffered a similar experience – I did not feel good about myself, having placed him in danger for want of reading a few lines of guide book. It was a sweaty and relieved pair of chastened walkers that eventually reached Coledale Hause, backsides and trousers covered in scree dust. It just shows that even after 20 years of fell walking with hundreds of walks completed, I can still fall prey occasionally to a lack of planning. I had wanted drama that day, but this most certainly was not on the agenda. I can only repeat Wainwright's advice to avoid this route, which can only become more unstable over time. It's not pleasant and was the one downside to a great day in the fells. By avoiding my mistake and taking the grassy route down, you will have all the pleasure of this route, with none of the pain.

A sense of 'joie de vivre' returned when we realised that we were safe and that a few more years of life stretched out before us. It's a bit of a slog from here over Sand Hill, but keep ploughing on and your reward will be the familiar diminutive summit of Hopegill Head. This was my second visit to Hopegill Head on the same hills break. On the first the weather had been dull and the views poor. So it was with some gratification for us that we now sat on Hopegill Head with a clear and distant view. We did not stay on the summit overly long, because we had the prospect of a long awaited new peak and another secret Lakeland route.

I have often looked down at Ladyside Pike from Hopegill Head and thought how graceful and slender its summit ridge appeared. Long before I had even thought about *Secret Lakeland* as a project, I had been meaning to traverse the narrow ridge between Hopegill Head and on to Ladyside Pike. I had looked at the ridge in winter, when the final notch leading to Hopegill Head was corniced by snow and looked fearsomely dangerous. Now at last I had perfect conditions to complete this mini ambition and it did not disappoint. There is feeling of leaping into the unknown leaving the summit of Hopegill Head towards the initial steep descent. All is rock here and fearful plunges over Hobcarton Crag, and yet in calm and dry conditions there is little to cause concern and a lot to cause excitement and joy. At one point great slabs of brittle rock cross the path in a scene of high drama, while the approaching ridge on to Ladyside Pike entices. The ridge is narrow but devoid of difficulties. As you begin to climb Ladyside Pike a wall is crossed and the final climb is a delight. Ladyside Pike is a grand little summit, with a surprisingly large cairn and a wonderful feel of space and depth around, not to mention a dramatic view back towards Hopegill Head. Above all, a wonderful little piece of secret Lakeland, with no-one to disturb us during our half an hour on the summit. It is strange in some ways, that this well-defined summit at over 2300 feet is not a Wainwright fell, but just a subsidiary of the 'true' Wainwright, Hopegill Head. Such is the arbitrary and unchangeable nature of the 214 Wainwright Fells. Unlike the Scottish Munros (mountains over 3000 feet), which keep having mountains added and subtracted from the list on an almost yearly basis, due to ever more accurate height surveys and arbitrary considerations, the Wainwrights will always be 214 fells because the criteria for a Wainwright has and could only be set by the great man himself. Nit-picking individuals such as the author can argue that Ladyside Pike is in a different league to some 'true' Wainwrights, such as Little Mell Fell and Ling Fell, but any court of hills law would be bound to throw out as unsound any attempt to create a 215th Wainwright. Good thing too really, as it keeps the Wainwright baggers away!

It is no wonder this graceful summit has such a feminine name. Some mountains are female in character and some more masculine. One could not imagine Eel Crag being called Ladyside Pike, it is too broad shouldered and muscular. The ridge leading from Hopegill Head to Ladyside Pike is mainly rocky, while the ridge leading on towards the bulk of Swinside, is smooth and grassy. Our route branched away from the wall, where it joined a new fence, just before reaching Swinside. The next 800 feet of height were lost remarkably quickly, the descent here being exceptionally steep but all on grass. I cannot imagine ever wanting to ascend this way, although it is described as a route of ascent in the *Wainwright Guide to the North-Western Fells*. To Stan and I though, it was a perfect and quick way down after a long day on the fells. Such was the sustained steepness that bottom would prove more effective than feet as the mode of downward travel. I can only salivate at the prospect of the ride one might have down these slopes under a covering of snow. I will have to come back just to try it!

This high speed descent deposits you at a gate, which is crossed into a small no-man's land of rough grass before another gate submerges the walker in the Swinside Plantation of Whinlatter Forest. Wainwright, like many of us, was somewhat contradictory and ambiguous in nature when it came to the subject of man-made afforestation. He detested what he saw as the despoliation of the Ennerdale Valley, to produce the rows of uniform pine trees that became Ennerdale Forest. On the other hand, he seems to have had some time for other forest enterprises, such as Dodd and Whinlatter. To throw my own tuppence in, I would rather not see any further afforestation in the National Park, but consider that those areas of forest that already exist are well established and as such are now part of the Lake District that we know and love. Maybe it is just because I have never known anything else, but I simply cannot imagine Whinlatter without its forest or Dodd without its skirt of trees.

As we entered the forest it looked about as good as it ever would. The vivid light and colour of an early May evening caressed the flanks of Graystones and Whinlatter. Walking through the forest was a constant interchange of dark canopy and dazzling, open air light. Oddly enough there were a number of sheep and young lambs within the forest. Odd, because one would expect them enclosed in a field, particularly at lambing time. It made for a slightly surreal atmosphere, with the mother sheep calling from some unseen dark patch of dense forest, only to have the call returned from some other dark corner, by the young lamb. Stan and I passed by quickly, feeling like intruders. It seemed such a contrast from the harsh morning light and open spaces of the miners road into Coledale, as if this were another day altogether. Great mountain days often have such contrasts. From the delightful Hobcarton Bridge, it was still some three miles back to the car at Braithwaite, but my pre-planning of this walk had showed me that it was almost possible to follow the forest tracks all the way back to the car. There would be just one small section of proper road walking at the end of a walk that had been without a car carrying road for almost its entire length. Although our ambition had not taken into consideration our mounting fatigue and hunger; we finally came to the conclusion that following the forest tracks was no longer a practical – or more importantly a quick – way to reach our destination. Decision made we stopped at the well-known Whinlatter car park viewpoint to enjoy the classic scene over Bassenthwaite Lake and Skiddaw, all the tourists by now long since gone as we reflected on a classic day in the fells. We continued down the road looking up as the treetops caught the last rays of evening sunshine, soon enough reaching the car park and the end of one of the grandest outings in this book. This magnificent walk was proof, if proof were needed, that there is far more to the Coledale group of fells than the admittedly classic, but at times very popular, Coledale Round.

A Stag in the Fells

A good friend does not necessarily make for a good walking companion in the hills. Friendship is not enough, if there is not also a basic love of countryside, drama and of course the high places. So it has always been with a little trepidation that I have introduced a new friend to fell walking. My own fell walking career began with my brother Peter, who has now, temporarily I hope, had to give up fell walking. Our fascination with the Lake District blossomed together and I realised that while we did have the odd argument, we were pretty much on the same wavelength when it came to our appreciation, becoming love, of the fells. We began with gentle low level walking, serving our apprenticeship before tackling the higher fells. After two years of this, I introduced my best mate Stan to the fells. I was 21 at the time and figured that being my best mate he would enjoy the experience like I had. His apprenticeship was a lot shorter, tackling the Old Man of Coniston on only his second day of Lake District walking. His initial feelings about the hills were not helped by a lack of sleep, due to my brother's snoring. I mistook his tiredness and lack of conversation for a lack of hills love. Fortunately I was wrong in this judgement and Stan has been my close walking companion ever since. The highest compliment I can pay him is that I equally enjoy walking with him as I do walking solo. There can be no higher esteem.

Almost fifteen years passed with Peter, Stan and I walking together in the Lake District, Scotland and Wales, before we decided to invite my other best friend Kevin along. His first experience of fell walking, in 2004, was on a chilling winter's day climbing Angletarn Pike and Brock Crags. That day he endured frequent, face numbing, snow showers. A severe trial of hills love and I am glad to say he passed. Now in April 2011, another friend – Stan's brother Bob – was about to experience either a loving or loathing of the fells.

April 29th 2011 will go down in history as being the date of the Royal Wedding of William and Kate. Now I neither consider myself a royalist or an anti-royalist. I do however think that in terms of the charity work they do, the tourism they bring in to the country and the sense of history and tradition, there is something to be said for having a Royal Family. Whatever one's thoughts, it cannot be denied that the extra public holiday given for the Royal Wedding provided an excellent opportunity for some fell walking, on fells largely bereft of other walkers! It was an opportunity too good to miss.

The four of us set off into the North-Western Fells that day, with our sights set on Whiteside and Hopegill Head. It was the first day of Stan's stag weekend. At 40 he had found true love, with a lovely lady called Liz and I was thrilled for him and thrilled also that I was to be his best man. But before my wedding duties came the traditional ritual of the Stag weekend. I'm not quite sure what has happened in the 16 years that have passed since I got married, but it no longer seems acceptable for a Stag do to be just a merry night out with your friends. These days it has to be a weekend, or even a week in some cases. However, with Stan being the lover of high places he is, the Stag weekend was to be held in the Lake District and involve, at least during the day, some fell walking. This in turn meant that Stan's nearest and dearest male friends would be joining us in the Lake District and more importantly on the fells. The only member of the party never to have walked in the fells was Stan's brother Bob.

I have known Bob for years, almost as long as I have known Stan, and he is a great guy. Now he would follow in Stan and Kev's footsteps to take what I call the 'hills love' test. My expectations of someone new to the hills can sometimes be very high, putting too much pressure perhaps on someone to enjoy it the way I do. It may seem a bit fanatical but having someone on a walk with you that cares not whether they are there or somewhere else, detracts from the experience for the rest of the party. So the jury was still out on Bob's 'hills-love'. In terms of his fitness levels Bob's pedigree was good, very good. In fact it worried me. I had become used to quite stately progress up the fells, with plenty of stops, sometimes to appreciate the landscape and sometimes just to get my breath back. Although I am certainly not unfit. I don't think an unfit person could do day after day of fell walking as I can. But I am certainly not what I would call fit. Where others may have a six pack, I have a one pack, my belly. Bob on the other hand is as lithe and lean as a piece of meat trimmed of all its fat. On top of that he loves running, thinking nothing at all of knocking off 10 km runs on his lunch break. Running is something I very rarely do; if I have to break into a run, it will generally be strictly out of necessity only. With Kev and Stan both also trim and fitter than me, it concerned me that although I was the most experienced of the party (along with Stan to be fair), I might end up lagging behind like some middle aged novice. If I am honest too, a selfish part of me wanted to enjoy the walk at the same pace and in the same way I would normally. Is there anything wrong in being selfish about one's passions?

Prior to setting off, I could not resist a little joke at the new boy's expense, a bit like the initiation for newcomers at secondary school. Two cars, carrying four men, pulled into the car park at Lanthwaite Green, from where we were to tackle a hopefully secret Lakeland route onto Whiteside, followed by another similarly secret route back down. We had firstly pulled Bob's leg by trying to convince him that the man-made duck pond at Tebay Services was in fact one of the famous lakes of the Lake District. That was a pretty poor effort and, unsurprisingly, he did not buy it. Something altogether more convincing was required. It was hard to imagine how Bob must have felt getting out of the car to do his first hill walk. It was something that was so organically natural for me to do, so much a part of my life, of my very essence, that the remembrance of it being wholly new seems like another life altogether. I could though recall a vague memory of adrenalin, tinged with fear, as I contemplated the high places for the first time. This remembrance was now the key to my little joke. From Lanthwaite Green, Whiteside must look daunting enough for someone who had never climbed a fell before. But of course Bob did not know which fell was Whiteside and so it occurred to me to try and convince him that the giant Grasmoor, which towers above the roadside here, and presents a seemingly sheer craggy face, was actually our objective for the day. So I pointed my walking pole casually to Grasmoor, in pretence that its craggy face did not in fact still scare the hell out me, and traced a line for Bob that we were supposedly going to take onto the fell. Bob had no reason to think that Grasmoor was not Whiteside and Kev and Stan quickly realised the bait I had set out and joined in with chat about how sheer Grasmoor's front was, but with a bit of luck Bob would be safe. Bob is a fairly inscrutable character. He does not wear his heart on his sleeve as I do and would make a great poker player. However, I'll swear that behind his calm exterior I sensed the presence of fear. We are all friends though, so it would have been wrong to maintain the pretence for too long before putting him out of his misery. I guess I am lucky that Bob is such a calm guy, or he might have done more than just smile at me and shake his head, when I revealed that we were pulling his leg.

So the four of us set off across the flat grassy path that starts this walk and leads to Liza Beck and, thanks to Stan, I actually found myself ahead of the pack. This was not because Stan was unfit, but because of his time honoured habit of taking about five times as long to get ready as everyone else. Having finally got all his walking gear on, he then had to cake himself in a face pack of sun cream, before finding he had lost the lid of the bottle, taking yet more time to locate it. My lead was however short lived – after we crossed the bouldery beck and began the steep haul onto Whin Ben, the natural order of cardiac fitness began to take shape. Bob began to stride ahead with the confidence of all those miles of running in his legs. I liked to think that at this stage he was the hare and I was the tortoise and I would bide my time for later in the day. Compensation for the haul onto Whin Ben is had from the retrospective views to the craggy, whaleback hulk of Mellbreak and Crummock Water. On a good day we could have seen out to Solway and the first hills of Scotland, but even though it was too hazy for that, Bob still appeared to be enjoying the views and the new experience.

The flat and grassy top of Whin Ben is a wonderful, comfortable place for a stop. The white path, snaking its way between the brown heather and curving round to Whiteside itself, beckons you onwards, while the views over crags to the 'V' shaped valley, that is home to Gasgale Gill, are dramatic. Leaving the delights of Whin Ben, the path soon encounters a rocky knobble calling for a little mild scrambling. At this point Bob began to appear a little hesitant and I detected the signs of fear and anguish that I had exhibited when doing the likes of Sharp Edge for the first time. It was easy for Stan, Kev and I to forget just how new this was to Bob. Kev loved the scrambly places, as did Stan, whilst I had lots of experience but still hovered between fear and enjoyment depending on how bad the obstacle was. Bob however had no precedent for this. No bank of experience of how to find a good line, or how to place hands and feet. He had been thrown in at the deep end and we had to guide him carefully onwards. At times he said that he could not make out the route onwards, when it seemed obvious to our trained eyes. So far Bob had been following a well-defined route and it is easy to see how someone new to all this could become confused when the path became narrower, or various bits of path split off here and there. It was not a time for mickey taking. I know only too well how the fear of what may lay ahead can overcome the actual reality beneath one's feet and at such times fell walking can cease to be enjoyable. We took it in turns to lead Bob up the striated rocks towards the summit of Whiteside. At about 2000 feet, a little wander from the path to the edge of the fell side provided fearsome views down the gullies of Gasgale Crags to the silver thread of Gasgale Gill far below.

Eventually the path began to level out and there appeared to be more sky ahead than land. One had that peculiar realisation that the summit could not be far away. A sudden but detectable change came over Bob. The shadows of mild terror appeared to have fallen from his eyes, to be replaced by a new, joyous sensation: that of approaching one's first summit. This feeling spreading through the party was viral; we were all

Kev on Gasgale Crags (across the way the Dove Crags route onto Grasmoor is seen)

delighting in Bob's pleasure. To see the look on his face on reaching his first Wainwright summit, indeed his first summit of any kind, was certainly memorable for us all. Bob is not one for massive displays of emotion (unlike the author), but the irrepressible smile on his face spoke volumes. I could have wished the view was clearer for him, but he did not care. A few seconds after he had reached the summit, we crowded round him for a group hug, a moment of unbridled celebration. I have had many profound moments on my own, but this shared experience ranks with the best of them.

The ridge from Whiteside to Hopegill Head is, in my opinion, one of the finest high level ridge routes in the Lake District. The path becomes rocky and narrow in places, with a little mild but generally optional scrambling. One can take the option of keeping to the crest of the ridge over slabby rocks, or bypass this along ledge like paths. There is no real danger, only perceived danger, but all the time the fearful drops down Gasgale Crags emphasise the situation and add a little adrenalin to proceedings, while ahead, ever present, Hopegill Head appears to rear up sharply. However, I could sense that once again the fear of the unexpected had got the better of Bob, as he gingerly stepped along every bypass route he could find, trying to avoid the crest. Not that I blame him. This is a place where a head for heights is needed and I would have been the same when I first started walking in the Lake District.

It was great that Bob carried on to the summit of Hopegill Head and thereby completed his second Wainwright. Once again I could sense a growing appetite for the fells. Bob did however display a certain naivety when he suddenly asked 'Where do I go to the toilet?' At least he cared enough to ask, unlike some. Surely he did not expect there to be some kind of portaloo on the fells?! We enquired whether he meant number one's or number two's. When he replied that he just wanted a wee, we told him – astonished at having to explain – as long as he doesn't do it on the path and out of decency find a place where no-one can see you, then that would be fine. At least he asked!

Our return route began by reversing the track along Gasgale Crags. To prove my theory that the fear of unknown danger can be worse than the actual reality under foot, Bob seemed a lot more confident retracing his steps back along the top of the crags, even venturing onto the crest at one or two places. It is only through such trials and tests that each fell walker comes to know his or her limit. Some might eventually progress to full scale climbs on Scafell Crag. For myself I reached that limit on Jack's Rake and unless someone pays me, I will probably never do it again. Bob was undergoing that early period of finding a personal boundary. Unfortunately, it is often only when you've scared yourself half to death that your personal limit is discovered.

Until now we had only met three solo walkers. Each time, instead of the usual comments such as 'Which route have you taken?' or 'Where are you heading for?', we had a conversation with each person we met that started along the lines of 'Not watching the wedding then?', to which all parties agreed it was too good an opportunity for a day in the fells. The route so far had been quiet, but it was to be quieter still in descent. In fact on leaving the east top of Whiteside we encountered no-one until we got back to the car. At first it heads gradually down sweeping flanks of heather and grass, across Whiteside's benign, easy angled tail, allowing quick progress to be made, in theory at least. As we descended, we encountered a fierce crosswind making it difficult to plot a straight course downwards. Wind to my mind can be the worst of the elements for a walker. You can reach the summit in rain, snow and mist, but the wind can physically prevent any further progress or at least make it so unpleasant as to sap the walker's resolve to continue; its constant buffeting and searing chill factor can be at best an irritant, at worst a killer. This wind bucked the trend though in that its characteristics were for once playing in our favour, it was a reasonably warm wind and was either blowing from the side or behind us and therefore, for the most part, blew us helpfully down the fell side towards the conspicuous hump of Dodd.

Dodd Pass is a curious place. As Wainwright points out, it is not dissimilar to Trusmadoor in the Northern Fells, although I would say that it is a bit grander and craggier than Trusmadoor. There is a faint path snaking its way through crag and scree on to the summit of Dodd. At the start of a day and in that early flush of enthusiasm, we would have wanted to get to the top of Dodd. However, once the mind has settled on descending and thoughts turn to the end of the walk, it is hard to get much motivation for more climbing, even though it was only another 200 feet. Of course had this been the only option to get back to the car we would just have got on with it, but at this stage we were in energy conservation mode plus I sensed that Bob, even though he was the fittest of the group, was beginning to feel the physical effects of his first fell walk. There are a number of subsidiary summits in Lakeland that are rarely visited and Dodd on the flanks of Whiteside is one of these. I have made a mental note to return and bag Dodd once I have completed my secret Lakeland labour of love. For now though there were two route choices, one a gentle and largely grassy traverse round the flanks of Dodd, or a more direct route down Cold Gill. I must admit the grassy traverse was an attractive proposition, but it would add another mile on to the walk back to Lanthwaite. The Cold Gill route was far more direct and the general consent was to take it and get down.

A faint path leads round the back of Dodd, heading towards the Cold Gill route and a triangular sheepfold. This path is narrow at times and set at a slight angle, the perfect place in fact to twist an ankle after a long day on the fells, so best to watch one's feet. The sheepfold sits hemmed in by Whiteside's huge backside completely overshadowed and insignificant – undoubtedly secret Lakeland, although not Lakeland at its most scenic. Now the route heads straight down Cold Gill. There is little and sometimes no path and at times it is a question of choice as to which side of the gill to walk. We tended to stick to the left side. Cold Gill is not much of a spectacle. It does not leap and bound in cataracts and waterfalls as other gills do. Instead it trickles and oozes into boggy banks and at times is so shy about its faults that it completely disappears below ground. The route down Cold Gill is certainly secret, but it is not what I would call a pleasant section of walking. Here there is loose scree, some bits of bog and a claustrophobic feeling. Bob was also hobbling and confided in me that his new boots were giving him discomfort in the toes and heels, the precursor of blisters. To his credit he got on with the walk and did not moan. In hindsight, though, it may have been better to have taken the longer and grassier route. Our route was a shortcut distance wise, but poor terrain slows you down and it is questionable as to whether the grassy route around Dodd, although longer, may have proved about the same in terms of time taken. Eventually our route joined the low level path to Lanthwaite, where the terrain was much improved and there was a rather lovely walk, in evening sunshine, back to the car. We all went to bed early that night, preparing ourselves for the main stag event the next day.

The Lake District has seldom looked more beautiful than it did on Saturday April 30th 2011. The sun shone, with just a few cotton wool clouds for company. The wind was light, but fresh. A little overnight rain had cleared the air and good views were anticipated. The walk we had planned catered for the fact that it was Stan's stag event in the evening and we wanted to be back in Keswick by 5pm and into the town by around 6pm for the first drinks. It was a walk more planned out of the need to get back early and also to still do a walk for this book, rather than a walk planned for classic scenery and drama. A simple and pleasant round of Graystones and Broom Fell from Embleton Church. There would be no crags or narrow ridges to worry the newcomer Bob today, just rolling grass and heather. However, as is sometimes the case, the walk did in fact prove to be one of the most cherished walks of my 20 odd years so far in the fells and far surpassed in beauty my expectations when planning the walk. It would be all too easy to relegate this walk to a poor weather day but far more rewarding to save it for good weather and enjoy its intimate delights and quiet, timeless charm.

This walk begins at Embleton Church, once a rather sombre grey building with a tiny tower, but recently given an altogether more joyous demeanour by having been whitewashed. Almost directly opposite the church is a narrow leafy lane, a quiet road leading steadily upwards and making for an easy and pleasant start to the walk. Pastoral intimacy had replaced the rugged grandeur of the previous day's walk. The stream of Tom Rudd Beck accompanies the lane, although to begin with you will struggle to see it, as it shyly hides behind the trees and beneath the line of the road. The mill pond mentioned by Wainwright is slightly easier to see. The road soon breaks out of the confines of the trees and crosses Tom Rudd Beck, which can now be clearly seen as a small boulder strewn stream. The road does a second sharp zig-zag before a gate which marks the start of the path to Graystones. All is pleasant and verdant, the type of terrain where trainers could easily replace walking boots. Already the clearer air brought Solway and the Galloway Hills into view and the pastoral nature of the walk was brought into perspective when a vole ran across the path in front of us.

Soon the terrain became rougher and wilder and the path just a thread through bracken. Just before the first tributary of Tom Rudd Beck and the larch trees that Wainwright mentions, is a tiny little dip in the folds of the hills. This is nothing on the map, but on a perfect late April day, with the pale blue sky above and the larks singing, it was the perfect spot for a halt. It was not that we desperately needed a halt, as we had only been walking a gentle 45 minutes or so. It was more that the four of us seemed to share the combined thought that here was a place so removed from the everyday buzz and stress of life and so tranquil, that it called us to just take things easy for a few minutes and lose ourselves in the peace. There was a subtle, sleepy spell over this little hollow. Three of us closed our eyes and succumbed and had Stan not been more interested in taking photos with his new expensive camera, who knows when this little group would have been aroused from slumber.

After some careful navigation and the crossing of a fence by a gate, the path trends up towards the dry stone wall that leads to the summit. Now Stan and Kev both know how obsessive I am about the minor details in the Wainwright guides, such as fenced bogholes and tiny springs of water. I am often the butt of jokes regarding this and so today I thought that I would play to the gallery. Wainwright mentions that at the foot of the final steep haul onto Graystones, there is the dry bed of an old reservoir. I decided to mention this to the others with an air of extreme enthusiasm and then began to look intently for the remains of this reservoir, like an archaeologist trying to find the outline of an old Iron Age fort. Then to add to this leg pulling, I began to take a series of pictures of pretty much nothing, except a flat piece of grassy land, with a regular edge that must have been the reservoir bank. I mockingly went down on one knee to get the right angle for these photos and it was at this point that the others realised that I had not gone insane, but was playing a little joke. Mind you even caricatures have a basis in truth.

Although it is a steep pull from the dried up reservoir to the summit, in clear weather the views back towards Solway drive you on to climb higher and higher. The summit of Graystones is an elevated platform and another perfect place to recline in good weather. The views are good without being great. On a clear day the long arm of the Galloway Coast is well seen across the Solway Firth, and there is a sizeable chunk of the Cumbrian plains in the foreground. Perhaps the finest aspect though is the beautiful scene of the Lorton Vale, backed by the dark, craggy slopes of Mellbreak. We had met no-one on ascent and just one solitary walker on the summit. I pondered how often I had been that solitary walker and would have been a little put out to find a group of four walkers crowding in on me. Perhaps there is a little hypocrisy in that.

Most walkers approach Graystones as a ridge walk from Broom Fell and this was how I first bagged the fell. Our route continued along the usual ridge to Broom Fell, going steeply down to Widow Hause, where the shadows of the dark Darling How plantation made for some welcome shade. The broad grassy path then climbs its way to Broom Fell. I could sense that Bob was now relaxing into the atmosphere of the place and that this was perhaps more like the kind of hill walking terrain he had expected. It was as something of a pleasant surprise when he suddenly asked whether he could run to the top of Broom Fell. As I have said, Bob loves running and this was perfect terrain for a run. I told him that the fells were all about being as free as possible and that there was no need to ask permission to run up the flanks of Broom Fell, as long as he did not expect me to join him. Kev had the idea of Bob timing himself to the summit and after a gap of about a minute or so we would follow him, walking as quickly as we could, to see how much slower our quick marching ascent was compared to Bob's running one. Bob duly set off, steady and rhythmic to begin with but then more faltering as the gradient increased until, as he disappeared out of sight, he appeared to be almost slowing to walking pace, although still at a pace overall far in excess of what we could expect to achieve. As soon as Bob vanished the three of us set off. With similar enthusiasm and some vigour, we marched urgently upwards, but as the slope steepened and lactic acid began to fill our muscles, the rate of ascent slowed dramatically to a simpering pathetic crawl. The summit cairn coming into view provided a renewed final burst of energy, before this gaggle of panting fell walkers reached the summit collapsing against the huge cairn in a sweaty heap. We had timed our ascent at three minutes thirty five seconds and were keen to see how much faster Bob had been. It would be interesting to see how we might compare to a fell runner or someone of similar fitness. Imagine our dismay then when Bob revealed that he had unfathomably forgotten to time his run! Although we were perhaps a little put out at Bob, having slogged and damn near given ourselves coronaries for no apparent reason, the overall feeling on Broom Fell was one of camaraderie. When I knew that the four of us were going to be fell walking for Stan's stag do, I was determined that I wanted to get a photo of the four of us on a summit for this book. A very kind lady duly obliged.

The Stag party

The easy descent from Broom Fell soon took us back to Widow Hause. From here grassy slopes branch off down towards the Wythop Moss, a vast flat and boggy expanse that I had long had a somewhat unfathomable desire to visit. It appears bleak and forlorn under dark clouds although my first crossing of the Wythop Moss was to prove in direct contrast from my expectations. During the years it had wielded a strange fascination over me; I had imagined a solo crossing, perhaps with clouds and mist skirting the fells above and a morass of bog to be negotiated underfoot. It was not something that called to me for its beauty or ease of terrain. It was more the call of a challenge, a desire to do something a bit different and above all to explore wilderness. However, its crossing proved a direct contrast to my preconceptions. Firstly, I was not alone but with a larger group than I had ever walked with before. Secondly, it was a glorious spring afternoon, following on from one of the driest and warmest Aprils I could remember. The crossing was therefore unusually dry underfoot. What really stuck in the mind were the colours. The coarse grass of the Moss shone a brilliant gold, like a field of ripe corn. Instead of gloomily rejecting us, it embraced us with its wild beauty. The four of us all sensed a special feeling as we crossed the Moss. For me there was a kind of spiritual calm and timeless peace about the place, a dazzling radiance of light that was seductive to the senses. I am sure on other days and under differing conditions, the Moss could be all the things I had initially imagined it would be, but for this one day it was a little hidden gem of Lakeland.

The crossing of the Wythop Moss ends beneath the heathery flanks of Ling Fell, a great pudding of a fell to climb, but a positive delight to walk beneath. That day the grassy lane that leads past Burthwaite Wood could have been bottled up and called 'Essence of Spring'. The trees lining the lane were of the most sumptuous, luxuriant green. The quiet roads back to Embleton Church were also a delight to walk, passing verdant fields, filled with the chorus of new born lambs.

So had Bob enjoyed his first experience of fell walking and the Lake District? It is true that Bob is not a man of many words and tends to ponder and choose his words wisely. As we sat outside the pub back in Keswick, the first of many that night, before alcohol took control of our faculties Bob stared up in wonderment at Skiddaw's majestic façade – now lit up by glorious evening sunshine – and said, somehow surprised at the bold magnificence on display, 'You know that's a great mountain and I want to climb it'. In his eyes finally was the understanding of why his little brother had been heading back to the same place so consistently for more than 20 years. In his own unassuming way, somewhat unexpectedly, he had formed his own bond with the fells.

Barf Direct

Wherever does the name Barf come from? Rest assured it has nothing to do with a slang word for being sick. The truth is decidedly less unpleasant. From what I can gather Barf is simply a variation on the word Barrow. So effectively there are two fells in the North-Western group whose names have the same origin. Barrow could either mean an ancient burial ground or more simply a grove. One thing is for certain about Barf. It is the odd man out in the fells north of Whinlatter Pass, which are generally of rounded appearance with an absence of crags; fine rambling country, but devoid of drama. Barf bucks the trend. From Thornthwaite, Barf rises very steeply in over a thousand feet of crag and scree ridden chaos, all compacted into just half a mile of land. The majority of walkers avoid this seemingly impregnable face and climb the fell via the back door route through Beckstones Plantation. However, for those with a strong disposition towards scrambling, or lunacy, there is I kid you not, a direct route to Barf's summit.

You may not believe me, but I do occasionally take the family to the Lake District. In fact, in August 2011, my wife Jenny, the three children and I spent two weeks in our eight berth tent, staying at the delightful Lanefoot Farm site near Braithwaite. Apart from a night where a hurricane force wind threatened to lift the tent clean off the ground requiring us to hammer down tent pegs at three in the morning, this was a grand holiday. The craggy face of Barf could be seen every time I strolled around the campsite and it called mockingly to me that I had yet to climb it. With just three months to go to my book deadline, I had better either do it now or forget it. Virtually every night I went for a short walk at dusk, either on my own or with my twelve year old son, and every night I found myself picking out the line of the direct route up Barf and studying Slape Crag, the crux of this climb. At times, generally after a pint or two of cider, I thought it did not look too difficult, at other more sober times I got adrenalin pangs just contemplating it. Now when I am with the family in the Lake District, I try not to take liberties with the solo walking urges. That holiday my youngest daughter Gemma, aged four, climbed her first three Wainwright fells (Dodd, Hallin Fell and Barrow), my daughter Hannah, aged eight, reached eight Wainwrights and my son Tim, aged twelve, got well into double figures. All the time Jenny could sense, with the knowledge that comes from 20 years living with a hills obsessive, that

I wanted to do the direct route on Barf. As there was no way she was doing it, let alone the children, she let me go off very early one morning, as long as I promised that I would return within four hours, so that we could have most of the day as a family.

Making an early start on a route that was far from popular more or less guaranteed solitude, something of a rare commodity in the Lake District in August. So I had high hopes of having the climb to myself. The Bishop of Barf is familiar to any fellwalker worth his or her salt, as well as countless tourists who see its knobbly white-washed profile on the side of Barf and wonder how it got there. So distinct is it from its surroundings that it's clearly seen from across the Vale of Keswick and the Skiddaw range of fells. There is a story behind the Bishop of Barf, which according to local legend marks the place where the Bishop of Derry was killed while riding his horse. You might ask yourself what on earth a man of the cloth was doing on a horse in such a perilous situation. Well I am sure many of my readers will have found themselves doing stupid challenges when under the influence of alcohol and this Bishop was no exception. Perhaps in his inebriated state he convinced himself that God would be on his side even more than usual. Whatever the case, having made a bet that he could ride up the hill, he somehow managed to get up the first couple of hundred feet of toil and then, not surprisingly, had a fatal fall. The Bishop and his horse are said to be buried beneath a smaller whitewashed stone, called the Clerk, which lies in the copse of wood at the base of the fell. Sometime after the alleged incident took place in 1783, the Bishop rock was painted white in honour of the Bishop and his faithful steed, first by the staff at the nearby Swan Hotel and then in more recent times by the Keswick Mountain Rescue Team.

The Clerk stands at the base of the scree and marks the start of this climb. The first two hundred and fifty feet of ascent to the Bishop comprise laborious scree and progress is slow on this ever shifting conveyor belt. Climbing this initial section gave me immense admiration for the Keswick Mountain Rescue volunteers, who carry the whitewash up to paint the Bishop whenever his pure white vestments start to fade. Not the most straightforward painting and decorating job you could take on it has to be said, although they do a fine job of it. At last the Bishop is reached and it is again worthy of comment that the people who paint the Bishop have actually bothered to paint his back profile, given that it cannot be seen from anywhere other than standing precariously next to him.

The next two hundred feet of climbing is short but testing, up a flaky scree gully, which tends to come away in one's hands and is set on even steeper ground than the initial climb to the Bishop. When scrambling it is most reassuring to feel in control of every movement, of every foot and hand placing. Here, however, nothing can be relied upon and indeed I read a couple of months after completing the climb that someone had fallen here and had to be rescued, having suffered quite severe injuries. So please take care. Scree finally ends at about 850 feet, to be replaced by thick and largely pathless heather. Here is found the solitary rowan tree that Wainwright mentions and states that having won such a secluded situation 'it is mortifying to find the slender trunk of the tree elaborately carved with the initials of a number of earlier visitors'. Even here one cannot escape humanity's obsession with leaving its mark, like a dog that pees against a tree. Shortly after the rowan tree, at a welcome little piece of level ground, I finally had a rest. A form of desperate adrenalin fuelled self-preservation had kept me going thus far. I knew I still had Slape Crag, the crux of the climb, ahead of me. For a few moments though I just wanted to forget past and future and revel in the now of my situation, with a plunging sweep in front of me down to Bassenthwaite Lake.

During the evenings at Lanefoot Farm studying the direct route up Barf, Slape Crag had become like a Nemesis and now that Nemesis was directly ahead of me. Thankfully you don't have to climb the actual crag, but instead there is a traverse left across its base, which ends with an exposed but not too difficult little section, with dizzying views over the lake below. Once above Slape Crag pat yourself on the back, for if you have got this far then you will make it to the summit. More steep heather and a short rocky escarpment finally lead to easier ground. There are two false summits before the actual summit of Barf, the first of which gives a grandstand view down on the climb completed. On most of the tough, scrambly walks in this book I have had Stan with me to keep me going. So it was with an added sense of achievement that I reached Barf having conquered the direct route on my own. It did not matter that hundreds, perhaps even thousands, had climbed Barf direct before. For a few moments I felt like Hillary on Everest.

All too soon a party of people heading from Lord's Seat towards Barf burst the bubble of my reverie and I became just another fellwalker in this popular area. I'd had my solitude, my moment in the sun; it was time to head down, via the familiar Beckstones Plantation route, to rejoin my family at Lanefoot Farm. Barf is only a small fell, but it packs a hell of a punch.

Mighty Grasmoor

Grasmoor is a fell of contrasting appearances. From Eel Crag it appears simply as a rounded dome and many walkers, including me, will have first climbed it as a quick out and back detour from Eel Crag. Of completely different character is the face shown to Lanthwaite Green, by Crummock Water. From here its conical shape, soaring sweep of crags and scree make it one of the most dramatic mountain faces in the district. Those familiar with Scotland's Buachaille Etive Mor, the sentinel of Glencoe, will perhaps concur with me that Grasmoor from Lanthwaite shares something of the same arresting and seemingly unassailable outline. Grasmoor would always want to be seen from this angle. This aspect of Grasmoor also provides a number of interesting and varied routes up or down the fell, routes where one way or another you will attain a whole different understanding of Grasmoor and give the mountain its rightful dues.

When Wainwright states tongue in cheek that a climb 'is probably less difficult than the North Wall of the Eiger', it is hardly a ringing endorsement for an easy, carefree ascent. I have taken the walker's route beneath the Eiger Nordwand and craned my neck to look up its 6000 feet sheer face – the degree of difficulty far exceeds anything in these Isles, obviously. The mere mention of the Eiger by comparison however, speaks volumes for the dramatic intimidating appearance of what is one of greatest challenges for any walker in the district, Grasmoor direct from Lanthwaite Green.

A tough timetable of walks to complete this book meant that Stan and I found ourselves contemplating Grasmoor direct while sitting at the breakfast table, with a less than ideal forecast. It spoke of a dry morning, gradually clouding over and leading to rain in the afternoon. We knew that provided we got to the summit of Grasmoor before things misted over for the day, we would be in familiar surrounds and could make our escape via Coledale Hause and Gasgale Gill, using GPS and compass if need be. However, we all know how unreliable mountain weather can be. What if the rain came early? Neither of us fancied a new and exposed scramble in rain and thick mist.

As we parked up at Lanthwaite Green, a watery sun was doing its best to keep the clouds at bay, but was fighting a losing battle. The milky nature of the sky spoke of the worsening weather to come. A few months earlier I had joked with the newcomer Bob, that we were taking him up

Grasmoor direct for his first ever Lakeland walk. Now as I contemplated this imposing mass of scree and crag, those words of jest came back to haunt me, saying 'Go on then, let's see how you fancy climbing me now. Really funny prospect eh?'

The initial grassy sward of path leading to the base of the climb was very much in contrast to what lay ahead. Upon reaching the steep pull of scree marking the start of Grasmoor direct, one half wishes for a continuation of smooth grassy path. Perhaps an outing in the Caldbeck Fells would have been better today? The scree starts steeply and gets steeper, but there is a vague path heading through the worst of it, although you will still at times find yourself clawing at heather or, even worse, without any heather to claw at desperately try to defy gravity and maintain upward progress. Just as the loose soil and gravel begins to become an ugly chore, things become a little rockier, with a kind of builder's rubble type surface beneath you, as you ease your way up to a conspicuous rock gateway marked in the Wainwright guide at 1500 feet. Finally there was a little seat of heather where we took a well earned rest. Approximately 500 feet of exposed scrambling lay ahead, before the Pinnacle that marks a slight easing of the terrain. This is the crux of the climb. We were committed now, for going back down seemed it anything more treacherous than carrying on up.

A grassy rake now leads for about 100 feet of climbing to the terrace Wainwright marks at 1600 feet. It is here that the exposure really starts to kick in. It was exhilarating and frightening at the same time, which I suppose was a degree better than just plain frightening. A level terrace carries what appears to be a sheep track, although I find it hard to believe that a sheep would choose this dramatic, almost inaccessible location for a spot of lunch. Although saying that, Stan did once tell me he saw a sheep stuck on a ledge near the top of Lord's Rake on Scafell. It seems hunger can drive you to almost anything. Leaving behind this oasis of calm in the midst of fearfulness, you head up some greasy rocks towards Fat Man's Agony. Having gained a stone or two in recent years it had been the thought of Fat Man's Agony that gave me most trepidation in the planning of this walk. What if I could not make it through and was stuck halfway up Grasmoor till I lost sufficient weight to carry on, like Winnie the Pooh in Rabbit's doorway. Luckily although it is a rocky scramble, Fat Man's Agony would only truly be agony for someone of extreme girth.

It was odd how once I passed through Fat Man's Agony, my frame of mind improved. Perhaps it was just that the terrain became slightly easier, or maybe that the arête we passed over was in such an amazing situation,

The grass does not last long before the masochistic haul of Grasmoor Direct

with a bird's eye view of the car park and Crummock Water far below. This arête is exposed but relatively easy, or to paraphrase AW it is less difficult than, say, Sharp Edge. The Pinnacle at 2000 feet is a divine place, with a sense of exposure and drama that belies its modest altitude. It is still another 800 feet to the summit along a curving and at times steep ridge, but once Grasmoor End is reached at 2400 feet you are back to simple fell walking again. Up till now we had scarcely noticed the weather, so engrossed and focused had our minds become on the glories and difficulties of the task. All I could tell you was that it had not yet rained. However, on taking a decent stop at Grasmoor End we could clearly see that a steady deterioration had occurred since we had begun the walk. Milky sky had become leaden grey sky. The highest peaks were drawing down shutters of mist for the day. The mist was toying with Grasmoor above us and had descended over the summit by the time we reached it. It was a pity to have no view, but we contented ourselves with the wonderful (in retrospect) exposed plunges we had contemplated on the ascent. The way back via Coledale Hause and Gasgale Gill was a very different experience. No exhilarating sense of height and space. No danger, except in losing direction. We became instead cocooned within our waterproof clothing, ensconced in a world of mist and fine rain, seeing only the next few feet in front of us. I'll swear though that we both had smiles on our faces all the miserable way back to the car. I suppose that means, in summing up that Grasmoor direct, tough and exposed though it is, may well be one of the more severe routes in this book that tempts me back.

The last of anything that has been enjoyable is always bound to have a degree of poignancy, whether it is the last page of a good book, the last event of the season in your favourite sport or perhaps the last tick on a list of mountains or mountain walks. Inevitably the last walk I did in my research for this book was tinged with poignant moments and with a bitter sweet sense of nostalgia. As at many times, I was blessed with fair weather, this time on a day in early October. I guess a last walk in driving rain would not perhaps have evoked anything other than a desire to get back to the car. I am a firm believer in choosing a grand outing for the last walk in any list of walks. For my Wainwright round, I chose Mellbreak for the final summit of the 214. For my final walk for this book, I chose a tour of Grasmoor that included a secret, at times thrilling ascent with a beautiful and elegant line of descent.

The little car park at Lanthwaite Green had proved a popular starting point on my journey through the secrets of the North-Western Fells. For this finishing walk it was fitting to have my long time companion Stan with me. The route began by following the same grassy sward of a path, slanting up through the bracken that had led to the start of the Grasmoor direct route. This time we headed away from thoughts and memories of the direct route, as we took a rough but perfectly tolerable path above Gasgale Gill beneath the huge wedge of Grasmoor. Our path had signs of neglect and a lack of use, with the occasional patch of scree covering it over for a few yards and the bracken gradually encroaching. It is a route that has fallen out of use for all but the discerning minority of walkers, who prefer to get away from the familiarity and crowds found on popular routes. This path has been superseded by an altogether more developed path on the other side of Gasgale Gill, which is now commonly used as a route to and from Coledale Hause. A group of ten or so walkers were headed along that route, separated physically from us by a few hundred feet of space and the rushing waters of the gill, effectively in an entirely separate wilderness sphere. Our route headed level for two thirds of a mile in grand surrounds, with the rotten gullies of Gasgale Crags on Whiteside dominant and imposing across the gill and the picturesque charms of Crummock Water and its environs behind. Over a thousand feet of mountain architecture hung over us on either side of Gasgale Gill, making us feel like insignificant specks on the landscape

The inevitable part of this approach to Grasmoor is that these early, easy steps will at some stage be replaced by a healthy dose of slog. It is quite difficult to determine where the route heads up and away from the low level path. One could head up just about anywhere, as there are no crags or dangers, but it is best to take advice from the recently revised Wainwright guide here (second Chris Jesty edition) and look for the green strip of moss heading up, to avoid wading thigh deep through heather. We rounded a few bends in the track before sighting the strip – it is fairly obvious once seen. Not that this early mossy part of the climb is particularly easy or pleasant, it is merely less unpleasant than the heather alternative. There is pretty much no path from here to the top of Grasmoor. Keep going though for there are rewards aplenty when the ridge of Dove Crags narrows and starts to properly form ahead of you. A look over the precipice reveals the hidden glories of Dove Crags. Here is a seldom seen hanging valley, whose grassy floor sits at nearly 2000 feet and is dominated by a semicircle of dark, sun starved crags. There are no paths in this lonely upland coomb and it must rank as one of the wildest and least trodden places in the district. One day I mean to go down into this grassy hollow and look in awe at the crags around me. To just sit and take it in – that in itself is surely the greatest privilege of all, the freedom to roam such a magnificent landscape.

Unlike the Grasmoor direct route from Lanthwaite, the Dove Crags ridge is almost devoid of awkwardness. I did say almost though, because you will have to contend with a rock slab at about the 2,200 feet contour. It is only about fifteen feet of scrambling, but the slab is greasy when wet and set at a rather awkward angle that gives the feeling that the feet are never quite secure. Take care here not to veer over too far towards Dove Crags, better if anything to head away from them. Half way up this rock step, I found that my walking pole, which I had forgotten to secure to my rucksack, was encumbering my progress. So I decided to fling the pole up towards the top of the slab, only for it unsurprisingly to conform to the laws of gravity and return like a boomerang to hit me in the face, ending its flight at the bottom of the slab. I had to climb back down the slab to retrieve it and then climb back up again for my sins against Sir Isaac Newton. I now know the rock slab rather well! Stan had witnessed the whole thing from the top of the slab and let out a torrent of knowing sarcasm about how it was a pointless gesture hurling the pole. I let out something profane and unrepeatable back at him. So it is with best friends.

From the slab to the top of Grasmoor the sense of height gradually increases to a heady crescendo. There are no more difficulties but the plunging views back to Gasgale Gill and the gulf of nothingness between you and Gasgale Crags lend a sense of excitement and thrill to the later stages of this climb. This time there was no mist to dampen our triumphal march to the summit, albeit approached from a somewhat confusing angle. There was only a pale blue sky, streaked with the odd fair weather cloud. This was how any walker, any author, would want the last summit to be. The massive cairn on the highest inches of the fell was visited, but this is not the best place to appreciate the grandeur of Grasmoor. Yes the summit view includes a myriad of Lakeland summits, but those close around are cut from the midriff downwards by the broad rim of the fell. To get a sense of depth, a tremendous sense of depth, the Crummock Water side of the wall shelter is the spot for me. It was by

Relaxing on the Dove Crags ascent of Grasmoor (looking across to Gasgale Crags)

now three o'clock on this October afternoon and we were lucky indeed to have the wall shelter to ourselves. The summit of Grasmoor is generous enough that the dozen or so people around it that day could all have their space, although that did not stop a couple of them from annoyingly standing directly behind our sheltered spot for a few minutes, before realising that we were going to be as immovable as the rocks around us. I sometimes wait for people to move on, but I do so from a distance, perhaps a hundred yards or more away. I can still see them and will know when they have gone, but they will not be aware of me or of any time pressure from me. It is rude to hang over people, as if in a queue for school dinners.

The couple soon got the message as we continued to recline in the lee of the wind. It was warm here, perhaps the last significant memory of warmth before the long descent into winter. This was a place to linger. A full 2600 feet below us, Crummock Water was a thrilling mixture of deep blue water and dazzling, shimmering crests of light, where the sun's rays hit the rippling waters. A small flat patch of land, four or five luxuriant green fields and a farmhouse, stood out against the chaotic outline of Rannerdale Knotts. The Fellbarrow Group looked friendly and welcoming, bathed in the autumn sunshine. The mighty giants of the Western and Southern fells beckoned me on to the next chapter of my secret Lakeland journey. Stan suggested the idea of finishing the walk in the dark and hanging around on the summit for as long as possible and given the weather conditions, I readily agreed. As the shadows lengthened and the fells began to pull over their bed covers for the night, we reluctantly left the summit of Grasmoor. However, this was not quite the end. There was one more secret Lakeland route; a classic route for descent and classic conditions to descend in.

From the summit of Grasmoor and even from the wall shelter, one wonders where the Lad Hows ridge is. There seems to be only open space between Grasmoor and the Whiteless Pike ridge. So concealed is the Lad Hows ridge that it is only upon reaching a subsidiary south-westerly cairn that it can be seen. And what a glorious sight it is, a slender ridge, with a wonderful easy path atop it, curving gracefully down to the valley floor. Its initial stages are as airy and gorgeous ridge walking as one could ever wish for. As we descended, the ridge gradually shifted in colour from a heart rending golden to the deep purple shades of dusk and the great sweep of Whiteless Pike began to dominate to the left. I am sure the Lad Hows route would be a fine climb to the summit of Grasmoor, but it is surely even better in descent.

As the fells around gradually faded to dark outlines against a sky lit by a crescent moon, it was inevitable that thought and conversation turned from the first third of our secret Lakeland adventure – now complete – to the next section. As I get older and I hope a little wiser, I try not to look back too much on life. Regrets are pointless and the past should only be mulled over to learn from one's mistakes and make a better future. If it was not for that whimsical emotion called nostalgia, I might be doing quite well in my quest to look forward and not back. It was with nostalgia now that I remembered those wonderful secret routes onto Skiddaw and Blencathra; the joys of making independent lines of ascent on the Coledale and Newlands fells; the delight of seeing my friend Bob reach his first Wainwright fell; the thrills and masochism of Easy Gully on Pavey Ark, Barf direct and Doddick Gill. All was now sprinkled with the magic dust of reminiscence.

Secret Lakeland part one had been a success. I had found solitude in spades, acres of loneliness, a Lakeland that the crowds forgot. Now it was forward to the next third of the challenge and the Southern and Western Fells. Here are concentrated many of the highest and most celebrated of the Lakeland Fells including Pillar, Great Gable, High Stile, Bowfell, Crinkle Crags and of course Scafell and Scafell Pike. Here also the terrain is generally rougher and craggier than that of the areas described in this volume. I can expect more scrambling and awkward situations and perhaps somewhat less rolling moorland and grassy fells. The routes have already begun to seep into my planning; I am itching to do them and itching to tell you about them. So farewell for the next two years, I hope that you enjoy these walks as much as I have. It would have been nice to have met some of you on one of the many routes in this book, discerning walkers that you are. Perhaps we could have shared in the intimate delights of Hause Gill on Knott, or the heady joys of the Shelf Route on Eel Crag. Unlikely now though, as I hunt out some more hidden gems in the south and west, ever guided by that master fell walker Wainwright and those old friends the *Pictorial Guides.* Unlikely but not impossible however, as I somehow think I will miss the walks and fells in this volume too much to be able to resist their tug completely for another two years. A list is good. A plan is good. They both provide a framework for the future, in my case the next four years and two volumes of scribbling. Become too much of a slave to a list or plan though and we lose some of that very freedom that we spend so many hours of our lives yearning for.

Appendix – Table of Walks

This table has been designed firstly as an index of the walks in this book for ready reference and secondly to provide a reference to where each walk can be found in Wainwright's *Pictorial Guides*.

I have also given details of whether, in my opinion, the walk is better safety wise or aesthetically in ascent or descent, or indeed whether it should only be used as a route of ascent for safety reasons.

Finally I have provided a grade for each of the routes described. This ranges from a '1' grading for an easy walk on mainly grassy terrain and without any difficulties or obstacles, to a '4' for a walk that requires scrambling and where the terrain is tough and uncompromising. A key is provided below for each grading.

I have included a column for you to date your first ascent or descent of each route. In my opinion as these route 'ticks' are not summits being reached, you can still claim having 'ticked off' a route, whether you have done it in ascent or descent. This is more about enjoyment and discovery than specific criteria!

Key for Walk Grading

1 – Easy and mainly grassy terrain with gentle inclines and usually tracks or paths to follow.

2 - Has some tracks or paths although some sections may be pathless and boggy. It may involve considerable ascent or descent.

3 – Pathless and rough terrain. It may involve a little scrambling or some optional scrambling.

4 - Lots of scrambling, sense of exposure or awkward rough terrain.

Section One - Northern Fells

Route	Pages in this book	Where found in AW's Northern Fells Guide	Better in Ascent or Descent	Grading	Date done
1. Skiddaw Little Man via South-West Arete	19-22	Skiddaw Little Man page 8	Ascent	3	
2. Skiddaw via Sale How	23-25	Skiddaw page 21	Descent	1	
3. Skiddaw via North-West Ridge	26-29	Skiddaw page 15	Ascent	2	
4. Skiddaw Little Man from Applethwaite	30-31	Skiddaw Little Man page 9	Descent	3	
5. Skiddaw via Barkbethdale	31-33	Skiddaw page 17	Ascent	2	
6. Skiddaw via Bakestall	34	Skiddaw page 20	Descent	2	
7. Skiddaw via Southerndale	35-38	Skiddaw page 15	Ascent	2 to 3	
8. Skiddaw via Hare Crag	39	Skiddaw page 21	Descent	2	
9. Binsey from Bewaldeth	42-44	Binsey page 4	Ascent or descent	1	
10. Binsey from High Ireby	44-45	Binsey page 6	Descent	1 (if you avoid getting lost)	
11. Knott from Fell Side	48-50	Knott page 7	Ascent	2 to 3	
12. Knott from Mosedale via Carrock Mine	51	Knott page 9	Descent	2	

Route	Pages in this book	Where found in AW's Northern Fells Guide	Better in Ascent or Descent	Grading	Date done
13. Knott from Mosedale via Coomb Height	51-52	Knott page 9	Ascent or descent	2	
14. Knott from Orthwaite	53-55	Knott page 5	Ascent	2	
15. Great Sca Fell from Longlands via Charleton Gill	55-57	Great Sca Fell page 7	Descent	1	
16. High Pike from Fell Side	57-58	High Pike page 8	Ascent	1	
17. High Pike via Potts Gill Mine	60-61	High Pike page 9	Descent	1	
18. Carrock Fell from Mosedale	61-63	Carrock Fell page 7	Ascent	2 to 3	
19. Carrock Fell via Carrock Beck	65-66	Carrock Fell page 9	Descent	1	
20. Long Side from Dodd Wood car park	67-70	Long Side page 4	Ascent	1 becoming 3	
21. Lonscale Fell via north-east buttress	71-73	Lonscale Fell page 5	Ascent only	3	
22. Lonscale Fell via Lonscale Crags (route C)	74-75	Lonscale Fell page 4	Ascent or descent	2	
23. Lonscale Fell via Burnt Horse Ridge	75-76	Lonscale Fell page 6	Descent	2	
24. Blencathra via Gategill Fell	78-80	Blencathra page 13	Ascent	2 to 3	
25. Blencathra via Doddick Fell	81-83	Blencathra page 21	Ascent	2 to 3	

Route	Pages in this book	Where found in AW's Northern Fells Guide	Better in Ascent or Descent	Grading	Date done
26. Bannerdale Crags East Ridge	85-86	Bannerdale Crags page 6	Ascent	2	
27. Bowscale Fell via Bowscale Tarn	87	Bowscale Fell page 7	Descent	2	
28. Blencathra via Blease Gill	89-91	Blencathra page 12	Ascent only advisable	4	
29. Blencathra via Roughten Gill	91	Blencathra page 9	Descent	3	
30. Blencathra via Doddick Gill	93-94	Blencathra page 20	Ascent only advisable	4	
31. Blencathra via Middle Tongue	95-96	Blencathra page 16	Descent	3 to 4	

Note – Lonscale Fell via Whit Beck (described on page 73 and 74) has been excluded from the main list as it is not shown as a route in the Wainwright's Northern Fells guide. It is however as wild and secret as anything in this book, would score a 3 grading and is for ascent only.

If you do it, you can put your date of ascent here _____

Section Two - Cental Fells

Route	Pages in this book	Where found in AW's Northern Fells Guide	Better in Ascent or Descent	Grading	Date done
32. Loughrigg Fell Exploration	101-108	Loughrigg Fell pages 3 and 4	Ascent or descent	1	
33. Ullscarf from Wythburn via Harrop Tarn	110-112	Ullscarf page 6	Ascent	2	
34. The Central Spine	112-116	Ridge Routes High Tove page 4, High Seat page 7, Bleaberry Fell page 10	N/A	2 to 3	
35. Bleaberry Fell via Goat Crag	116-118	Bleaberry Fell page 6	Ascent	3	
36. Steel Fell via north ridge	121-122	Steel Fell page 5			
37. Silver How from Elterwater	126-127	Silver How page 5	Ascent or descent	1	
38. Grange Fell from Rosthwaite	129-131	Grange Fell page 4	Ascent	2	
39. Grange Fell east ridge	132-135	Grange Fell page 5	N/A	2 to 3	
40. High Rigg Traverse	141-143	High Rigg pages 2 and 3	Best done north to south leaving summit till the end	2	
41. Blea Rigg via Whitegill Crag	144-146	Blea Rigg page 8	Ascent	3 with short section of 4	
42. Pavey Ark via Easy Gully	146-147	Pavey Ark page 7	Ascent only advisable	4	

Route	Pages in this book	Where found in AW's Northern Fells Guide	Better in Ascent or Descent	Grading	Date done
43. Harrison Stickle via Pike Howe	148	Harrison Stickle page 9	Descent	2	
44. Eagle Crag using Route A	149-151	Eagle Crag pages 3 and 4	Ascent only	3	

Section Three - North Western Fells

Route	Pages in this book	Where found in AW's Northern Fells Guide	Better in Ascent or Descent	Grading	Date done
45. Robinson from Buttermere	157-161	Robinson page 7	Ascent	2	
46. Robinson from Hassness	165-167	Robinson page 8	Ascent	2	
47. Robinson from Gatesgarth	168	Robinson page 9	Descent	2	
48. Robinson from Newlands Church	168-171	Robinson page 5	Ascent	3	
49. High Spy from Grange	172-174	High Spy page 6	Ascent	2	
50. Graystones from Armaside	177-180	Graystones page 6	Ascent or descent	1	
51. Sale Fell from Beck Wythop	180-182	Use map on Sale Fell page 8	Ascent or descent	1	
52. Knott Rigg from Keskadale	183-185	Knott Rigg page 4	Ascent	2	
53. Grisedale from Thornthwaite or Whinlatter Visitor Centre	190-193	Grisedale Pike page 9	Ascent or descent	2	
54. Wandope via the Addacomb Ridge	196-197	Wandope page 6	Ascent recommended, very steep in descent	3	
55. Wandope via Third Gill	198-200	Wandope page 5	Ascent only advisable	3	
56. Eel Crag (Shelf Route)	200-203	Eel Crag pages 7 and 8	Ascent only advisable	3	

Route	Pages in this book	Where found in AW's Northern Fells Guide	Better in Ascent or Descent	Grading	Date done
57. Eel Crag (Tower Ridge)	203-204	Eel Crag pages 7 and 8	Ascent only advisable	4	
58. Hopegill Head from Whinlatter	206-208	Hopegill Head page 9	Descent	2 to 3	
59. Whiteside from Lanthwaite Green	211-212	Whiteside page 8	Ascent	2	
60. Whiteside via Cold Gill	214-216	Whiteside page 6	Descent	3	
61. Graystones from Embleton Church	216-218	Graystones page 5	Ascent	2	
62. Broom Fell via Wythop Moss	219-220	Broom Fell page 4	Descent	2	
63. Barf from Thornthwaite	221-223	Barf page 6	Ascent only advisable	4	
64. Grasmoor Direct	224-226	Grasmoor page 6	Ascent only advisable	4	
65. Grasmoor via Dove Crags	227-229	Grasmoor page 5	Ascent	3	
66. Grasmoor from Rannerdale	230-231	Grasmoor page 8	Descent	2	

Also from Sigma Leisure:

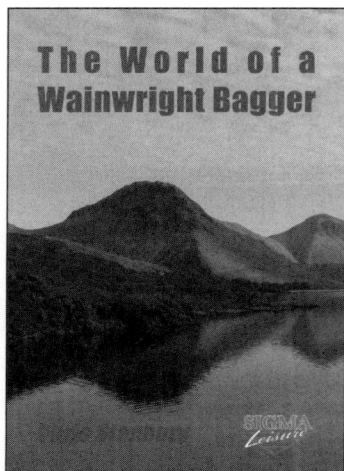

The World of a Wainwright Bagger
Chris Stanbury

Chris Stanbury provides an insight into the world of a 'Wainwright Bagger', inspiring those new to The Wainwrights, to those who have done most of the fells with a series of essays giving a flavour of the enjoy- ment to be found in completing Wainwright's 214 fells.

£8.99

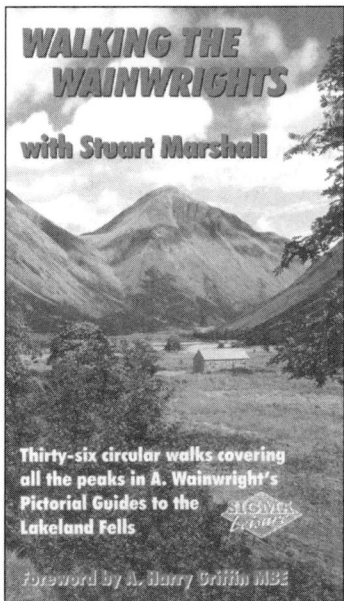

Walking the Wainwrights
Stuart Marshall

This book links all 214 peaks in the late Alfred Wainwright's seven-volume Pictorial Guide to The Lakeland Fells. Clear route descriptions are presented with two-colour sketch maps.

"An excellent, concise manual on how to tackle the 'Wainwrights' in an intelligent way." – A. Harry Griffin MBE

£8.99

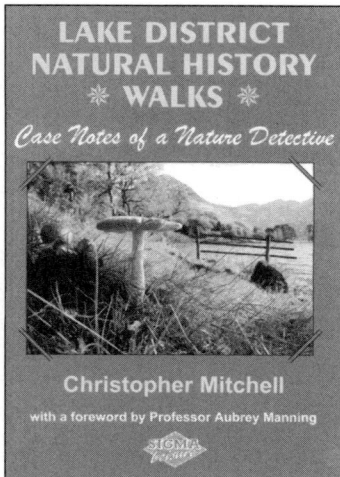